中国-东盟法律研究中心

重庆市人文社会科学重点研究基地

最高人民法院东盟国家法律研究基地

>> 本书是中国-东盟法律研究中心规划课题成果

中國 — 东盟法律评论

CHINA-ASEAN LAW REVIEW

（2017 Myanmar Volume）

第七辑 二〇一七年（缅甸法专辑）

■ 主　　编:张晓君　【缅甸】吴温敏

■ 主办单位
中国西南政法大学
中国—东盟法律研究中心
本辑合作单位
缅甸联邦最高检察院

■ Chief Editors　Zhang Xiaojun　U Win Myint (Myanmar)
■ Sponsors
Southwest University of Political Science and Law of China
China-ASEAN Legal Research Center
Co-Sponsor
The Union Attorney General's Office of the Republic of the Union of Myanmar

■ 执行编辑: 徐忆斌　钟　佳　罗媛媛

■ Executive Editors: Xu Yibin　Zhong Jia　Luo Yuanyuan

厦门大学出版社　国家一级出版社
XIAMEN UNIVERSITY PRESS　全国百佳图书出版单位

中國—东盟法律评论

韦柠滨

Bình luận pháp luật Trung quốc - Asean.

越南—中国—东盟法律信息咨询中心主任陈大兴用越南文字为
《中国—东盟法律评论》题写刊名

Journal Undang Undang Asean China

冯正仁

马来西亚联邦法院前大法官、第五届"中国—东盟法律合作与发展高层论坛"
组委会主席冯正仁先生以马来语为《中国—东盟法律评论》题写刊名。

柬埔寨司法部大臣昂翁·瓦塔纳用高棉语为《中国—东盟法律评论》题写刊名

China. ASEAN Legal Research Centre plays vital role in legal communication and cooperation between China and Myanmar

17.12.16

H.E. Mr. Win Myint
Deputy Attorney General
Union Attorney General's Office
Republic of the Union of Myanmar

缅甸联邦最高检察院副检察长吴温敏为中心题词

Many thanks for
China-ASEAN Legal Research Center
to provide the strenthing legal caperaton
between Indonesia and China

Nanning. China
6th. Dec. 2017

Indonesia Attorney General

H. M PRASETYO

印尼最高检总检察长 穆罕默德·普拉赛特为中心题词

中国—东盟法律研究

中心：

法学之花盛开！

徐步 题
驻东盟大使
二〇二四二月七日

Advisory Committee

■China

Zhang Mingqi	Vice President of China Law Society
Liu Xuepu	Vice Director of the Standing Committee of the People's Congress of Chongqing
Fu Zitang	President of Southwest University of Political Science and Law
Wu Zhipan	Vice President of Beijing University
Wang Han	Vice President of Northwest University of Political Science and Law
Yang Guohua	Professor of School of Law, Tsinghua University

■ASEAN Countries

Chan Sotheavy	Secretary of State of Ministry of Justice of Cambodia
Colin Ong	President of Arbitration Association of Brunei Darussalm
Maitree Sutapakul	Justice of the Supreme Court of Thailand
Muhammad Hatta Ali	Chief Justice of the Supreme Court of Indonesia
Tan Sri James Foong	The former Justice of the Federal Court of Malaysia
U Win Myint	Deputy Attorney General of the Union, Republic of the Union of Myanmar
Chaleuan Yapaoher	Minister of Prime Minister's Office of Laos and Governmental Spokesman

序

很久之前我就对《中国-东盟法律评论》有所关注,这是一本透过聚焦东盟各国法律事件,分析各国法治处境,反映东南亚各国司法法治现状的优秀著作。此书由中国西南政法大学、中国-东盟法律研究中心主编,一年发行一卷,每一卷讲述一个东南亚国家的法律,如今这已经是第7卷了。最新的这一卷《中国-东盟法律评论》重点关注缅甸法律系统和法治现状。无独有偶,好事成双,恰逢这一期著作的发行与缅甸联邦政府致力于法治改革的步伐相一致,目前缅甸政府正在积极致力于国家法治建设,废除旧的法律,颁布一系列新的法律。

同时,我也发现第7卷《中国-东盟法律评论》是在中国-东盟法律研究中心的大力支持下,由缅甸留学生共同努力,创作出来的智慧结晶。缅甸留学生优秀成果的背后离不开西南政法大学受人尊敬的张晓君教授与其他专家学者的悉心指导。本书的重点放在对缅甸最新法律热点事件的研究、分析和评论。细读过后不难发现,这不仅是一本有利于专家学者研读的法律著作,还是一本让不同群体读者对缅甸法律系统感兴趣的百科全书。

在中国-东盟法律研究中心的支持下,这卷由缅甸留学生创作的《中国-东盟法律评论》填补了缅甸法律评析的空白。现如今,用国际通用语言英语撰述缅甸法律系统的书籍少之又少,因此,在一定程度上说,这本书对缅甸法治的发展有一定的贡献。我认为这绝对是一本值得读者细致阅读的法律评论类书籍。在这里,我也向中国-东盟法律研究中心的各位官员,向关注缅甸法治发展的专家学者,向为本书发行做出突出贡献的各位老师,致以我最崇高的敬意!

缅甸联邦总检察长办公室副检察长
H. E. U Win Myint
本文翻译:郭小杰

FOREWORD

I have known that the legal review has been issued annually, reflecting the judicial and legal aspects, events and situations in South-East Asian Countries in rotation by the China-ASEAN Legal Research Center and Southwest University of Political Science and Law of China. It is the seventh time that the Research Centre issues the *China-ASEAN Law Review*. This time of issuing the review is the concern of Myanmar Legal System and Myanmar current legal situation. This occasion of being able to issue this legal review of Myanmar is coinciding with the time of Myanmar endeavoring to do law reform, in which Myanmar is currently repealing old laws and enacting the new law in urgent need.

I realize that this review is the collective effort of Myanmar students with the supervision of very respectful and prudent professor Zhang Xiaojun, other professors and lecturers from Southwest University of Political Science and Law and with the encouragement of China-ASEAN Legal Research Center. This review has placed emphasis on the legal current issues presenting consideration, analysis and giving comments on these issues which are currently assumed to arise. This legal review will be very useful and beneficial not only for the academicians but also for those who are interested in Myanmar legal system.

This review compiled and written by Myanmar law students with the guidance of China-ASEAN Legal Research Center, filling up the gap in Myanmar law reviews because nowadays, books or legal reviews written in English about Myanmar laws are quite rare. In addition, this book, therefore, will contribute to some extent to the legal development in Myanmar.

By virtue of this, I can recommend that it is one of the legal reviews that is worth reading. Accordingly, I would like to express my deep appreciation to the officials concerned from China-ASEAN Legal Research Center for their kind interest in Myanmar and sponsorship for publication.

H. E. U Win Myint,
Deputy Attorney General,
Union Attorney General's Office
The Republic of the Union of Myanmar

目 录

编 者 按

　　本卷《中国-东盟法律评论》为东盟国家法律制度专刊,主要收录了来自缅甸密支那大学法学院和缅甸联邦总检察长办公室的学者和官员的八篇文章,他们也都是西南政法大学招收的法学博士研究生。这些文章从条约法、检察官法、民事婚姻家庭法、合同法、仲裁法、劳动法、投资争端解决等角度,对缅甸主要法律制度作了介绍和评述。

　　缅甸总检察长办公室官员 Aung Ye Lwin 的文章《缅甸条约批准程序》,首先分析了条约批准在一般国际法中的概念和作用,特别是维也纳条约法公约的规定。他指出,现代国家可以选择批准或签署使条约生效,大多数现代条约都规定了条约的生效程序。批准是对条约的确认,是缔约国规定的义务,但签字只表明签署国有意受条约约束。在此基础上,他介绍了条约在缅甸宪法中生效的具体规定,缅甸采用的是条约批准生效模式。

　　由于缅甸联邦共和国和中华人民共和国的法律制度不同,因此两个国家检察官的职责和权力也是不一样的。缅甸联邦总检察长办公室行政官员 Ei Khine Zin Aung 的文章《缅甸联邦共和国检察官职能与中华人民共和国检察官职能比较研究》,通过对两个国家检察官及其最高管理机构的简要介绍,引出文章的核心内容:具体分析和研究比较了缅甸和中国检察官在其国内法律机构和法律程序中的不同职责和职能,最后总结指出尽管两个国家的检察官职能有所差别,但其维护法治的最终理念应是不变的,每个检察官都应秉持公正的精神,打击犯罪分子,维护人民和国家的正当利益。

　　随着"一带一路"建设不断推进,中缅在科技、文化、经济等领域的民事交往与合作不断深化,缅甸密支那大学法学院助教 Khin Htar Win 撰写了《缅甸民事诉讼法的基本原则》一文,重点介绍和分析了缅甸民事诉讼法的基本原则。他详细分析了缅甸民事诉讼法中的管辖权、起诉、判决、法令、执行和审判监督的基本原则,指出缅甸民事诉讼法最初源于印度法律,受到英国惯例和程序的影响,法律制度具有对抗性。同时他也分析了缅甸现行的民事诉讼法存在无法适应现状的问题,表示最高联邦法院将审查和修订其民事诉讼法。

目前,缅甸存在诸多劳动问题,尤其是最低工资和流动劳动者问题。在劳动力市场方面,除了投资增加产生的对熟练工人的需求,同时也产生了规范劳动力市场的法律法规的需求。为了保护劳动者的权利,建立良好的雇佣关系,促进组建独立的劳动组织,缅甸联邦共和国立法机关根据《缅甸宪法》第24条颁布了《缅甸劳动法》。缅甸密支那大学法学院助教 Khwar Nyo Oo 的文章《缅甸劳动法评论》着重介绍了缅甸一些重要的劳动法律法规,他指出《缅甸劳动法》是对部分劳动法律规定予以修改,并按照国际标准制定的新法律法规。

缅甸密支那大学法学院讲师 May Thu 的文章《合同构成要素研究——以〈缅甸合同法〉为研究对象》,以《缅甸合同法》为写作素材,以规则研究为切入点,通过列举《缅甸合同法》中规定的有关合同的基本原则,具体阐释和分析了有效合同形成的六大基本要素:要约和承诺、意思自治、缔约能力、合法的对价与标的、非法律规定绝对无效类合同和法律要求的书面形式。最后,作者总结出缅甸合同法律框架应持续更新以适应国际上合同法律的发展。

联邦总检察长办公室法律咨询部商业合同司官员 Thin Thin Oo 的《缅甸仲裁法》一文,针对缅甸 2016 年实施的《仲裁法》,系统阐述《仲裁法》改革的背景、框架结构、基本内容及改革前后的法律制度变化。文章全面展示仲裁法的管辖权、仲裁员的选任、仲裁的程序等内容,重点论述了《仲裁法》的改革进步和不足的地方。最后针对缅甸的仲裁制度的完善,提出建设仲裁机构或仲裁委员会等建议。

缅甸联邦总检察长办公室立法审查和咨询司行政官员 Moe Cho 的文章《缅甸投资争端解决机制的法律研究》,围绕缅甸外商投资争端解决机制,阐明缅甸的投资争端解决方式主要包括诉讼、仲裁、谈判、调解等,并且提倡建立以谈判友好解决、调解为主,仲裁、诉讼为辅的投资争端解决机制。该文详细分析了缅甸各种争端解决方式的存在现状、制度运行的程序、各程序之间的关系和协调。同时指出投资者在缅甸投资遇到投资争端时可以选择国际仲裁和国内仲裁,合理利用民事诉讼法也能够维护其合法权益。最后,其认为新的仲裁制度和司法制度已经能够为投资者提供足够的制度机制保障,缅甸已成为投资的理想东道国。

西南政法大学中国-东盟法律研究中心项目官员罗媛媛和缅甸联邦总检察长办公室立法审查和咨询司行政官员 Moe Cho 的文章《缅甸婚姻制度法律评论》为在缅甸与缅甸公民缔结婚姻关系的外国人提供相应的法律知识和建

议。他们指出,缅甸婚姻不以双方国籍为基础,而是以婚姻双方的宗教为基础,宗教徒之间的婚姻以及非宗教人士与宗教徒之间的婚姻,甚至外国人与缅甸宗教教徒的婚姻,既要依据宗教的相关规则和习俗缔结,也要遵守缅甸2015 年《缅甸一夫一妻法》的规定。

The Ratification Procedure of Treaty in Myanmar

Aung Ye Lwin[*]

Abstract: A modern country may choose to ratify or sign a treaty to make it enter into force, and most modern treaties specify the procedure for its entry into force. Ratification is the confirmation of a treaty and sets obligations for states parties. The signing only indicates the intention of the signatories to be bound by the treaty. This paper first analyzes the concept and function of treaty ratification in general international law, especially the provisions of the Vienna convention on the law of treaties. Secondly, it introduces the specific provisions on the entry into force of the treaty in Myanmar constitution. Myanmar adopts the model of treaty ratification to make treaties enter into force.

Keywords: Ratification, Confirmation, Signature Intention

Introduction

The purpose of this article is to consider the function of ratification in the modern practice of states. States are free to choose for themselves the procedure for the entry into force of a compact between them. Thus there is no doubt that if an international agreement expressly stipulates for entry into

* Aung Ye Lwin, Doctoral Student of School of International Law of SWUPL/Union Attorney General's Office, Staff Officer, Building No. 25, Naypyitaw, Myanmar, E-mail: aungyelwin2011 @ gmail. com.

force by signature or ratification or some other manners, the prescribed procedure must be complied with. Nor again, is there any doubt that in cases where it is clearly implied that the parties intended to use some particular procedures to bring a treaty into force, such implication is no less decisive than an express provision. In most modern treaties, it is either expressly stated or clearly implied by what procedure they are to come into force.

Conception and function of ratification

Ratification is the term for the final confirmation given by the parties to an international treaty concluded by their representatives. Although a treaty is concluded as soon as the mutual consent is apparent from acts of the duly authorized representatives, its binding force is, as a rule, adjourned until ratification is given. As long as ratification is not given, the treaty is, although concluded, not perfect. Some maintain that, as a treaty is not binding without notification, it is the latter which really contains the mutual consent, and really concludes the treaty.

Before ratification, they maintain, no treaty has been concluded, but a mere mutual proposal to conclude a treaty has been agreed to. But this opinion does not accord with the facts. For the representatives are authorized, and intend, to conclude a treaty by their signatures. Government acts, as a rule, on the view that a treaty is concluded as soon as their mutual consent is clearly apparent. They make a distinction between their consent, given by representatives, and their ratification, to be given subsequently; they do not confuse the two by considering their ratification to be their consent. It is for that reason that a treaty cannot be ratified in part, that no alterations of the treaty are possible through the act of ratification, that a treaty may be tacitly ratified by its execution, that it is always dated from the day when it was duly signed by the representatives, and not from the day of its ratification, and that there is no essential difference between such treaties as need, and such as do not need, ratification.

Moreover, there is no legal obligation to ratify a treaty and there are additional reasons why the signature of a treaty cannot be regarded as a mere formality. In signing a treaty, a state exercises an influence upon many of its important procedural clauses, such as those relating to accession, to reservations, to conditions of entry into force, and the like. Likewise, according to a widely accepted view, signatory states, even if they have not yet ratified a treaty, may validly exercise the right of objecting to reservations appended by any other state wishing to become a party to the treaty. It is occasionally maintained that ratification is a confirmation of the treaty as distinguished from confirmation of the signature expressing the consent of the parties. This view is probably inaccurate. Its indirect implication which, as suggested above is contrary to practice is to reduce the legal value and effects of the signature.

Requirement of ratification

Ratification, in principle, is not always essential. Although it is now a generally recognized customary rule of international law that treaties regularly require ratification, even if this is not expressly stipulated, there are exceptions to the rule. For treaties concluded by such state functionaries have the power to exercise within certain narrow limits the treaty-making competence of their state, do not require ratification, but are binding at once when they are concluded, provided that the respective functionaries have not exceeded their powers. Further, treaties concluded by Heads of States in person do not require ratification, provided that they do not concern matters in regard to which constitutional restrictions are imposed upon Heads of States.

Again, it may happen that the parties provide expressly, for the cause of a speedy execution of a treaty, that it shall be binding at once without ratifications being necessary. The practice of dispensing with ratification and expressly providing that the treaty shall enter into force upon signature has become a prominent feature in the procedure of conclusion of treaties. This applies in particular to exchanges of notes, which constitute about one-third of international agreements. However, express renunciation of ratification is valid only if given by representatives duly authorized to make such renunciation. If the representatives have not received a special authorization to dispense with ratification, their renunciation is not binding upon the states which they represent.

It has been asserted that apart from those compacts which bear the little treaty or convention, ratification is only required where it is provided for but this affirmation is too comprehensive. Since all international compacts are contracts and therefore treaties in the wider sense of the term, the title which a particular compact bears cannot decide the question whether it does or does not, require ratification. The answer to the question depends upon the contents of the compact. Thus a protocol or declaration, or exchanges of notes, in so far as they merely add some minor point or record agreement on the interpretation of a clause in a treaty, do not require ratification unless this is specially stipulated. The same applies with regard to agreements providing for a *modus vivendi* and the like, whatever title they may bear. However, apart from these exceptions, treaties require ratification unless they contain a provision to the contrary, whatever title the instrument may bear.

Form of ratification

No rule of international law exists which prescribes a necessary form of ratification. Ratification can be given tacitly as well as expressly. Tacit ratification takes place when a state begins the execution of a treaty without expressly ratifying it. It is usual for ratification to take the form of a document duly signed by the heads of state concerned, and their secretaries for foreign affairs. It is usual to draft as many documents as there are parties to the convention, and to exchange these copies between the parties. Occasionally the whole of the treaties is recited *verbatim* in the ratifying documents, but sometimes only the title, preamble, date of the treaty and the names of the signatory representatives are cited. As ratification is only the confirmation of an already existing treaty, the essential requirement in a ratifying document is merely that it should refer clearly and unmistakable to the treaty to be ratified. The citation of title, preamble, date and names of the representatives is, therefore, quite sufficient to satisfy that requirement.

Who can effect in ratification

Ratification is effected by those organs which exercise the treaty-making power of the states. These organs are normally the heads of states or their governments but they can accord the municipal law of some states, delegate the power of ratification for some parts of their territory to other representatives. Thus the viceroy of India was empowered to ratify treaties with certain Asiatic monarchs in the name of the King of Great Britain and Emperor of India.

In case the head of a state ratifies a treaty although the necessary constitutional requirements have not been previously fulfilled (for instance, where a treaty has not received the necessary approval from the parliament of the said state) the question arises whether such ratification is valid, or null and void. When the head of the state has exceeded his powers, the state concerned cannot, as a rule, be held to be bound by the treaty.

According to international law, states have the capacity to make agreements, but since states are not identifiable human persons, particular principles have evolved to ensure that persons representing states have indeed the power so to do for the purpose of conducting the treaty in question. Such persons must produce what is termed "full powers" according to Article 7 of the Vienna Convention, before being accepted as capable of representing their countries. "Full powers" refers to documents certifying status from the competent authorities of the state in question.

Article 7 of the Vienna Convention on the law of treaties, 1969 provided as follows:

(1) A person is considered as representing a state for the purpose of adopting or authenticating the text of a treaty or for the purpose of expressing the consent of the state to be bound by a treaty if

(a) He produces appropriate full powers; or

(b) It appears from the practice of the states concerned or from other circumstances that their intention was to consider that person as representing the state for such purposes and to dispense with full powers.

(2) In virtue of their functions and without having to produce full powers, the following are considered as representing their state:

(a) Head of states, head of government and ministers for foreign affairs, for the purpose of performing all acts relating to the conclusion of a treaty;

(b) Heads of diplomatic missions, for the purpose of adopting the text of a treaty between the accrediting state and the state to which they are accredited;

(c) Representatives accredited by the states to an international conference or to an international organization or one of its organs, for the purpose of adopting the text of a treaty in that conference, organization or organ.

On the other hand, article 14 (1) of the *Vienna Convention on the Law of Treaties*, provided that consent to be bound by a treaty expressed by ratification, acceptance or approval. The consent of a state to be bound by a treaty is expressed by ratification when

(a) the treaty provides for such consent to be expressed by means of ratification;

(b) it is otherwise established that the negotiating states were agreed that ratification should be required;

(c) the representative of the state has signed the treaty subject to ratification; or

(d) the intention of the state to sign the treaty subject to ratification appears from the full powers of its representative or was expressed during the negotiation. Article 14(2) of *Vienna Convention on the Law of Treaties* provided that the consent of a state to be bound by a treaty is expressed by acceptance or approval under conditions similar to those applied to ratification.

The legal basis to enter into international treaties

Ratification defines the international act whereby a state indicates its consent to be bound to a treaty if the parties intended to show their consent by such an act. In the case of bilateral treaties, ratification is usually accomplished by exchanging the requisite instruments, while in the case of multilateral treaties the usual procedure is for the depositary to collect the ratifications of all states, keeping all parties informed of the situation. The institution of ratification grants states the necessary time-frame to seek the required approval for the treaty on the domestic level and to enact the necessary legislation to give domestic effect to that treaty.

Most multilateral treaties expressly provide for states to express their consent to be bound by signature subject to ratification, acceptance or approval. Providing for signature subject to ratification allows states time to seek approval for the treaty at the domestic level and to enact any legislation necessary to implement the treaty domestically, prior to undertaking the legal obligations under the treaty at the international level. Once a state has become party to a treaty at the international level, its international responsibility is engaged.

Generally, there is no time limit within which a state is requested to ratify a treaty which it has signed. Upon entry into force of the treaty for a state, that state becomes legally bound under the treaty. Ratification at the international level, which indicates to the international community a state's commitment to undertake the obligations under a treaty, should not be confused with ratification at the national level, which a state may be required to undertake in accordance with its own constitutional provisions before it expresses consent to be bound internationally. Ratification at the national level is inadequate to establish a state's intention to be legally bound at the international level. The required action at the international level, i. e. , the deposit of the instrument of ratification, must also be undertaken.

Some multilateral treaties impose specific limitations or conditions on ratification. For example, when a state deposits with the secretary-general an instrument of ratification, acceptance or approval of, or accession to the Convention on Prohibitions or Restrictions on the Use of Certain Conventional Weapons which may be deemed to be excessively injurious or to have indiscriminate effects, 1980, it must at the same time notify the secretary-general of its consent to be bound by any two or more of the protocols related to the Convention. In the case of the Optional Protocol to the Convention on the Rights of the Child on the Involvement of Children in Armed Conflict, 2000, when a state deposits an instrument of ratification, approval, etc., it must at the same time also deposit a binding declaration under article 3 (2) in which it sets forth the minimum age at which that state will permit voluntary recruitment into its national armed forces and a description of the safeguards that it has adopted to ensure that such recruitment is not forced or coerced.

Provisions of constitution law and other related law in Myanmar

In Myanmar, we practice the dualistic theory approach in the ratification process of international treaties or conventions. According to section 108 of the *Constitution of the Republic of the Union of Myanmar*, the Pyidaungsu Hluttaw (Parliament):

(a) shall give the resolution on matters relating to ratifying, annulling and revoking from international, regional or bilateral treaties, agreements submitted by the president;

(b) shall confer the authority on the president to conclude, annul and revoke any kind of international, regional or bilateral treaties, agreements without the approval of the Pyidaungsu Hluttaw.

On the other hand, section 209 of the *Constitution of the Republic of the Union of Myanmar* provides that the president—

(a) shall enter into, ratify or annul international, regional or bilateral treaties which require the approval of the Pyidaungsu Hluttaw, or revoke from such treaties;

(b) may enter into, ratify or annul international, regional or bilateral treaties which do not require the approval of the Pyidaungsu Hluttaw, or revoke from such treaties.

Moreover, according to section 59 of the law relating to the Pyidaungsu Hluttaw, it provides that the Hluttaw shall decide in respect of the ratification, annulling or withdrawing of the international, regional, bilateral treaties, agreements submitted by the president. And then, section 60 of the law relating to Pyidaungsu Hluttaw, it provides that the Hluttaw may confer power to the president to carry out conclusion, annulling or withdrawing of certain category of treaty or agreement without obtaining the approval of the Hluttaw among the international, regional or bilateral treaties and agreements. The treaties and agreements which shall be submitted by the president for the decision of Hluttaw under section 59 are as contained in schedule I. The treaties and agreements which are entitled to be carried out by the president under section 60 are as contained in schedule II.

Schedule I

The treaties and agreements which are entitled to be carried out with the approval of the Hluttaw:

1. The matter relating to determining the territorial boundary.

2. The matter for ending the war.

3. The matter that requires enacting the domestic law.

4. The matter relating to the defense and security of the Union.

5. The matter of war reparation.

6. The matter undertaking to provide or incur the Union fund except the matters for which fund is sanctioned and determined by the Hluttaw.

7. The matter carried out in accord with any international law.

8. The matters of international conventions and agreements, regional contracts and agreements.

9. The matter relating to tax and revenues.

10. The matter relating to exploration of natural energies, natural resources.

11. The matter relating to the project of electricity.

Schedule II

The treaties and agreements which are entitled to be carried out by the president without the approval of the Hluttaw [Section 61 (b)]:

1. The matter relating to representatives of diplomatic, consular and other affairs.

2. The matter relating to participation in international, regional and bilateral conferences, seminars, meetings, associations and other organizations.

3. The matter relating to international and regional treaties, agreements,

conventions and bilateral agreements.

4. The matter of performance of the dams，embankments and irrigation works managed by the Union.

5. The science and technological research matter.

6. The matter relating to narcotic drugs and psychotropic substances.

7. The matter for construction of the deep-sea port.

8. The matter for construction of the Union roads and bridges.

9. The matter for friendship.

10. The matter of non-alignment.

11. The matter of non-aggression.

12. The matter relating to economy and commerce.

13. The matter relating to conservation of environment.

14. The matter for prevention of biological and chemical weapon.

15. The matter for non-use of the poisonous gas in military operation.

16. The matter for prohibition of the nuclear-test.

17. The matter for granting asylum in the Union.

18. The matter for extradition of offender to the relevant state and request from the relevant state.

19. The matter for prohibition and prevention of hijacking of plane or vessel and committing terrorism.

20. The matter for protection of the victims of war.

21. The matter arising from the main treaty concluded with the approval of the Hluttaw.

22. The matter for borrowing money within the sanctioned stipulation of the Hluttaw.

23. The matter relating to marine and air navigation.

24. The matter of posts，telegraphs，telephone，fax，e-mail，Internet，intranet and similar means of communication.

25. The matter for cultural exchange.

26. The matter of production and distribution of electricity.

27. The matter for providing assistance and cooperation relating to technical know-how and economic expertise.

28. Other matters performed with the approval of the Union Government

except the matters contained in Schedule I.

Therefore, according to above provisions, the treaty and agreement of the international, regional, bilateral treaties, agreements which are listed in Schedule I can be ratified, annulled or withdrawal by the president with the approval of Hluttaw (Parliament). As far as, the listed in schedule II of the treaty and agreement of international, regional, bilateral treaties, agreements can be done by the president without the approval of Hluttaw (Parliament).

Practice of treaty ratification in Myanmar

When a state wishes to ratify, accept, approve or accede to a treaty, it must execute an instrument of ratification, acceptance, approval or accession, signed by one of three specified authorities, namely the head of state, head of government or minister for foreign affairs. There is no mandated form for the instrument, but it must include the following:

(1) Title, date and place of conclusion of the treaty concerned;

(2) Full name and title of the person signing the instrument, i.e., the head of state, head of government or minister for foreign affairs or any other person acting in such a position for the time being or with full powers for that purpose issued by one of the above authorities;

(3) An unambiguous expression of the intent of the government, on behalf of the state, to consider itself bound by the treaty and to undertake faithfully to observe and implement its provisions;

(4) Date and place where the instrument was issued; and

(5) Signature of the head of state, head of government or minister for foreign affairs (the official seal is not adequate) or any other person acting in such a position for the time being or with full powers for that purpose issued by one of the above authorities.

In the case of bilateral treaties, ratification is usually accomplished by exchanging the requisite instruments, while in the case of multilateral treaties the usual procedure is for the depositary to collect the ratifications of all states, keeping all parties informed of the situation. The institution of ratification grants states the necessary time-frame to seek the required approval for the treaty at the domestic level and to enact the necessary legislation to give domestic effect to that treaty. [Arts. 2 (1) (b), 14 (1) and 16, *Vienna Convention on the Law of Treaties* 1969]

In exceptional circumstances of depository, the practice of the UN secretary-general is to accept a letter from a permanent representative to the United Nations, accompanied by a fax of the signed instrument, confirming that the original is "in the post". But if the instrument should not be received within a few days, the secretary-general may refuse to treat the state as having ratified.

The lead ministry or authority for the treaty or convention may wish to undertake the following:

(1) Translation of the treaty or convention and ancillary documents into the national language;

(2) Collection of all relevant documentation;

(3) Survey of the existing legal and institutional framework to determine which legislative and administrative measures need to be taken to implement the treaty or convention;

(4) Cost-benefit analysis of becoming a party to the treaty or convention, including implementation of the measures identified;

(5) Assessment of whether the legal regime established by the treaty or convention would be beneficial to the state.

And then, the lead ministry/authority for the treaty or convention will consult with the Union Attorney General's office and the relevant Ministry. Union Attorney General's office tenders the legal advice upon the treaty or convention and makes the opinion whether the treaty or convention will need to submit the Hluttaw or not. The Union Attorney General's Office also makes the opinion that this treaty or convention sends to cabinet or not. Lastly, the lead authority submits the treaty or convention to the meeting of cabinet which has composed of president, vice president, all of ministers. After passing the meeting of cabinet, the head of state or head of government or foreign minister signs and sends the instrument of ratification or depositary. I have mentioned the form of instrument of ratification and the instrument of full power in below as Annex 1 and 2.

The procedure for participating of treaty or convention in Myanmar

Treaty and convention can be generally separated into two parts; bilateral treaties and multilateral treaties. In the case of bilateral investment treaties, the contracting parties firstly negotiate about the crucial points of treaties which are legal clause, preamble, the co-operation scope, and the responsibility, the dispute settlement mechanism, the term of word, termination period, and modification clause. After negotiation of the contracting parties, they prepare and adopt the internal process to comply with the obligations of bilateral treaties. And then, the lead ministry/ the negotiating ministry sends that to the Union Attorney General's Office and other relevant ministry to get legal advice and to prepare the obligation of bilateral treaties. The Union Attorney General's Office tenders the legal advice upon the important point of this bilateral treaties and gives the advisory opinions whether this treaty need to submit the Hluttaw's approval or not and whether this treaty to present the cabinet meeting. Mostly, the lead ministry always does next procedure to comply with the advisory opinion of the Union Attorney General's Office. And then, the lead ministry renegotiates about the variance between them. The contracting parties make the final draft of bilateral treaty. After making the final draft, the lead ministry and other contracting party sign this bilateral treaty. In the arena of the investment, Myanmar has signed more than 10 bilateral investment treaties. Among them, most of the treaties expired but some has been enforcing until.

In another kind of multilateral treaty, there are generally classified two kinds of multilateral treaties such as United Nations multilateral treaties, ASEAN multilateral treaties. In case of multilateral treaty, the founder member firstly drafts the treaty and then negotiates between them. To become a party in such treaties is the signing of that treaty. Most of multilateral treaties contain signature provisions indicating the place of signature, date of opening for signature, period of signature, etc. Such treaties also list the methods by which a signatory state can become party to them, e. g. , by ratification, acceptance, approval or accession.

Multilateral treaties often provide that they will be open for signature only until a specified date, after which signature will no longer be possible. Once a treaty is closed for signature, a state may generally become a party to it by means of accession. Some multilateral treaties are open for signature indefinitely. A signing state does not undertake positive legal obligations under the treaty upon signature. However, signature indicates the state's intention to take steps to express its consent to be bound by the treaty at a later date. Signature also creates an obligation, in the period between signature and ratification, acceptance or approval, to refrain in good faith from acts that would defeat.

Some treaties provide that states can express their consent to be legally bound solely upon signature. This method is most commonly used in bilateral treaties and rarely used for multilateral treaties. In the latter case, the entry into force provision of the treaty expressly provides that the treaty will enter into force upon signature by a given number of states. Of the treaties deposited with the secretary-general, this method is most commonly used in certain treaties negotiated under the auspices of the Economic Commission for Europe, e. g. , article 4(3) of the *Agreement concerning the Adoption of Uniform Conditions for Periodical Technical Inspections of Wheeled Vehicles and the Reciprocal Recognition of Such Inspections*, 1997. Countries may become contracting parties to the agreement: by signing it without reservation to ratification; by ratifying it after signing it subject to ratification or by acceding to it. Myanmar acceded to the *Vienna Convention on the Law of Treaties* in 1998. So, all of treaties processes are in line with this convention.

Conclusion

All formulations of the rule of the mode of entry into force of treaties make the issue dependent in the first place upon evidence of the intentions of the parties. The examination of the present practice of states has shown that whenever states intend to bring treaties into force by some procedure other than signature, their intention is evidenced by express provisions or by cogent implication. The same applies usually to cases where states intend to bring treaties into force by signature. The treaties in which the intentions of the parties as to the mode of entry into force are not thus evidenced are not numerous; but they cannot all be said to be of "minor importance". They are not all in the form of exchanges of notes, nor do they all go under the names of "modus vivendi", "arrangement", or "additional protocol". Neither are they all concluded without the use of formal full powers. What is common to these treaties is that—almost without exception the parties intended to become bound by signature. The fact that intention has not been expressed in any way is only explained by the existence of a general belief among those who concluded these treaties that, in the absence of express or clearly implied intentions to the contrary, treaties—by virtue of a rule of international law—enter into force by signature.

In multilateral treaties, the consensus between the parties may be established and expressed by the traditional procedure of deposits of instruments of ratification following signature. But it may equally well be evidenced simply by deposits of instruments of ratifications. There is a certain interval between the signature of the treaty and the exchange of the instruments of ratification. It is this interval that is often referred to as the primary purpose of the procedure of ratification. It enables the competent executive authorities of the states to undertake a "fresh examination" of a treaty, to receive the advice of government departments and others concerned, and, what is most important, to submit the treaty to the legislature for approval, if this be required under the constitutional law or practice of the state.

Annex. 1

MODEL INSTRUMENT OF FULL POWERS

(To be signed by the Head of State，Head of Government or Minister for Foreign Affairs) FULL POWERS _____ I，[name and title of the Head of State，Head of Government or Minister for Foreign Affairs]，HEREBY AUTHORIZE [name and title] to [sign* ① , ratify, denounce, effect the following declaration in respect of，etc.] the [title and date of treaty，convention，agreement，etc.] on behalf of the Government of [name of State]. Done at [place] on [date].

[Signature]

_____

Annex. 2

MODEL INSTRUMENT OF RATIFICATION ,ACCEPTANCE OR APPROVAL

(To be signed by the Head of State，Head of Government or Minister for Foreign Affairs) [RATIFICATION /ACCEPTANCE/APPROVAL] _____ WHEREAS the [title of treaty，convention，agreement，etc.] was [concluded，adopted，opened for signature，etc.] at [place] on [date]，AND WHEREAS the said [treaty，convention，agreement，etc.] has been signed on behalf of the Government of [name of State] on [date]，NOW THEREFORE I，[name and title of the Head of State，Head of Government or Minister for Foreign Affairs] declare that the Government of [name of State]，having considered the above-mentioned [treaty，convention，agreement，etc.]，[ratifies，accepts，approves] the same and un-

---

① Subject to the provisions of the treaty，one of the following alternatives is to be chosen：[subject to ratification] or [without reservation as to ratification].

Reservations made upon signature must be authorized by the full powers granted to the signatory.

dertakes faithfully to perform and carry out the stipulations therein contained. IN WITNESS WHEREOF, I have signed this instrument of [ratification, acceptance, and approval] at [place] on [date].

[Signature]

References

- L. Oppenheim, International Law: A Treaties, Vol. I, 8th edition, 1966.
- The Constitution of the Republic of the Union of Myanmar, 2008.
- The Law Relating to the Pyidaungsu Hluttaw(Parliament),2011.
- Treaty Handbook, United Nations, 2012.
- Vienna Convention on the Law of Treaties, 1969.

缅甸条约批准程序

Aung Ye Lwin*
编译　孟　真**

摘要：现代国家可以选择批准或签署并使条约生效,大多数现代条约都规定了条约的生效程序。批准是对条约的确认,并为缔约国规定的义务。签字只表明签署国有意受条约约束。本文首先分析了条约批准在一般国际法中的概念和作用,特别是维也纳条约法公约的规定。其次,介绍了条约在缅甸宪法中生效的具体规定,缅甸采用的是条约批准生效模式。

关键词：批准,确认,签订意图

本文旨在考虑条约批准在现代国家实践中的功能,国家自主选择条约生效程序。因此,毫无疑问地,如果一份国际条约明确规定条约经签署、批准或其他行为生效,那么该法定程序必须被遵循。同样,毫无疑问地,在缔约方默示应通过特殊程序使条约生效的情况下,该默示效力如明示条款。在大部分现代条约中,要么明确规定要么默示规定条约生效程序。

批准的概念与功能

批准是指缔约方对于其加入的国际条约的最终确认。尽管被授权代表表示一致时条约可视为签署,但是一般来说,直到国家批准该条约后该条约才具有约束力。只要条约未被批准,即使已签署该条约,该条约也具有效力上的瑕疵。有主张称,条约不能未经通知而具有约束力,因此,批准才体现了缔约国意思表示一致,这才是真正签订条约。

他们主张,未经批准条约不视为已缔结,仅仅是双方达成缔结条约的提议

---

*　西南政法大学国际法学院博士生/缅甸联邦最高检检察官。
**　西南政法大学 2014 级本科法学专业实务人才实验班。

被采纳。但此观点与实践不符。对于被授权代表,他们在缔结的条约上签字即代表缔结意图。一般来说,政府颁布与缔结条约有关的法案即意味着相互意思表示一致。他们的保留意见由代表提出,其后再批准。在这种情况下,通过考虑是否批准来达成意思一致。这就是条约不能部分批准的原因,未经改变的条约也可能通过批准,条约可经实行而默示批准,生效日期往往追溯至代表签署之日,而不是签署后批准之日,这种未经批准的条约与经过批准的条约在本质上并没有不同。

并且,缔约方没有法定义务批准条约,而且也有理由解释为什么签署条约不能仅仅视为一个礼节。在签署条约过程中,缔约国家会对重要的程序性条款产生影响,如非缔约国的加入、条款的保留、生效条件等等。同样地,根据普遍接受的观点,即使签署国未批准条约,其依然可以合法地行使反对其他任何想加入条约的国家提出的附加保留的权利。一般认为批准是对条约的确认,区别于签署表示缔约方的意见一致。这个观点可能不准确。它的间接含义是暗示上述行为与实践相反并且使签署的法律价值与影响降低。

批准的必要条件

原则上批准不总是必要的。虽然根据没有明文规定的国际习惯法的规定,条约通常需要批准,但也存在除外条款。对于这种由有缔约能力的国家工作人员缔结的条约,无须批准,只要未超过工作人员职权范围即为有效。进一步讲,只要宪法没有对国家元首的相关权利进行限制,国家元首亲自签署的条约无须批准。

还存在这样一种情况,缔约方若需要立即执行条约,该条约可未经批准具有约束力。实践中免除批准程序并明确规定条约经签署生效已成为条约缔结程序的显著特点。这尤其适用于约占比三分之一国际协定的换文。然而,只有代表在被充分授权的情况下,明示拒绝履行批准才是有效的。未经特别授权的代表豁免批准程序,其所作的决定不代表国家行为。

有人主张除这些带有条约或公约的合同外,批准只在规定的情况下才需要,但是这个确认非常广泛。若所有的国际合同都是合同,那么条约应作广义上的解释,特殊合同适用的标题不能决定其是否需要批准,应由合同的内容决定。因此,议定书或宣言或者换文,除特别明文规定外,对于仅仅增加次要的观点以及记录的条款解释无须批准。这同样适用于无论怎样被命名的临时协定。然而,除了这些特殊情况,除非包含相反条款,无论怎样被命名,条约需经批准生效。

批准的形式

没有国际法规定批准的必要形式。批准应根据规定进行。国家未经批准实行条约视为默示批准。批准一般以国家元首或外交部签署文件的形式进行。一般起草和缔约方数量相等的文件,并在缔约方间交换。有时整个条约会被批准文件全部列举,但是有时只列举标题、序言、日期和签字国代表既然批准只是对存在条约的确认,那么对于文件批准最重要的要求就是需要清楚地提及条约以及不弄错条约。因此,引用的标题、序言、日期与代表名称对于批准是必备要件。

谁能影响批准

行使国家缔约权力的机构可以影响批准。这些机构通常是国家元首或其政府首脑,但他们可以根据某些国家的国内法,将其领土的某些部分的批准权下放给其他代表。因此,印度总督有权以大英帝国王和印度皇帝的名义批准与某些亚洲君主达成的条约。

如果一个国家的元首批准了一个条约,但是之前还没有履行必要的宪法要求(例如,如果一个条约没有得到该州议会的批准),那么这样的批准是有效还是无效的呢?当国家元首滥用权力时,一般来说,条约对该国无约束力。

根据国际法,国家有能力达成协议,但由于国家不同于可识别的人,用来确保国家代表享有执行有关条约实权的特定原则已发展起来。这些人必须根据1969年《维也纳条约法公约》第7条享有"全权"才可以代表其国家。"全权"是指有其国家当局证明其身份的文件。

1969年《维也纳条约法公约》第7条规定如下:

(1)任一人员如有下列情况之一,视为代表一国议定或认证条约约文或表示该国承受条约拘束之同意:

(a)出具适当之全权证书;或

(b)由于有关国家之惯例或由于其他情况可见其此等国家之意思系认为该人员为此事代表该国而可免除全权证书。

(2)下列人员由于所任职务无须出具全权证书,视为代表其国家:

(a)国家元首、政府首长及外交部长,为实施关于缔结条约之一切行为;

(b)使馆馆长为议定派遣国与驻在国间条约约文;

(c)国家派往国际会议或派驻国际组织或该国际组织一机关之代表,为议定在该会议组织或机关内议定之条约约文。

《维也纳条约法公约》第14(1)条规定,以批准接受或赞同表示承受条约约束之同意。遇有下列情形之一,一国承受条约拘束之同意,以批准表示之

条约规定以批准方式表示同意;

另经确定谈判国协议需要批准;

该国代表已对条约作须经批准之签署;或

该国对条约作须经批准之签署之意思可见诸其代表所奉之全权证书,或已于谈判时有此表示。《维也纳条约法公约》第14(2)条规定,一个承受条约拘束之同意以接受或赞同方式表示者,其条件与适用于批准者同。

加入国际条约的法律基础

批准定义了一项国际行为,即当事各方表示同意通过此种行为表明其接受条约约束的国际行为。就双边条约而言,批准通常通过交换必要的文书来实现;而对于多边条约而言,通常的程序是由保管方收集所有国家的批准书,并向所有缔约方通报情况。该批准制度给予缔约方必要的时间,以便其在国内履行必要批准程序,并进行必要的立法以使该条约具有国内效力。

大多数多边条约明确规定各国同意以签字形式表示批准、接受或核准条约。以签字形式表示批准给各国充分时间在国内批准条约,并在承担国际条约所规定的法律义务之前,给各国时间在国内进行执行条约必要的立法工作。一旦一个国家成为条约的缔约方,其国际责任即产生。

一般而言,一个国家批准其签署条约的时间不限。条约对一国生效后,该国就受到条约的约束。向国际社会表明国家承诺履行条约义务的国际一级的批准不应与国家一级的批准相混淆,后者把国家可能需要根据其宪法规定进行批准表示其同意受到国际约束。国家一级的批准不足以表明该国愿在国际上受法律约束的意图,还必须采取国际一级的必要行动,即交存批准书。

一些多边条约对批准规定特定的限制或条件。例如,当长交存一份批准书,接受或核准或加入"禁止或限制使用具杀滥伤作用的常规武器公约"(1980),它必须同时通知秘书"公约"有关的两项或多项议定书的约束。就2000年"关于儿问题的儿童权利公约任择议定书"而言,当一个国家交存批准书或核准书等时,它必须同时将根据第3条第(2)款的规定,划定自愿入伍的最低年龄,并说

明其采取的安全保障措施是为了保障征员，不是强制的。

缅甸宪法和其他相关法律的规定

在缅甸，批准国际条约或公约的程序采用二元论学说。根据《缅甸共和国宪法》第 108 条，Pyidaungsu Hluttaw（议会）：

（a）应就批准、废除和撤销国际、区域或双边条约，总统提交的协定，提出决议；

（b）授权主席未经 Pyitaungsu Hluttaw 批准，缔结、废除或撤销任何国际、区域或双边条约协议。

另一方面，《缅甸共和国宪法》第 209 节规定，总统——

（a）应缔结、批准或废除需要 Pyidaungsu Hluttaw 批准的国际、区域或双边条约，或撤销这些条约；

（b）可以缔结、批准或废除不需要 Pyidaungsu Hluttaw 批准的国际、区域或双边条约，或者撤销这些条约。

此外，根据关于 Pyidaungsu Hluttaw 的法律第 59 条，Hluttaw 应就批准、取消或撤回总统提交的国际、区域或双边条约和协定作出决定。然后，与 Pyidaungsu Hluttaw 有关的法律第 60 条规定，Hluttaw 可授权总统未经议会同意情况下，缔结、取消或撤回某些类别的条约或协议。总统根据第 59 条提交 Hluttaw 决定的条约和协议载于附表一。有权由总统根据第 60 条实行的条约和协定载于附表二。

附表一

经 Hluttaw 批准可施行的条约和协议：

1. 有关确定领土边界的事宜。

2. 结束战争的问题。

3. 需要制定国内法的事宜。

4. 有关国家防卫和安全的问题。

5. 战争赔款问题。

6. 承诺提供国家资金或国家招商的事项，但基金需由 Hluttaw 批准和决定的除外。

7. 根据国际法实施的事宜。

8.有关国际公约和协定、区域合同和协议的事项。

9.有关税收和收入的问题。

10.有关探索自然能源、自然资源的问题。

11.有关电力的事宜。

附表二

未经 Hluttaw［第 61(b)条］批准,总统有权执行的条约和协定:

1.与外交、领事和其他事务代表有关的事项。

2.涉及参加国际、区域和双边会议、研讨会、峰会、协会和其他组织的事宜。

3.有关国际或区域条约、协定、公约和双边协定的事项。

4.由国家管理的水坝、堤坝和水利工程问题。

5.科学技术研究事项。

6.有关麻醉药品和精神药物的问题。

7.深海港口建设事宜。

8.国家道路和桥梁建设事宜。

9.邦交事宜。

10.不结盟的问题。

11.不侵略事宜。

12.有关经济和商业的问题。

13.有关环境保护的事宜。

14.预防生化武器的事宜。

15.在军事行动中不使用有毒气的问题。

16.禁止核试验的问题。

17.给予国家庇护的问题。

18.向有关国家引渡罪犯的事项和有关国家请求引渡事宜。

19.关于禁止和防止劫机、航空器以及恐怖主义的事宜。

20.关于保护战争受难者的问题。

21.需 Hluttaw 批准的条约相关事项。

22.在 Hluttaw 规定的制裁范围内资金借贷事宜。

23.有关海洋和空中航行的事宜。

24.邮寄、电报、电话、传真、电子邮件、互联网、内联网和类似通信方式事宜。

25. 文化交流的问题。

26. 发电和分配问题。

27. 提供关键技术和经济知识援助与合作的事宜。

28. 除附表一所载事项外,国家政府批准的其他事项。

因此,根据上述规定,附表一所列的国际、区域、双边条约或协定可经议会批准,由总统批准、撤销或由撤回。就附表二所列的国际、区域、双边条约或协议而言,可由总统在未经 Hluttaw(议会)批准的情况下完成。

缅甸条约批准的实践

当一个国家希望批准、接受、赞同或加入条约时,必须由三个特定国家领导人之一签署批准书、接受书、核准书或加入书,这三个特定国家领导人为国家元首、政府首脑或外交部长。该文书没有规定的格式,但必须包含以下内容:

1. 有关条约的标题、日期和缔结地;

2. 签署该文书的人的全名和头衔,如国家元首、政府首脑或外交部长或任何其他当时担任此职位的人或由上述人员授予全权证书的人;

3. 国家代表明确表示受条约约束,并忠实地遵守和执行其条款;

4. 文书签发的日期和地点;和

5. 国家元首、政府首脑或外交部长(官方印章不可以)或任何其他当时担任类似职位或由上述人员授予全权证书的人的签字。

就双边条约而言,批准通常通过交换必要文书来实现,而对多边条约,通常的程序是由保管人收集所有国家的批准书,并向所有当事方通报情况。批准制度规定了必要的时限,以便缔约国在国内进行批准程序,并进行必要的立法以使该条约具有国内效力。[1969 年《维也纳条约法公约》第二(1)(b)条、第 14(1)条和第 16 条]

在特殊情况下,联合国秘书长可接受常驻联合国代表的来信,来信可附已签署文书的传真,确认原件是"在该文件中"。但是,如果在几天内未能收到文书,秘书长可能拒绝将该国视为已经批准。

条约或公约的主要部门或权力机构可能希望进行以下工作:

(1)将条约或公约及其辅助文件翻译成本国语言;

(2)收集所有相关文件;

(3)调查现有法律和体制框架,以确定需要采取哪些立法和行政措施来执行条约或公约；

　　(4)成为条约或公约缔约方的成本效益分析,包括已确定措施的实施；

　　(5)评估条约或公约确立的法律制度是否有利于国家。

　　然后,条约或公约的主管部门/权力机构将与国家司法部长办公室和相关部门进行磋商。国家司法部长办公室就条约或公约征求法律意见,并就该条约或公约是否需要提交 Hluttaw 发表意见。国家司法部长办公室也应对该条约或公约是否送交内阁发表意见。最后,主要机构将条约或公约提交给由总统、副总统、各部长组成的内阁会议。通过内阁会议后,国家元首或政府首脑或外交部长签署并发送批准书至保管方。笔者将在附件一和附件二中展示批准书和全权证书的格式。

缅甸缔结条约或公约的程序

　　条约和公约一般可分为两种:双边条约和多边条约。就双边投资协定而言,缔约方首先就法律条款、序言、合作范围和责任、争端解决机制、终止期等关键条款进行谈判,修改条款。缔约方协商后,他们根据内部程序履行双边条约。然后,主要部门/谈判部门向国家司法部长办公室和其他相关部门提供法律意见,并拟定双边条约的义务。国家司法部长就这一双边条约的关键内容发表法律意见,并就该条约是否需要提交 Hluttaw 批准以及该条约是否提交内阁会议发表意见。大多数情况下,主管部门总是会执行下一个程序来遵守国家司法部长办公室的建议。然后,主管部门就它们之间的分歧重新谈判。缔约方提出双边条约的最终草案。最终草案定稿后,主管部门和其他缔约方签署双边条约。在投资领域,缅甸已签署 10 多个双边投资条约。其中大部分条约已经过期,但有些至今仍有效。

　　对于多边条约,通常分为两类,如联合国多边条约、东盟多边条约。对于多边条约,发起国首先起草条约然后各国进行协商。签署该条约的国家为缔约方。大多数多边条约包括签署条款,明确签字地点、签署日期、签署期限等。这些条约还列出签字国可以成为缔约国的方式,如批准、接受、核准或加入。

　　多边条约通常会规定,只有在规定日期之前才可以签字,改日后再签名将无效。一旦条约签署完毕,其他国家通常可以通过加入方式加入条约。一些多边条约无限期地开放签署。签字国在签署协议时不承担正式的法律义务。但是,签署表明该国在签署后同意受条约的约束。签署还在签署后批准、接受或核准前的期间创建一项义务,以避免可能失败的善意行为。

一些条约规定,各国可以只通过签署便受条约约束。这种方式在双边条约中最为常用,很少用于多边条约。在后一种情况下,条约中有关条约生效的条款明确规定,条约将在一定数目的国家签署后生效。在交存秘书长的条约中,这种方式最常用于由欧洲经济委员会主持谈判的某些条约,如"关于采用定期技术检查轮式车辆统一标准的协定"第4(3)条,以及相互承认此类检查。各国可以成为协议的缔约方:无保留地签署批准、在签署之后批准或者同意加入。缅甸于1998年加入了维也纳条约法公约。所以,所有条约进程都符合这个公约。

结　论

条约生效方式首先依赖于证实当事方意图的证据。对各国现行做法的研究表明,只要国家打算通过签名以外的某种程序使条约生效,其意图就可以通过明示条款或令人信服的暗示来证明。这同样适用于意图通过签字使条约生效的情况。双方关于生效方式约定不明确的条约并不多;但他们不能说都是"次要的"。它们并不是全部以交换书的形式出现,也不是全部以"临时协议""安排"或"附加议定书"为名。如果没有正式的全权证书,它们也不会缔结。这些条约的共同之处在于——几乎毫无例外,当事方打算受到签名的约束。意图没有以任何方式表现的情况只能存在于这些条约缔结者拥有普遍原则:在没有与明确表示或明确暗示相反的意图的情况下,条约根据国际法通过签字生效。

在多边条约中,各方之间的协商一致可以通过签署后交存批准书的传统程序来确定和表达。但同样也可以简单地通过批准书的存放来证明。条约的签署与交换批准书之间有一段时间间隔。正是这个间隔期间经常被认为是批准程序的首要目的。它使各国行政主管部门能够对条约进行"新鲜审查",接受政府部门和其他有关方面的意见,并且最重要的是将条约提交立法机关批准,如果这是宪法或国家惯例要求的话。

附件一

全权证书的批准书示范文书

(由国家元首、政府首脑或外交部长签署)全权证书 _____ ,(国家元首、政府首脑或外交部长的姓名和职务名称),特此授权(姓名和职务)代表(国家名称)的政府签署 * [1],批准,谴责,实施下列关于(⋯⋯的)条约、公约、协定等)的声明。于(日期)(地点)完成。

签　名

附件二

批准、接受或核准的示范文书

(由国家元首、政府首脑或外交部长签署)[批准/接受/核准] _____ 鉴于(条约,公约,协定等的标题)于(日期)在(地点)缔结、接受、开放签署,并鉴于上述(条约,公约,协定等)是于(日期)由代表(国家名称)的政府签署的,因此,(国家元首、政府首脑或外交部长的名字和头衔)宣布(国名)政府在审议了上述(条约、公约、协定等)后(批准、接受、认可)并忠实履行其规定。为证实,我于(日期)在(地点)签署了[批准、接受和核准]书。

签　名

Comparison the Functions of the Public Prosecutors between the Republic of the Union of Myanmar and the People's Republic of China

Ei Khine Zin Aung[*]

Abstract：As the legal systems of the Republic of the Union of Myanmar and the People's Republic of China are different，the duties and powers of the public prosecutors and public procurators are not the same. The article describes the prosecutors of the two countries and their highest governing bodies to bring out the central content of this article：namely introducing the different responsibilities and functions of prosecutors in different legal institutions and legal procedures of Myanmar and China.

Keywords：The public prosecutor，Responsibility，Function

Introduction

The prosecutor is the chief legal representative of the prosecution in countries with either Common Law legal system or Civil Law legal system. In Common Law jurisdiction，they usually only involved in a criminal case. They are typically employed by an office of the government. In Civil law jurisdiction，they are typically civil servants who possess a university degree in

---

* Ei Khine Zin Aung，Doctoral Student of School of International Law of SWUPL/Union Attorney General's Office，Staff officer，Building 25, Nay Pyi Taw，Myanmar，E-mail：ekza86 @ gmail. com.

law, and additional training in the administration of justice. In this Article,
I focus on the duties and functions of public prosecutor in Myanmar and the
duties and functions of public procurator in China.

Myanmar legal system is a unique system and partly belong to English
Common Law Legal System. In the Republic of China, Law is mainly a Civil
Law System. As the legal systems of these two countries are different, the
duties and powers of the public prosecutors and public procurators are not
the same. A public procurator is a position in the People's Republic of
China, analogous to both detective and public prosecutor. Although there
are different duties and powers between them, they have the same duty. It
is that they carry out to safeguard the Constitution and to protest the
interest of the public in their country. In this article, I will present the
different duties and powers of the public prosecutors and public procurators
in both.

Historical background

The history of public prosecutor in Myanmar is long. The public
prosecutor came up with together the Union Attorney General's Office. So
firstly the history of Union Attorney General's Office should be observed.
Since the end of the First Anglo-Myanmar War in 1826, the British
introduced a legal system modified with the Common Law legal system for
criminal and civil cases in Myanmar. The Government Advocate General,
Government Advocate and Public Prosecutor are appointed to conduct case
for and on behalf of the Government in both criminal and civil cases.

When Myanmar regained her independence in 1948, the office of the
Attorney General was constituted under the Attorney General of the Union
Act, 1948 where an Attorney General, Government Advocates and legal
draftsmen were appointed.

In 1962, when the Revolutionary Council took over the state
responsibilities, an Attorney General was appointed on 7th March, 1962
under the Declaration No15. His main functions were to appear for and on
behalf of the Government in civil and criminal cases and to tender legal

advice to the Revolutionary Council and the Government.

On 15th March, 1972, Declaration No. 97 was issued under which the existing machinery was abolished and a new machinery was substituted. After that, the Ministry of Justice was formed by Notification No. 2 on 31st March, 1972. There emerged a new Attorney General's Office which was responsible for the prosecution, tendering legal advice, legislative drafting and legal translation.

When the Socialist Republic of the Union of Myanmar came into existence under the 1974 Constitution, the Council of People's Attorney swhich was formed by the Pyithu Hluttaw also formed respective State/ Divisional and Township law offices. To supervise these law offices, the Central Law Office was established and substituted in the place of the Attorney General's Office.

When the tate Law and Order Restoration Council took over the responsibilities of the State in 1988, the Attorney General Law was promulgated on 26th September, 1988. This Law is still apply to 26th February, 2001. The Attorney General Law, 2001 was promulgated. This law was amended on 2nd January, 2003.

Currently, the Constitution of the Republic of the Union of Myanmar has been adopted by the Referendum on 29th May, 2008. The Attorney General of the Union Law was promulgated in accord with section 443 of the Constitution of the Republic of the Union of Myanmar on 28th October, 2010. The Union Attorney General has appointed under section 237(a) of the Constitution of the Republic of the Union of Myanmar 2008 and section 5 of the Attorney General of the Union Law, 2010 by the President with the approval of Pyidaungsu Hluttaw (the Parliament).

Deputy Attorney General (DAG) has also appointed under Section 239 (a) of the Constitution of the Republic of the Union of Myanmar 2008 and Section 6 of the Attorney General of the Union Law, 2010 by the President. Term of the Office of UAG and DAG is the same as that of the President.

At present, Myanmar public prosecutor service is a government institution governed by the Attorney General of the Union (AGU). The Attorney General of the Union (AGU) published the Attorney General

Rules with the consent of the Union Government under section 41(a) of the Attorney General Law by Declaration No 8/2016 on 7th January, 2016. Under this Rule, public prosecutor means the law officer who is appointed by the Attorney General or the person who is particularly given the duty by the Attorney General. Moreover, public prosecutor can conduct on behalf of the Attorney General or various law office in various levels of the Courts or the Constitutional Tribunal or the Election Tribunal or any tribunal which is organized by any law.

When the British annexed Myanmar, Myanmar exercised the common law legal system. Since that colonies time, the role of Union Attorney General's Office had emerged. At that time, the role of public prosecutors play in criminal case and civil case to conduct on behalf of the Government. They are called government lawyers. After independent, public prosecutors had to conduct government lawyer as well as legal draftsman. In revolutionary council time, the public prosecutors had conducted on behalf of government in civil and criminal case and then they conduct tendering legal advice, legislative drafting and legal translation. From the time Myanmar exercise the democracy system in 2010, public prosecutors do not need to conduct the legislative drafting. They have conducted vetting the legal draft, translating the laws, rules, regulation, etc, tendering legal advice and prosecution. The public prosecutors' duty which has never been changed is the prosecution which is the main duty of public prosecutor.

The Chinese legal system is a socialist system of law based primarily on the Civil Law model. Procuratorial system is exercised in Civil law inquisitorial rather than common law adversarial system. China uses a procuratorial system. The office of a procurator is called a procuracy or procuratorate. The terms are public procurator from Latin and originate with the procurators of the Roman Empire.

After the People's Republic of China (PRC) was founded in 1949 by the Chinese Communist Party (CCP), the Organic Law of the Central People's Government stipulated the establishment, status, functions and powers of the prouratorates, which was the legal basis of the system of procuratorates in the new China. Organic Law of the People's Procuratorate of the People's

Republic of China was adopted at the Second Session of the Fifth National People's Congress on July 1，1979，promulgated by Order No. 4 of the Chairman of the Standing Committee of the National People's Congress on July 5，1979 and effective as of January 1，1980；amended according to the Decision on the Revision of the Organic Law of the People's Procuratorates of the People's Republic of China adopted at the Second Meeting of the Standing Committee of the Sixth National People's Congress on September 2，1983.

In China，the Constitution has been promulgated in three times. The current Constitution of the PRC was enacted in 1982. From Article129 to Article 135，Section 7 of these Constitution provided about the people's procuratorates.

Public Procurators Law of the People's Republic of China was promulgated on 28th February，1995 and amended on 30th June，2001. The Supreme People's Procuratorate is the highest state organ for legal supervision，which includes functions of both bringing criminal prosecutions and ensuring that government agencies act in accordance with the law. A public procurator shall be appointed or removed from the post in accordance with the limit of authority for，and procedures of，appointment or removal as prescribed by the Constitution and laws.

Since 1949，China had exercised the procuratorate system. The people's procuratorates are the Chinese criminal prosecution authorities. They are not part of the administrative part of the government. They are a branch of its own. Another additional task of the people's procuratorates is the legal supervision.

The organization of the Union Attorney General's Office(UAGO)

The Union Attorney General's Office（UAGO）is an organization composed principally of law officers or public prosecutors acting as government lawyers. The UAGO is currently organized as the Legislative Vetting Department，the Legal Advice Department，the Prosecution Department，the Administration Department and the Head Office. And

then, the UAGO is constituted with 14 Region and State Advocate General
Offices, 72 District Law Offices and 330 Township Law Offices. The public
prosecutor usually begin their careers in one or more of our 330 township
office and then move to one of 72 district offices, 14 region and state offices
and sometimes head offices.

The organization of the Supreme People's Procuratorate

The Supreme People's Procuratorate (SPP) shall establish a number of
procuratorial departments and professional agencies as needed. The SPP
consists of 15 functional departments as well as a political work department,
a retiree bureau and five subordinate institutions.

The functional departments include the general affairs office,
investigation supervision department, prosecution department, anti-
embezzlement and bribery administration, negligence of duty and rights infringement prosecution department, prison and detention department, civil
and administration department, reporting and charges prosecution
department (also known as the Reporting and Charges Center of the SPP),
criminal appeals department, railway transportation prosecution
department, department for the prevention of crimes committed by taking
advantage of one's positions, law and policy research office, supervision
bureau, foreign affairs bureau, planning, finance and equipment bureau.

The political work department itself consists of officers of publicity, education and training as well as the general affairs office.

Subordinate institutions refer to the organ service center, the
Procuratorate Daily, China Procuratorate Publishing House, procuratorate
technology information research center, procuratorate theory research
institute and the state procurators college.

The people procuratorate at various local levels shall be divided as
people procuratorte of provinces, autonomous regions and municipalities
directly under the central government, people procuratorate of counties,
cities, autonomous counties, municipal districts. People procuratorate at the
provincial or county level may set up people procuratorate as their agencies

in industrial and mining area, agricultural reclamation areas, forest zones, etc.

The procurator-General shall be elected and removed by the National People Congress. Deputy Procurator-General, a member of the Procuratorial committee, procurators of the supreme people procuratorate shall be appointed and removed by the standing committee of the National People Congress upon the recommendation of the Procurator-General. People Procuratorate of all levels shall each have chief procurator, a number of deputy chief procurators and procurators. The chief procurators of the people's procuratorates of provinces, autonomous regions, and municipalities directly under the Central Government and their branches shall be elected and removed by the people's congresses. Deputy Chief Procurator, a member of procuratorial committee and procurators at this level shall be appointed and removed by the standing committee of the people congress of corresponding levels upon the recommendation of Chief Procurator. The chief procurators of people's procuratorates of autonomous prefectures, cities directly under the provincial governments, counties, cities and municipal districts shall be elected and removed by the people's congresses at corresponding levels. The deputy chief procurators, members of procuratorial committees and procurators shall be appointed and removed by the standing committees of the people's congresses at corresponding levels upon the recommendation of the chief procurators. People's procuratorates at all levels shall have a number of assistant procurators and clerks. The assistant procurators and clerks shall be appointed and removed by the chief procurators of people's procuratorates at all levels.

Duties and Powers of the Public Prosecutor in Myanmar

The Union Attorney General's office serve the Government of Myanmar's main legal advisory body. This Office is led by the Union Attorney General of Myanmar. The Attorney General is Myanmar's most powerful legal officer as a member of executive. The Attorney General provides legal advice to the President and the Hluttaw, analyses

international treaties, drafts and amends laws, and represent the
government in judicial proceedings. The Attorney General also directs the
public prosecutors' office and ensures that cabinet actions are legally valid,
in line with the constitution and international law. The Attorney General is
responsible to the President of the Union. The Attorney General is nominated by
the president and is elected by the Hluttaw. The public prosecutors in the various
levels of law offices under the Office of the Attorney-General of the Union shall
carry out the functions and duties delegated by the Attorney-General of the Union
in accord with the stipulations.

Public prosecutors serving in the Union Attorney General's Office have
to move to one office to another office around the country. Sometimes they
serve in Head Office. During the period of serving in Head office, they have
to conduct the duty of department which they serve in. There are four departments in Head office.

In department 1, the Legislative vetting department of UAGO, there
are four divisions- called legislative vetting and advising division, rules, regulations, orders and directives vetting and advising division, legal
translation and vetting division and constitutional division.

The duties and functions of public prosecutors serving in legislative
vetting and advising division are to advice and vet draft laws which are sent
to the Union Attorney General's Office in order to amend, substitute, repeal
and promulgate necessary new laws. Draft laws advised by the Union
Attorney General's Office are of four types, namely; draft law amending the
existing law, draft law substituting the existing law, draft law repealing the
existing law and the new draft law. Situation of consideration is different according to the nature of various draft laws and the Union Attorney General's
Office has to observe the content of the relevant law thoroughly. Advising
the draft laws is based on whether they are in conformity with the
constitution or whether they are contrary to the existing laws or whether
they are in conformity with the time or not. Moreover, if the provisions
contained in the draft law are in connection with international conventions
and agreements, the Union Attorney General's Office vets whether they are
in conformity with these conventions and agreements or not. If a draft law is

in connection with international organizations, necessary coordination should be made with these organizations.

The duties and functions of public prosecutors serving in rules, regulations, orders and directives vetting and advising division are to vets rules, regulations, by-laws, orders, notifications, directives and procedures drafted for the implementation of the laws under their administration by the relevant government departments and organizations based on the provisions of the relevant law. If necessary public prosecutor advises and reply to add and modify.

The duties and functions of public prosecutors serving in legal translation and vetting division are to translate Myanmar Laws into English for the awareness of foreign investors including foreigners. Moreover, they translate rules, procedures, ordinances, declarations, notifications, orders and directives to be issued by the Union Government into English when so assigned. Treaties of International Conventions and Agreements to be concluded with any foreign State or with any regional organization translated from Myanmar to English or vice versa are also vetted when so requested by the relevant government department and organization.

The duties and functions of public prosecutors serving in constitutional division are to advice with the guidance of Attorney General of the Union when the President of the Union or the President of Hluttaw or Union level organization requests legal advice in respect of constitutional affairs. They conduct in accordance with the guidance of Attorney General to submit the special condition in relevant with legal affair to the meeting of Hluttaw. They do research to answer when the proposal or question concerning with the Union Attorney General's Office arises in Hluttaw. Some proposal or question are need to answer combination with other relevant Ministry. They have to do other duties which the Attorney General assign.

Department 2, the legal Advice Department are formed with three divisions, namely; International Law and ASEAN Legal Affairs Division, Commercial Contract Division and General Legal Advice Division. The public prosecutors who serve in International Law and ASEAN Legal Affairs Division tender legal advice relating to the following international or regional agreements when so requested by the relevant Government Departments and Organizations:

- International conventions and regional agreements;
- Human Rights Conventions;
- Agreements on Demarcation and Border Area Management;
- Air Service Agreements;
- Memorandums of Understanding, Memorandums of Agreement and Non-Commercial Assistance Project Documents;
- Conventions on Rights of the Child and the Women;
- Environmental Conventions;
- ASEAN agreements;
- Conventions on Prevention and Elimination of Narcotic Drugs;
- Agreements on Assistance by non-governmental organization from foreign countries;

Cooperation agreements on Trade, Investment, Science and Technology, Culture and other Non-Commercial Contracts.

The public prosecutors who serve in Commercial Contract division have to give legal advice relating to the following commercial contracts or agreements when so requested by the relevant Government Departments and Organizations.

- Joint venture agreements;
- Memorandums of Association and Articles of Association;
- Land Lease Agreements and Building Lease Agreements;
- Build, Operate and Transfer (BOT);
- Foreign Supply Contracts;
- Loan Agreements;
- Production Sharing Contract for the exploration and Production of petroleum gas (P. S. C Contract);
- Memorandum of Understanding and Memorandum of Agreements;
- Foreign Consultant Agreements;
- Local Sale Contracts;
- Construction Agreements;
- Tender Agreements;

• Other Commercial Agreements;

In the General Legal Advice Division, the public prosecutors have to give general legal advice which are not concerned with pre-trial legal advice. They:

(a) scrutinizes and replies the matters on general legal advice requested by the Government or the relevant government departments and organizations;

(b) scrutinizes and replies the matters on general legal advice when guidance is requested by various levels of Law Offices;

(c) scrutinizes and approves the copies of general legal advice sent by the State/ Division Law Offices and amend them, if necessary.

Department 3, the Prosecution Department is the oldest department in the Union Attorney General's Office. Since the formation of the Office of the Attorney General, this department is responsible for appearing on behalf of the Union in criminal cases and in civil cases in which the government is involved. This department has five divisions, namely: Prosecution Division of the Supreme Court of the Union, Criminal Appeal and Revision Scrutiny Division, Pre-trial Legal Advice Division, Prosecution Division for Union Level Departments and Civil Litigation Division.

In Prosecution Division of the Supreme Court of the Union, the public prosecutors appear as amicus curiae in original criminal cases, appeal cases, special appeal cases, revision and miscellaneous application cases in which the Union is involved and adjudicated at the Supreme Court of the Union.

In the Criminal Appeal and Revision Scrutiny Division, the duties and functions of public prosecutors are the implementation of the provision "filing appeal or revision if it is necessary to file appeal or revision to the Supreme Court of the Union on judgment, order or decision passed by any High Court of the Region or State, in cases relating to the Union" prescribed in section 12 (I) of the Attorney General of the Union Law.

They scrutinizes that it is necessary to file appeal against acquittal in criminal case passed by any High Court of the Region or State, when it is submitted by the Union Attorney General's Office or by the relevant Office of the Advocate General of the Region or State within 6 months of the limitation period.

If it is necessary to file after scrutinizing when it is submitted by the Union Attorney General's Office or by the Office of the Advocate General of the Region or State, in respect of judgment, order or decision passed by any High Court of the Region or State, in cases relating to the Union, they file revision and miscellaneous application to the Supreme Court of the Union within 60 days of the limitation period.

If they scrutinize to file special appeal against acquittal or dismiss order in the criminal appeal and revision cases adjudicated at the Supreme Court of the Union, special appeal is filed to the Supreme Court of the Union within 90 days.

If they know according to the completion report sent to the Union Attorney General's Office by the Department of the Special Investigation Bureau or any other means in respect of criminal cases appeared by such department, they carry out scrutinizing to file revision or miscellaneous application and scrutinizing documents contained in for filing appeal against acquittal order. And then, they scrutinize the Decided Case Form (Law Officer Case Conduction Form 5) for criminal appeal, revision and miscellaneous application sent by Offices of the Advocate General of the Region or State.

In Pre-trial Legal Advice Division, the public prosecutors have the duties to scrutinize and tenders legal advice on the matters directly requested by the government, relevant government department and organization and any prosecuting body to the Union Attorney General's Office for prosecution. When the matters occur to revise after scrutinizing the copies of confirmation on advice of Offices of Advocate General of the Region and State, they reply with remark to revise.

Public Prosecutors who are serving Prosecution Division for Union Level Departments appears, on the side of the Union, in applications to issue writs to the Supreme Court of the Union.

Under section 378(a) of the Constitution, it provides that the Supreme Court of the Union has power to issue the following writs as suitable:-

• Writ of Habeas Corpus;

- Writ of Madamus;
- Writ of Prohibition;
- Writ of Quo Warranto;
- Writ of Certiorari.

Among five kinds of writ, writ of Habeas Corpus as criminal miscellaneous application or the other writs as civil miscellaneous application are adjudicated at the Supreme Court of the Union. Adjudicating as such, Director, head of the division, himself gives argument for civil miscellaneous application (writ) or criminal miscellaneous application (writ) at the Supreme Court of the Union. In doing so, the writs of Certiorari are majority.

In Civil Litigation Division, public prosecutors scrutinize and tender legal advice on civil case in which any government department and organization is involved as the plaintiff or defendant. In respect of civil case in which any government department and organization is involved as plaintiff or defendant, it scrutinizes the submission as to whether or not to file appeal case, special appeal case, civil revision case, review or miscellaneous application case and, when it is necessary, it files them to the Supreme Court of the Union.

Department 4, the Administration Department, are formed, namely: Personnel Affairs and Inspection Division, Training and ICT Division, Budget and Accounts Division, Research and Logistic Division. In these four divisions, some staff officers are permanent. They don't need to move one office to another. Public prosecutors who are serving in these four divisions have to serve for two years or more in one time. After they serve two years, they can move to other Law Offices.

The Personnel Affairs Division carries out the functions and duties such as managing the matters of service personnel relating to the appointment of the service personnel of various levels of Law Office, confirmation, promotion, transfer, making departmental enquires, granting leave and retirement, appointing legal advisors and experts, arranging to confer medals of honour, preparing the lists of the strength of the Service Personnel of the Union Attorney General's Office and various levels of Law Office, arranging

Executive Committee's meeting and Seminars, performing the matters of security and greenness of the environment and keeping systematic records of the Union Attorney General's Office and various levels of Law Office.

The Inspection Division inspects various levels of Law Office in accord with the prescribed inspection plans. In doing so, this division performs the regular inspections, if necessary, performs the surprised inspections and special inspections. It supervises whether the relevant Law Offices implement or not the advice contained in the auditor reports of the Accounts Offices and carries out functions on matters which are necessary to take action arising out of the records of inspection.

The Training Division performs these functions as administrative arrangements of sending the recruiting officials and staff to attend the introductory courses to the Central Institutes for Civil Service, supervising and opening training courses and refresher courses to uplift the ability of law officers, facilitating the law officers to attend the local and foreign training courses, seminars and meetings.

ICT Division carries out the functions for the development of the office works through ICT, maintaining the records, service books and assessment cards of the service personnel of the Union Attorney General's Office and various levels of Law Offices, and performing the social welfare of the service personnel of the Union Attorney General's Office and various levels of Law Offices.

The Budget and Accounts Division performs the functions to prepare and request the estimated budget in time for the expenditure of the Union Attorney General's Office and various levels of Law Offices and to allocate the funds for them, to examine by keeping the check list whether the Law Offices use the allocated funds in conformity with the instructions for the Basic Accounts Departments or not and whether they send the monthly statement of accounts in time; to carry out matters for preparing budget accounts, transferring the budget head and depositing the surplus of the Union Attorney General's Office and to consider and permit the loans for hazard of fire, water and air and loans for rainy season ration.

The functions of the Research Division are preparing the lecture notes of

Legal Subjects to be taught in the training Courses opened in the Union Attorney General's Office and various levels of Law Offices, compiling, publishing, maintaining, distributing and selling Law year books, Myanmar law books of English version, law manuals, law journals and other legal research papers, doing legal research, studying and keeping the record of the amendments of laws, opening files of legal research, preparing dissemination plans for legal studies, supervising the library of the Union Attorney General's Office.

The logistic Division performs the functions as searching for the plots of land to build law offices, constructing various kinds of buildings, maintaining and renting the buildings, buying and distributing the stationary for the Union Attorney General's Office and various levels of Law Offices, buying and maintaining the vehicles for the Union Attorney General's Office and various levels of Law Offices and arranging ferry service for personnel of the Union Attorney General's Office.

The Public prosecutors in the four departments of the Union Attorney General's Office have to conduct the duties and functions of relevant divisions of departments. They move to other law offices after they serve for two years. But the public prosecutors who got degree from abroad and skillful staff officers are appointed in legal vetting and advising department, legal advice department and prosecution department permanently.

Various levels of Law Offices are formed under the Union Attorney General's Office as follows:
- Offices of the Advocate General of the Region or State
- Law Office of the Self-Administered Division
- Law Office of the Self-Administered Zone
- District Law Offices
- Township Law Offices
- Other Law Offices formed in accord with law

The Offices of the Advocate General of the Region or State are led by the Advocate-Generals of the Region or State. The Advocate-Generals of the Region or State is a member of the relevant Region or State Government. The Advocate-General of the Region or State shall be responsible to the

Attorney-General of the Union or to the relevant Chief Minister of the Region or State. Law Office of the Self-Administered Division, Law Office of the Self-Administered Zone and District Law Offices are led by the public prosecutors who are called law officer grade- 1. Township Law Offices and other Law Offices formed in accord with law are led by the public prosecutors who are called Law officer grade-3.

In the various levels of Law Offices, public prosecutors have the functions and duties to carry out justice by cooperation with police officers, lawyers and judges in the criminal proceedings. The criminal proceedings can be divided into three stages which are Investigation Stage, Trial State and Post trial Stage. In these three stage, Law Officers have to participate.

In the criminal proceeding, there are proceeding for cognizable offence and non-cognizable offence. Non-cognizable Offence cannot be investigated by police without the order of a Magistrate and it shall be directly complained to the court. In non-cognizable Offence, a police officer may not arrest without warrant. Non-cognizable offences are prescribed in schedule 2 of the Criminal Procedure Code, for example high treason, unlawful compulsory labour, dishonest misappropriation of property, punishment for cheating, etc. In cognizable offence, police- officer may, in accordance with the second schedule or under any law for the time being in force, arrest without warrant, for example, murder, rape, theft, robbery, etc. When a cognizable case occurs, it can be informed to the police station. The police-officer shall investigate it and may arrest the accused in accord with the provision of the Criminal Procedure Code and the manual of the Police Force.

Nobody shall be held in custody for more than 24 hours without the remand of a competent magistrate. If investigation cannot be completed within 24 hours, the accused is brought to the court for giving the remand. Before the accused is brought to the court, the public prosecutor in relevant law office checks the data about the accused. If public prosecutor founds that the accused is child, he or she recommends to release with bond or to send to the guardian with making discipline and then sends continuing to the court.

After completion of investigation, if there is sufficient evidence in the case, it shall be sent the case to the public prosecutor for giving pre-trial advice. At that time, public prosecutor shall tender legal advice necessarily and send back this case to the police officer. After that, the case shall be sent to the relevant court through the law office. Within the remand time police officer must request legal advice. The sufficient time must have for tendering legal advice. Although the police-officer has enough time to investigate, he or she sent the accused and case to the public prosecutor at almost end of remand time. In these circumstance, after the public prosecutor replies the pre-trial advice, he or she reports to the higher Law Office to cooperate with prosecution organ for taking action.

But if there is no sufficient evidence in the case, the accused shall be released and this case has to be submitted to the public prosecutor for closing. The public prosecutor shall scrutinize and make decision relating to the closing of the case which cannot be prosecuted. When the prosecution organization submit case to the Law Office for prosecution, after the public prosecutor shall check whether it has necessary witness list or whether it contains necessary documents or whether it is in conformity with pre-trial advice or not, it continue to send to the court.

The public prosecutor from the Union Attorney General's Office and various levels of Law Offices are responsible to conduct as government lawyer in hearing before the court in criminal ordinary case, appeal case, special appeal case , revision case, miscellaneous case including the government or the case which notified by the court to the law office to conduct as office communion. Therefore, the public prosecutor takes part in the trial stage. The public prosecutor shall conduct the cognizable offence before the court in accord with the UAG law. The public prosecutor examine with chief-examination the witnesses from the plaintiff side and then the accused themself or the defend lawyer may ask cross-examination these witness. When the witness answer differently with the chief-examination, the public prosecutor make sure by asking re-examination.

After all witnesses from plaintiff side are examined, the public prosecutor argues to charge the accused in provision of the relevant law. The court charges the accused by prima faci of evidence. If accused admits the guilty, he shall be convicted in provision of the relevant law charged and if accused deny the guilty, the court asks him to recall the prosecution witnesses whose evidence has been taken. If there is no prima faci of evidence, the accused shall be discharged. When the order of charge is not in conformity with law, public prosecutor may file revision to the relevant court.

At the final stage of trial, the court decides the case on the conclusive of evidence. If the accused is found guilty, the court shall convict him under the relevant law but he is not found guilty, he shall be acquitted. After that, the law officer shall report the completion of the case to the higher law office with his comment. In the post-trial stage, if the law officer considers that the judgment of the court is not in conformity with law, the case shall be filed as a revision or appeal case to the relevant court.

At the any stage of trial, when the aggrieved person submits the withdrawal of case, the public prosecutor shall scrutinize and make decision whether to withdraw the case or not.

The complainant has the right to hire a private lawyer for him although the public prosecutor appears for him and on behalf of the State. But the hired lawyer shall conduct the case under the direction of public prosecutor in accord with section 493 of Criminal procedure Code.

Therefore, in Myanmar, public prosecutor takes part in the whole case. For example, when a murder case occurs in one of Townships in Yangon, the police- officer shall investigate this case. The police-officer arrest the accused and detect evidences. Murder case is a non-bail able offence. So the police need to take remand, they sent the accused to take remand to the court with the recommendation of the public prosecutor. And then they need to take the pre- trial advice from public prosecutor. After public prosecutor check the case whether the evidences are sufficient or not, the case prosecute to the court with the recommendation of public prosecutor. In the trial stage, public prosecutor make leading the trial until it finish. If the order of the court is not conformity with Law, the public prosecutor may file as a revision or appeal to the higher level court. The public prosecutor take re-sponsible the case from the beginning to the end. When the public prosecutor who is responsible the case moves to another office before the court has not decided the case which he take responsible, the new public prosecutor who replaced in old one shall take responsible this case continuously.

Duties and Powers of Public procurators in China

The people procuratorates have the right to exercise procuratorial authority. They exercise this authority over case endangering jurisdiction and public security, damaging economic order and infringing citizens' personal and democratic rights and other important criminal case. They exercise this authority over civil case endangering the public interest. A public procurator is an officer of a state charged with both the investigation and prosecution of crime. They are not represent the government. They have the legal right to sue the government.

Article 129 of the Constitution of the People's Republic of China and Article 1 of the Organic Law of the People's Procuratorates of the People's Republic of China stipulate that 'the people's procuratorates of the people's Republic of China are state organs for legal supervision.' Under Article 131 of the Constitution of the People Republic of China, People procuratorate shall, in accordance with the law, exercise procuratorial power independently and are not subject to interference by administrative organs, public organizations or individuals. Under the Public Procurators Law of the People's Republic of China, the function and duties of Public Procurators are to supervise the enforcement of Laws according to law, to make public prosecution on behalf of the State, to investigate criminal cases directly accepted by the People's Procuratorates as provided by law, and to do other functions and duties as provided by law.

The supreme people's procuratorates is the highest procuratorial organ of the State and represents the state in independently implementing the right of prosecution. It is responsible to the Standing Committee of the National People's Congress. Its major tasks are to exercise leadership over local people's procuratorate at all levels and special people's procuratorates in implementing their supervision functions and ensure the unity and correct implementation of State law. The SPP consists of 15 functional departments; namely: the general affairs office, investigation supervision department, prosecution department, anti-embezzlement and bribery administration, negligence of duty and rights infringement prosecution department, prison and detention department, civil and administration department, reporting and charges prosecution department (also known as the Reporting and Charges Center of the SPP), criminal appeals department, railway transportation prosecution department, department for the prevention of crimes committed by taking advantage of one's positions, law and policy research office, supervision bureau, foreign affairs bureau, planning, finance and equipment bureau.

Every departments under the fundamental department of the SPP have respectively major tasks. Prison and detention department is responsible for providing guidance to executive organs in the legality of their activities of implementing penalties, reducing sentences, making release on parole, and allowing medical treatment on bail, the legality of the activities of prisons, detention centers and organs in charge of education through forced labor and supervising over extra time of custody;

Giving guidance on the investigation before trial of cases of malpractices in the execution of sentences and penalties, ill-treatment of those held in prison or detention centers, releasing without permission those in custody, negligence leading to the escape of those in custody, reducing sentences, granting release on parole and allowing medical treatment on bail as a result of giving favoritism and engaging in irregular practices;

Dealing with questions submitted by procuratorates of lower levels over difficult cases and studying and formulating rules and regulations for the prosecution work concerning prisons and detention centers.

Moreover, Chief and administration department is in charge of providing guidance over civil and economic dispute trials, administrative charges and supervision cases in the country; in accordance with procuratorial supervision procedures, putting forward protests to the SPP against verdicts of courts at various levels on civil, economic and administrative cases that have already been implemented but are indeed mistaken; appearing in court during the trial in the Supreme People's Court of civil, economic and administrative cases which the SPP is protesting;

Studying very difficult issues in the nation concerning the trial of civil and economic disputes and charges and supervision of administrative cases and putting forward solutions;

Undertaking inquires raised by lower prosecution bodies over difficult issues in the work of civil and administrative procuratorial organs; and studying and formulating rules and regulations concerning the work of civil and administrative supervision.

And then criminal appeals department is responsible for giving guidance to the work of prosecuting organs concerning criminal appeals and compensation; dealing with citizens' criminal appeals, dealing with appeals of criminals serving sentences or of their close relatives or legal agents; dealing with criminal appeal cases under the jurisdiction of prosecution organs and urging prosecution organs to investigate and report the results; making comprehensive reports on the situation of criminal appeals and compensation; handling criminal appeals and compensations; and studying and formulating rules and regulations concerning the work of criminal appeals and compensation.

Railway Transportation Prosecution Department is in charge of giving guidance to the prosecution work concerning railway transportation in the country; directly participating or organizing or coordinating the investigation of serious cases which have national impact and are being handled by prosecution bodies; giving approval to the arrest and charges in serious cases concerning railway transportation that are of national impact; studying and analyzing criminal activities and trends in railway transportation and putting forward policies of dealing with the situation; and studying and formulating rules and regulations concerning the work of prosecution in railway transportation.

Negligence of Duty and Right Infringement Prosecution Department is in charge of giving guidance on the investigation and inquisition of cases involving civil servants in the negligence of their duties or abusing their power to illegally detain people, extort confession through torture, retaliate through frame-up, search and to engage in other criminal activities that infringe upon the personal rights and democratic rights of citizens;

Taking part in the investigation of serious criminal cases of negligence of duties and infringement upon rights; directly investigating serious cases of negligence of duties and infringement upon rights that are of national significance; organizing, coordinating and leading the investigation of serious cases of negligence of duties and infringement upon rights which involve more than one province; studying and analyzing the rules and features of crimes of negligence of duties and infringement upon rights, and putting forward corresponding policies of dealing with them; handling inquires raised by lower prosecution bodies concerning serious and difficult issues in their work; and studying and formulating rules and regulations concerning the prosecution of cases of negligence of duty and infringement upon rights.

Reporting and Charges Prosecution Department is responsible for offering guidance to the work on reporting and bringing charges by the prosecution bodies in the country; handling reports and charges lodged by citizens; referring clues of reports and charges to proper organs and making preliminary investigation of clues of reports and charges that are not exactly clear as to which organ should be the handling body and therefore are difficult in being referred to the proper authorities; making comprehensive reports on the situation of reporting and charges; and studying and formulating rules and regulations on the work of reporting and charges.

Department for the Prevention of Crimes Committed by Abusing One's Power is responsible for offering guidance to the work of procuratorates in the prevention of crimes committed by people taking advantage of their job positions; studying and analyzing the rules and features of the prevention of crimes committed by people taking advantage of their job positions in the country and putting forward policies against bribery, embezzlement and negligence of duties; conducting work of prevention of crimes committed by minors; undertaking publicity of the legal system in the prevention of crimes committed by people taking advantage of their job positions; handling inquiries raised by lower level procuratorates concerning difficult issues in the prevention of crimes committed by people taking advantage of their job positions; and studying and formulating rules and regulations concerning the work of the prevention of crimes committed by people taking advantage of their job positions.

Investigation Supervision Department is responsible for offering guidance over arrests and investigation of the suspects of criminal cases in the country (including cases directly handled by prosecution bodies involving bribery, embezzlement and negligence of duties) and supervising the investigation of such cases; handling cases involving giving approval to arrests referred to by the SPP; undertaking the reply to inquires raised by lower prosecution bodies concerning difficult questions in approving arrests; giving guidance to the review and approval of arrests of minors who have committed crimes; and studying and formulating rules and regulations concerning the work of giving approvals to arrests.

Public Prosecution Department is responsible for giving guidance to the reviews of instituting legal proceedings, bringing charges in court and making protests against court verdicts and decisions concerning criminal cases in the country (including cases of crimes of bribery, embezzlement and negligence of duties directly investigated by prosecution bodies); offering guidance to the supervision of trial activities of people's courts; undertaking cases the SPP instituting legal proceedings or making protests and conducting duties in court in cases in which the SPP is protesting against the opening of trials by the Supreme People's Court;

Handling inquires raised by lower prosecution bodies concerning difficult issues in instituting legal proceedings; providing guidance to the work of instituting legal proceedings of cases involving minors; and studying and formulating rules and regulations on the work of bringing public charges.

Anti-Bribery and Embezzlement Administration is in charge of giving guidance to investigation and inquisition of cases handled by prosecution bodies in the country concerning bribery, embezzlement, misappropriation of public funds, improper source of huge funds, concealing deposits overseas, dividing up state-owned funds or confiscated properties among private individuals; taking part in the investigation of serious criminal cases of bribery and embezzlement; organizing, coordinating and leading the investigation of serious bribery and embezzlement cases; taking charge of coordinated investigation of serious bribery and embezzlement cases; studying and analyzing the rules and features of crimes of bribery and embezzlement in the country and putting forward policies of dealing with such crimes; handling inquires raised by lower level prosecution bodies concerning difficult issues on anti-bribery and embezzlement work; and studying and formulating rules and regulations concerning the work in anti-bribery and embezzlement prosecution.

Law and Policy Research Office is responsible for the study of the implementation of state laws, regulations and policies concerning prosecution work, putting forward suggestions correspondingly; undertaking the drafting of laws related to prosecution work; handling the drafting and negotiation of legal documents concerning judicial assistance and extradition agreements; making research in the applied theories on prosecution; providing suggestions on the drafts of state laws and administrative regulations when the SPP is asked to offer its opinions; giving judicial explanations on legal issues concerning prosecution; studying and planning the building of a legal system in prosecution work; undertaking the daily routine work of the Prosecution Committee of the SPP; offering guidance to the research of basic theories on prosecution work; providing guidance and leadership over inspection of the enforcement of law among prosecution bodies; collecting books and materials on prosecution work; editing and compiling laws, legal documents and almanacs on prosecution work; undertaking the routine work of the Special Consulting Committee of the SPP; and handling work of the SPP concerning Taiwan.

Supervision Bureau is responsible for providing guidance to the supervision work of all prosecution bodies in the country; inspecting the implementation of laws, regulations, decisions of the SPP or procuratorates of higher levels by prosecution bodies and their subsidiary organizations at various levels; handling charges and reports against members of prosecution bodies in their actions against disciplines; dealing with prosecution staff who have broken disciplines and their appeals against disciplinary decisions.

Foreign Affairs Bureau is responsible for the external exchanges and international judicial assistance of prosecution bodies and giving guidance to developing external exchanges by prosecution bodies in the country; in charge of contact and assistance of prosecution bodies in different parts of the country with those in Hong Kong and Macao; in charge of investigation of cases involving foreigners; coordinating and managing the drafting and negotiation of agreements between the SPP and foreign prosecution organizations; translating and compiling related materials and studying international judicial developments.

Planning, Finance and Equipment Bureau is responsible for giving guidance on planning and finance to prosecution bodies in the country; formulating long- and medium-term development plans concerning finance and equipment of prosecution bodies in the country and implementing such plans; distributing and managing funds for the work, equipment and capital construction of prosecution bodies; offering guidance to the plans of the prosecution system of the country on technical equipment, transportation, communication, armament and uniforms; reviewing and managing the funds for the various offices of the SPP and subsidiary institutions for their daily work, capital construction and foreign affairs activities; and handling the unified purchasing and allocation of their equipment of materials.

Moreover, the people procuratorates take part in criminal proceeding. There are four parts included in the criminal judicial procedure: filing a case, investigation, initiation of public prosecution and criminal trial. In the filing a case, the People's Procuratorates or the public security organs shall determine to file the criminal cases for investigation or trial. The People's Procuratorates investigate cases which are crimes of embezzlement and bribery, crimes of dereliction of duty committed by State functionaries, crimes involving violations of a citizen's personal rights and infringement of a citizen's democratic rights and other grave crimes committed by State functionaries by taking advantage of their functions by themselves.

Under Article 111 of the Criminal Procedure Law, a public security organ does not file the case which should be filed for investigation, the

People's Procuratorate shall request the public security organ to state the reasons for not filing the case. If the People's Procuratorate considers that the reasons for not filing the case given by the public security organ are untenable, it shall notify the public security organ to file the case, and upon receiving the notification, the public security organ shall file the case.

In the investigation stage, interrogation of the criminal suspect must be conduct by the investigator of the People Procuratorate or Public Security organ. If a people procuratorate deems it necessary to repeat inquest or examination that has been done by the public security organ, it may ask the latter another inquest or examination and may send procurators to participate in it. In investigation of the case directly accepted by the people procurator, the arrest or detention of criminal suspect is decided by the people procurator and executed by the public security organ. Interrogation of the criminal suspect must be conducted within 24 hours after the detention or arrest, and if it is found that the person should not have been detained or arrested, he must be immediately released. When a public security organ wishes to arrest a criminal suspect, it shall submit a written request for approval of arrest together with the case file and evidence to the People's Procuratorate at the same level for examination and approval. Where a people's procuratorate deems it necessary to arrest a detainee in a case directly accepted by it, it shall make a decision thereon within 14 days.

When a People's Procuratorate considers after full examination of the case transmitted by the public security organs as a result of the conclusion of investigation for prosecution or the case handled by itself as a result of conclusion of investigation, it shall initiate the public prosecution in the court.

After the full examination of the case transferred by the public security organ as a result of the conclusion of investigation with a recommendation to initiate a prosecution or the case as a result of the conclusion of investigation by itself,

if it finds that the suspect shall not be investigated for criminal responsibility, or the case is minor and the offender need not be given criminal punishment or need be exempted from it according to the law or the case does not meet the conditions for initiation of a prosecution after supplementary investigation has been conducted twice, the Procuratorate shall make a decision not to transfer the case to the People's Court for trial. In examining a case that requires supplementary investigation, the People's Procuratorate may remand the case to a public security organ for supplementary investigation or conduct the investigation itself. If the public security organ considers that the decision not to initiate a prosecution is wrong, it may demand reconsideration, and if the demand is rejected, it may submit the matter to the People's Procuratorate at the next higher level for review, it may submit the matter to the People's Procuratorate at the next higher level for review.

In the criminal trial, the People's Court makes trial of the cases filed by the People's Procuratorate for public prosecution. The People's Procuratorate appear before the court to support the public prosecution. Citizens of all nationalities have the right to use the spoken and written languages of their own nationalities in court proceedings. At that time, the people's court and people's procuratorates should provide translation for any party to the court proceedings who is not familiar with the spoken or written languages in common use in the locality. Under Article 64 of the Criminal Procedure Law of the People Republic of China, 2012, the People's Courts, the People's Procuratorates and the public security organs may, according to the circumstances of a case, issue a warrant to compel the appearance of the criminal suspect or defendant, order him to be released on bail pending trial or subject him to residential surveillance. People's procuratorates shall exercise supervision over the legality of the decision and enforcement of residential surveillance at designated places of residence.

If a People's Procuratorate discovers that in handling a case a People's Court has violated the litigation procedure prescribed by law, it shall have the power to suggest to the People's Court that it should set it right. If the Supreme People's Procuratorate finds some definite error in a legally effective judgment or order of a People's Court at any level, or if a People's Procuratorate at a higher level finds some definite error in a legally effective judgment or order of a People's Court at a lower level, it shall have the power to present a protest to the People's Court at the same level against the judgment or order in accordance with the procedure for trial supervision.

Before a People's Court causes a death sentence to be executed, it shall notify the People's Procuratorate at the same level to send an officer to supervise the execution. If a People's Procuratorate considers that the order on commutation of sentence or on parole made by a People's Court is improper, it shall, within 20 days from the date of receiving a copy of the written order, submit a written recommendation to the People's Court for correction. The People's Court shall, within one month from the date of receiving the recommendation, form a new collegial panel to handle the case and render a final order. The People's Procuratorates shall supervise the execution of criminal punishments by executing organs to see if the execution conforms to law. If they discover any illegalities, they shall notify the executing organs to correct them.

Conclusion

In two countries having different legal system, there are different powers of public prosecutor. But they have the same purpose. That is to implement the rule of Law. Public procurator in China can investigate the case by himself. It is not the interference of the duty of police. It make more powerful to emergence the right in grave cases.

If the polices do not perform to complete their duties, both public prosecutor and public procurator do not send the case to be continuous and ask the police to perform their all duties completely. If the interim order or final order of the court is not conformity with law, they must file appeal or revision to the higher level court. In the court proceeding, if the performance of the judge or lawyer is not conformity with law, they ask to record and notify to the higher level court.

China public procurators is only the legal supervisor in criminal case and civil case. The China public procurators are more powerful than the Myanmar public prosecutor. Myanmar public prosecutors have many responsibilities and accountabilities in criminal, civil case involving government, tendering legal advice, and other functions. Therefore to improve the skill of public prosecutors in Myanmar, every prosecutor must know existing laws, international law, commercial law, legislative drafting and other legal knowledge. Nowadays, in UAGO, many workshops, training, seminar are often hold for law officers in corporation with the International Organization. Some law officers are sent to abroad to obtain Master Degree and PhD Degree. Respect for human rights and the rule of law requires the UAGO to investigate and prosecute criminal offence with impartiality and functional independence. Within the UAGO, public prosecutor must be empowered to fulfill their professional duties with integrity in an independent, impartial and objective manner and in the protection of the public interest.

Especially the spirit of prosecutors must love justice and they have to make decision without fear and favor. UAGO needs much more qualified and unprejudiced public prosecutors. They can not only protect the innocent people and State but also combat the criminals with their legal knowledge. Country will get much benefit from their responsibility efficiently and effectively.

References

• Attorney General of the Union Act, 1948.
• The Constitution of the Socialist Republic of the Union of Myanmar, 1974.
• The Attorney General Law, 1988.
• The Attorney General Law, 2001.
• The Attorney General Law, 2010.
• The Attorney-General of the Union Law, 22/2010.
• The Constitution of the Republic of the Union of Myanmar, 2008.
• The Attorney-General of the Union Rules, 2016.
• The Organic Law of the People's Procuratorates of the People's Republic of China.
• The Constitution of the People's Republic of China, 1982.
• The Public Procurators Law of the People's Republic of China.
• Criminal Procedure Code (Myanmar).
• Criminal Procedure Law of the People's Republic Of China (2012).

缅甸联邦共和国检察官职能与中华人民共和国检察官职能比较研究

Ei Khine Zin Aung[*]

编译　钟舒婷^{**}

摘要：由于缅甸联邦共和国和中华人民共和国的法律制度不同，因此两个国家检察官的职责和权力也是不一样的。本文通过对两个国家的检察官及其最高管理机构的简要介绍，引出文章的核心内容：即阐释缅甸和中国的检察官分别在其国内的不同法律机构和法律程序中的不同职责和职能。

关键词：检察官，职责，职能

一、介　绍

检察官是普通法系或民法法系国家检察机关的主要法定代表人。在普通法系管辖区中，他们通常管辖及刑事案件。他们通常由某一政府部门雇用。在民法法系管辖范围内，他们通常是拥有大学法律学位的公务员，并且进行过司法管理的额外培训。在这篇文章中，笔者的侧重点在于检察官在缅甸的职责和职能以及检察官在中国的职责和职能。

缅甸的法律制度是一种独特的制度体系，部分隶属于英国的普通法法系。中国的法律主要是民法体系。由于这两个国家的法律制度不同，因此检察官和检察官的职责和权力是不一样的。检察官是中国的一个职位，类似于侦探和公诉人。虽然他们之间有不同的责任和权力，但他们有相同的义务。他们

　＊　西南政法大学国际法学院博士生/缅甸联邦最高检检察官。

＊＊　西南政法大学 2014 级本科法学专业实务人才实验班。

的义务是为了维护宪法，保护公民在本国的利益。在这篇文章中，笔者将介绍检察官在这两个国家间的不同职责和权力。

二、历史背景

缅甸检察官的历史很悠久，检察官和联合检察总长办公室同时出现，所以首先应该关注联合检察总部的历史。自 1826 年第一次益格鲁—缅甸战争结束以来，英国为缅甸的刑事和民事案件引入了一种以普通法法系为模板的修改版的法律制度，任命政府检察长、政府检察官和检察官代表政府对刑事案件和民事案件进行案件审理。

缅甸于 1948 年恢复独立时，根据 1948 年《联邦总检察长法》设立了总检察长办公室，负责任命为检察长、政府倡导者和法律起草人。

1962 年革命委员会接管国家时，在 1962 年 3 月 7 日根据第 15 号宣言任命了总检察长。他的主要职能是代表政府出席民事和刑事案件，并向革命委员会和政府提供法律咨询。

1972 年 3 月 15 日，发布第 97 号宣言，根据该宣言废除现有机构设置，并替换新机构。此后，司法部于 1972 年 3 月 31 日通过"第二号通知"成立。成立新的总检察长办公室，负责起诉、提起法律咨询、立法起草和法律翻译。

根据 1974 年《宪法》，缅甸联邦社会主义共和国成立后，由 Pyithu Hluttaw 组建的人民检察院也成立了各州/省和乡镇的律师事务所。为监督这些律师事务所，中央法律办公室成立并代替总检察长办公室。

1988 年，国家法律和秩序恢复委员会接管国家责任时，在 1988 年 9 月 26 日之前的案件颁布了《总检察法》。本法仍适用于 2001 年 2 月 26 日。2001 年颁布了《总检法》，该法于 2003 年 1 月 2 日修改。

目前，缅甸联邦共和国宪法已于 2008 年 5 月 29 日通过了公民投票。2010 年 10 月 28 日，根据缅甸联邦共和国宪法第 443 课颁布了《联邦总检察长法》。联盟总检察长的任命根据缅甸联邦共和国宪法第 237（a）条和 2010 年联邦总检察长法第 5 条的规定，经总统 Pyidaungsu Hluttaw（议会）批准。

副检察长（DAG）的任命与联邦总检察长（UAG）相同。联邦总检察长和 DAG 的任期与总统的任期相同。

目前，缅甸检察官服务是由联邦总检察长（AGU）管理的政府机构。根据总检法第 41（a）条，2016 年 1 月 7 日第 8/2016 号的声明，联邦总检察长根据联邦政府的同意 AGU 发布了总检察长规则。根据这项规则，检察官是指由总检察长指定的法律官员或特别由受检察长负责的人员。此外,检察官可以代表总检察长、各级法院、宪法审裁处、选举法、任何法律组织的任何法庭进行诉讼。

当英国吞并缅甸时,缅甸运用普通法系法律。自殖民地时期以来,联邦检察总长办公室的角色就已经出现。当时,检察官在刑事案件和民事案件中扮演的角色代表了政府的职能。他们被称为政府律师。独立后,检察官需执行政府律师和法律起草人的职务。在革命理事会时期,检察官在民事和刑事案件中代表政府行事,接着他们还提供法律咨询,进行立法起草和法律翻译工作。从 2010 年缅甸实行民主制度开始,检察官就不需要进行立法起草工作了。他们审查法律草案,翻译法律、规则和条例等,提出法律建议和起诉。从未改变的检察官职责是检察机关的检控职责,这也是他们的主要职责。

中国的法律体系主要是以民法模式为基础的社会主义法律体系。检察制度来源于民法法系纠问制,而不是普通法的对抗制。中国采用检察制度,检察官办公室被称为检察院。这些术语是来自拉丁文的检察官和起源于罗马帝国的检察官。

1949 年中国共产党成立以后,中央人民政府组织法规定了检察院的设立、地位、职能和权力,这是新中国检察院制度的法律基础。中华人民共和国人民检察院组织法于 1979 年 7 月 1 日在第五届全国人民代表大会第二次会议通过,于 1979 年 7 月 5 日由全国人民代表大会常务委员会主席令第四号发布,于 1980 年 1 月 1 日生效;1983 年根据第六届全国人大常委会第二次会议通过的《关于修改〈中华人民共和国人民检察院组织法〉的决定》《关于修改〈中华人民共和国人民检察院组织法〉的决定》进行了修改 。

在中国,宪法已经三次颁布。现行《中华人民共和国宪法》于 1982 年颁布实施。宪法第七节第 129 条至第 135 条作出有关人民检察院的规定。

《中华人民共和国检察官法》于 1995 年 2 月 28 日颁布,并于 2001 年 6 月 30 日修改。最高人民检察院是国家最高的法律监督机关,其中既包括提起刑事诉讼也包括确保政府机构依法行事的职能。根据宪法和法律规定的任免权限和程序,任命或者免除检察官职务。

自 1949 年以来,中国已行使检察制度。人民检察院是中国的刑事检察机关,不是政府行政部门的一部分,而是它自己的一个分支。人民检察院的另一项任务是进行法律监督。

三、联邦总检察长办公室的组织

联邦总检察长办公室(UAGO)是一个主要由作为政府律师的法律官员或检察官组成的组织。联邦总检察长办公室目前由立法审查部、法律咨询部、检察部、行政部和总部组成。然后,联邦总检察长办公室由 14 个地区和州检察长办公室、72 个地区法律办公室和 330 个乡镇法律办公室组成。检察官通常在我们的 330 个乡镇办事处中的一个或多个开始他们的职业,然后转移到 72 个地区办事处、14 个地区和州办公室,有时还有总部办事处。

四、最高人民检察院的组织

最高人民检察院根据需要设立若干检察机关和专业机构。最高人民检察院由 15 个职能部门以及一个政党工作部门,人事局和 5 个下属机构组成。

职能部门包括总务室,调查监督部门,检察部门,反贪污贿赂管理部门,疏忽职责侵权检察部门,监狱和拘留部门,民政部门,举报和收费检察部门(也称最高人民检察院的报告和收费中心),刑事上诉部门,铁路运输检察部门,利用职务犯罪防治部门,法律与政策研究室,监察局,外事局,规划、财务和设备局。

政治工作部门本身由宣传教育培训官员和总务室组成。

下属机构是指机关服务中心、检察院日报、中国检察院出版社、检察院技术信息研究中心、检察院理论研究所和国家检察院。

地方各级人民检察院分为省、自治区、直辖市人民检察院,县、市、自治县、市辖区人民检察院。省级或县级人民检察院可以设立人民检察院,作为工矿区、农垦区、林区的代理机构。

检察长由全国人大选举并罢免。检察委员会副检察长,最高人民检察院检察员由总检察长提名,由全国人大常委会任免。各级人民检察院分别设主要检察长,副检察长、检察官。省、自治区、直辖市人民检察院及其所在地检察长由人民代表大会选举和罢免。副检察长、本级检察委员、检察官由检察长推荐,由本级人民代表大会常务委员会任免。自治州人民检察院检察长,省、直辖市、县、市、市辖区检察长由本级人民代表大会选举并罢免。副检察长、检察委员、检察官,由检察长推荐,由本级人民代表大会常务委员会任免。各级人民检察院应当设有一批检察助理和文员,助理检察员和文员由各级人民检察院检察长任免。

五、缅甸检察官的职责和权力

联邦总检察长办公室为缅甸政府的主要法律咨询机构提供服务,该办公室由缅甸联邦总检察长领导,总检察长是缅甸权力最大的执法官员之一。总检察长向总统和缅甸联邦议会提供法律建议、分析国际条约、起草和修订法律、在司法程序中代表政府行事。总检察长还指导检察官办公室,并确保内阁行动在法律上符合宪法和国际法。总检察长对联邦主席负责,总检察长由总统提名并由联邦议会选出。在联邦总检察长办公室下的各种法律办公室下的检察官应该履行联邦总检察长按照规定授予的职责。

在联邦总检察长办公室工作的检察官必须在全国各地办事,有时候他们在总部工作。在总部任职期间,他们必须履行他们所服务的部门的职责。总部有四个部门。

在联邦总检察长办公室的第1个部门立法审查部门中,有立法审查和建议司,规则、条例、命令和指令审查和建议司,法律翻译和审查司以及宪法司四个司。

检察官在立法审查和咨询司工作的职责和职能是提供咨询和审查法律草案,送交联邦总检察长办公室,以修改、替代、废除和颁布必要的新法律。联邦检察总长办公室建议的法律草案有四种类型,即修改现行法律的法律草案、代替现行法律的法律草案、废除现行法律的法律草案和新的法律草案。根据各种法律草案的性质,审议情况有所不同,联邦总检察长办公室必须完全遵守有关法律的内容的规定。对法律草案提出意见的依据是它们是否符合宪法,或者它们是否违反现行法律,或者它们是否与时间一致。此外,如果法律草案中的条款与国际公约和协定有关,联邦总检察长办公室会审查他们是否符合这些公约和协定。如果法律草案与国际组织有联系,就应该与这些组织进行必要的协调。

检察官在规则、条例、命令和指令审查和建议司中的职责和职能根据有关法律的规定为相关政府部门和组织执行其管理和法律而起草的规则、案例、细则、命令、通知指令和程序。必要时检察官提出建议并进行回复添加和修改以上规定。

检察官在法律翻译和审查司中的职责和职能是将缅甸法律翻译成英文,以提高包括外国人在内的外国投资者的认识。此外,他们将联邦政府发布的规则、程序、条例、声明、通知、命令和指令翻译成英文。将与任何外国或任何区域组织缔结的国际公约和协定条约从缅甸语翻译成英文或从英文翻译成缅甸语,应按有关政府部门和组织的要求审查。

检宪法司中的职责和职能是在联邦主席或者联邦议会主席或者联邦层级的组织的主席在宪法事务方面请求法律意见时,在联邦总检察长的指导下提供意见。他们按照总检察长的指示,向联邦议会会议提交与法律事务有关的特殊情况。他们会在联邦议会中通过研究以回答与联邦检察总部有关的提案或问题。有些提案或问题对于回答与其他相关部门的合并有帮助。他们必须履行总检察长分配的其他职责。

联邦总检察长办公室总部的第二个部门——法律咨询部由三个司组成,即国际法和东盟法律事务司、商业合同司和一般法律咨询司。在有关政府部门和组织的要求下,在国际法和东盟法律事务司服务的检察官就下列国际或区域协定提供法律咨询意见:

(1)国际公约和区域协定;

(2)人权公约;

(3)关于标界和边界管理的协定;

(4)航空服务协议;

(5)谅解备忘录,备忘录和非商业援助项目文件;

(6)《儿童和妇女权利公约》;

(7)环境公约;

(8)东盟协议;

(9)《预防和消除麻醉品公约》;

(10)非政府组织援助外国的协议;

贸易、投资、科技、文化和其他非商业合同的合作协议。

在商业合同司提供服务的检察官在有关政府部门和组织的要求下,必须就以下商业合同或协议提供法律咨询。

(1)合资协议;

(2)公司章程和公司章程;

(3)土地租赁协议和建筑物租赁协议;

(4)建设,运营和转让(BOT);

(5)对外供应合同;

(6)贷款协议;

(7)石油天然气勘探和生产的产量分成合同(P.S.C合同);

(8)谅解备忘录和协议备忘录;

(9)外国顾问协议；

(10)当地销售合同；

(11)施工协议；

(12)投标协议；

(13)其他商业协议；

在一般法律咨询司,检察官必须提供与审前法律意见无关的一般法律建议,它们是:

(a)审议并答复政府或有关政府部门和组织要求的一般法律意见事宜；

(b)在各级法律办公室要求的指导下审查和答复一般法律咨询事项；

(c)审查并批准国家/部门法律办公室发送的一般法律咨询副本,并在必要时予以修改。

联邦总检察长办公室总部的第三个部门——检察部门是联邦合检察总部最古老的部门。自总检察长办公室成立以来,该部门负责代表联邦在刑事案件和涉及政府的民事案件中出庭。该部门有五个司,即联邦最高法院起诉司、刑事上诉和修订审查司、预审法律咨询司、联邦各级起诉司和民事诉讼司。

在联邦最高法院起诉司内,检察官在原国际刑事案件、上诉案件、特别上诉案件,联邦提起修订和参与并在联邦联最高法院裁决的申请案件中以法庭之友的身份出席。

在刑事上诉和修订审查司中,检察官的职责和职能是"在需要向联邦最高法院提起上诉或修改判决、命令或裁决时执行上诉或修改条款的规定,该判决、命令或裁决由地区或州的任何高等法院在关系到整个联邦的案件中通过",当由联邦总检察长办公室还是由区域总检察长办公室在 6 个月限制期限内提交的上诉文件,他们发现,有必要对该区域或州的任何高等法院通过的刑事案件提起上诉。在关系到整个联邦的案件中,对于任一地区或州高级法院通过的判决、命令、或裁决,在仔细检查由联邦总检察长办公室或地区或州的总检察长办公室提交的上诉文件后,如果有必要提起上诉,应在 60 日内限制期限内向联邦最高法院提交修正和申请文件。如果他们仔细审查后对联邦最高法院裁决的刑事上诉和修改案中的无罪释放或解除命令提出特别上诉,则应在 90 日内向联邦最高法院提出特别上诉。如果他们根据特别调查局向联邦总检察厅发出的完成报告或通过其他任何有关该部门出庭的刑事案件的合式知道相关事实,他们会审查修改或杂项申请文件并审查针对无罪释放令的上诉文件。然后,他们仔细审查由该地区或州总检察长办公室发出的判决案件表格(法律官员案件实施表格 5),以便提出刑事上诉、修改和杂项申请。

在审前法律咨询司,检察官有责任就政府、相关政府部门和组织以及任何起诉机构直接要求的事项进行审查并向联邦总检察长办公室提出法律意见,以便起诉。当仔细审查区域和州总检察长办公室的意见审查确认书副本后相关事项发生修改时,他们以评论的形式回复修改法律意见。

担任联邦级部门检察司的检察官就任何出现在联邦方面的申请,应向联邦最高法院下达令状。

根据"宪法"第 378(a)条,该条规定联邦最高法院有权发出下列令状:

(1)人身保护令;

(2)履行责任令;

(3)禁止书;

(4)现行保证书的令状;

(5)移审令。

在五种令状中,作为刑事杂项申请的人身保护令或作为民事杂项申请的其他文书在联邦最高法院裁决。如是本司司长作出的裁决,他本人应在联邦最高法院就民事杂项申请(令状)或刑事杂项申请(令状)提出论据。这种情况下,多数是移审令。

在民事诉讼司,公诉人就任何涉及政府部门和组织作为原告或被告的民事案件进行审查并提起法律意见。在涉及任何政府部门和组织作为原告或被告参与的民事案件中,审查是否提交上诉案件、特别上诉案件、民事修正案、审查案件或其他申请案件的呈文,将它们提交给联邦最高法院。

联邦总检察长办公室总部的第四个部门行政部的组成:人事和视察司、培训和信息和通信技术司、预算和账务司、研究和后勤司。在这四个司中,一些政府职员是固定的。他们不需要改变工作岗位、工作地点。在这四个司任职的检察官必须一次服务两年或两年以上。他们服务两年后,可以转到其他的法律办公室。

人事司履行管理涉及各级法律服务人员任职、确认、晋升、调动,制定部门查询、准予许可和退休、聘任法律咨询专家等服务人员,安排授予荣誉奖章、准备联邦总检察长办公室和各级法律事务处服务人员名单、安排执委会会议和研讨会、履行安全和绿色环境,并保持联邦总检察长办公室和各级法律办公室的系统记录的职能和职责。检查司根据规定的检查计划对各级法律办公室进行检查。检查司的做法是进行定期检查,必要时进行突击检查和特殊检查。它负责监督相关法律办公室是否执行会计师事务所审计报告中的建议,并履行检查记录所需采取的行动。

作为行政安排,培训司执行以下职能——派遣招聘官员和工作人员参加中央公共事务研究所的入门课程、监督和开设培训课程和进修课程,以提高法律干事的能力,协助法律干事参加当地和国外的培训课程、研讨会和会议。

信息和通信技术司通过信息和通信技术开展办公室工作,维护联邦总检察长办公室和各级法律办公室的服务人员的记录,服务记录和评估卡,并履行联邦总检察长办公室和各级法律办公室服务人员的社会福利。

预算和账务司履行的职能包括及时编制和要求联邦总检察长办公室和各级法律办公室的预算,并为其分配资金;通过保留检查清单确定各律师事务所是否按照基本会计部门的指示使用拨款资金,是否及时发送月结单;开展预算账户的准备工作,转移预算负责人并存储联邦检察长办公室的余额,考虑并允许发生火灾、水和空气危险以及雨季时定额贷款。

研究司的职能是准备在联邦检察总长办公室和各级法律办公室开设的培训课程中教授法律科目的讲义;编制、出版、维护、分发和销售法律年鉴、缅甸法律书籍英文版、法律手册、法律期刊和其他法律研究论文;进行法律研究;研究和保存修改的法律记录;开放法律研究档案、制定法律传播计划、监督联邦总检察长办公室图书馆。

后勤司执行的职能是为联邦总检察长办公室和各级法律办公室寻找地块建立法律办公室,建造各种建筑物,维护和租用建筑物,购买和分发文具,购买和维护车辆,并为联邦检察总局的人员安排渡轮服务。

联邦总检察长办公室四个部门的检察官必须履行有关部门的职责。他们在服务两年后转移到其他法律办公室。但获得国外学位和熟练的参谋人员的检察官在法律审查和咨询部门、法律咨询部门和检察部门中可以被长期任命。

联邦总检察长办公室下设各级法律办公室:

(1)该地区或国家的总检察长办公室

(2)自我管理部门的律师事务所

(3)自我管理区的律师事务所

(4)区法律办公室

(5)乡镇律师办公室

(6)依法成立的其他律师事务所

该地区或州的总检察长办公室由该地区或州的检察长领导。该地区或州的检察长是相关地区或州政府的成员。该地区或州的总检察长应对联邦总检察长或该地区或州的相关首席部长负责。自治司法律办公室、自治区法律办公室和地区法律办公室由被称为一级法律官员的检察官领导。依法组建的乡镇法律办公室和其他法律办公室由被称为三级法官的检察官领导。

在各级法律办公室,检察官在刑事诉讼中与警官、律师和法官合作履行司法义务和职责。刑事诉讼程序可分为调查阶段,审判阶段和后审阶段。这三个阶段,法律官员必须参与。

在刑事诉讼程序中,存在着可识别的犯罪的诉讼和不可识别的犯罪的诉讼。未经司法机关命令,警方不可调查不可识别犯罪行为而是直接向法院投诉。在不可识别的罪行中,警察不得在没有逮捕令的情况下逮捕。《刑事诉讼法》附表2规定了不可识别的犯罪行为,如叛国罪、非法强制劳动、不诚实盗用财产、惩罚欺诈行为等。在可识别的犯罪中,如谋杀、强奸、盗窃、抢劫等,警察可以按照第二节或根据当时有效的任何法律进行逮捕或无证逮捕。当发生可识别的案件时,可以通知派出所。警察应对其进行调查,并可根据《刑事诉讼法》和警察手册的规定逮捕被告。

任何人不得在没有主管裁判官还押的情况下被拘禁超过24小时。如果调查不能在24小时内完成,被告会被送到法院进行还押。在被告人被起诉前,相关法律部门的检察官需检查核实有关被告的信息。如果检察官发现被告是孩子,他建议保释或送交监护人进行纪律监管,然后继续送交法院。

调查结束后,如果案件证据充分,应将案件送交检察官提供预审意见。同时,检察官必须提供法律意见,并将此案送回警察局。之后,该案件将通过该警察局送交有关法院。在还押时间内,警务人员必须请求法律咨询,且须有足够的时间来寻求法律意见。虽然警官有足够的时间进行调查,但他们基本会在还押时间结束时将被告人和案件送交公诉人。在这种情况下,检察官答复预审意见后,他(或她)向上级法律办公室报告来与检察机关合作采取行动。

但是,如果案件中没有足够的证据,被告应该被释放,并且这个案子必须提交给检察官结案。公诉人应当审理和决定不能起诉的案件的结案。检察机关向相关法律办公室提起诉讼时,检察机关应当检查是否有必要的证人名单,是否含有必要的证件或是否符合预审通知后,继续送达法院。

联邦总检察长办公室和各级法律办公室的检察官负责在普通刑事案件、上诉案件、特别上诉案件、修改案件,包括政府在内的其他案件或者法院通知法律办公室进行办公室交流的案件中作为政府律师在法庭上进行听证。因此,检察官参与审判阶段,检察官应根据《联邦总检察长法》在法庭上识别可认知的犯罪。检察官和主审员从原告方审查证人,然后被告自己或辩护律师可以询问这些证人。当证人与主审员的答辩不一致时,检察官应通过重新审查核实情况。

在对原告方的所有证人进行审查之后,检察官主张在提供相关法律时指控被告。法院通过初步证据来指控被告。如果被告承认有罪,他将根据提供的相关法律被定罪;如果被告否认有罪,法院要求他召回已提出证据的控方证人。如果没有初步证据,被告应被释放。如果控告的指令不符合法律规定,公诉人可以向有关法院提出修改意见。

在审判的最后阶段,法院根据确凿的证据作出判决。如果被告人被认定有罪,法庭应根据有关法律将他定罪;若他没有被认定有罪,他将被宣判无罪。之后,法律官员应将案件情况及其相关法律意见通知上级法律办公室。在审判后阶段,如果法官认为法院的判决不符合法律规定,则应将案件作为上诉案件提交有关法院。

在审判的任何阶段,当受害人提出撤诉时,检察官应当审查并决定是否撤诉。

尽管检察官代表申诉人和国家出庭,申诉人有权为他自己雇用私人律师。但聘请的律师应根据《刑事诉讼法》第493条在检察官的指导下进行审理。

因此,在缅甸,检察官参与整个案件。例如,在仰光的一个乡镇发生谋杀案时,警察应调查此案。警方逮捕了被告,并查明证据。谋杀案是不可挽回的罪行。因此,警方需要采取还押方式,他们根据检察官的建议,将被告人押回法庭。然后他们需要接受检察官的审前建议。在检察官对案件证据是否充分进行核实后,他们根据检察官的建议将案件起诉到法院。在审判阶段,检察官领导审判直至完成。如果法院的命令不符合法律,检察官可以向上级法院提出重审或上诉。检察官从始至终负责案件。在法院尚未裁定某一检察官负责某一案件之前,未来负责该案件的该检察官移至另一个办公室后,新检察官应持续对此案负责。

六、中国检察官的职责与权力

人民检察院有权行使检察权。它们针对危害管辖权和治安、破坏经济秩序、侵犯公民的个人权利和民主权利等重大刑事案件行使权力。它们对危害公共利益的民事案件行使这一权力。检察官是负责调查和起诉犯罪的国家官员。他们不代表政府,他们有起诉政府的合法权利。

《中华人民共和国宪法》第129条和《中华人民共和国人民检察院组织法》第1条规定:"中华人民共和国人民检察院是国家的法律监督机关。"根据《中华人民共和国宪法》第131条的规定,人民检察院依法独立行使检察权,不受行政机关、社会团体和个人的干涉。根据《中华人民共和国检察官法》的规定，检察官的职责是依法监督法律的执行，代表国家提起公诉，对人民检察院直接受理的刑事案件进行调查，并履行法律规定的其他职能和义务。

最高人民检察院是国家的最高检察机关，代表国家独立实施检察权，它对全国人大常委会负责。它的主要任务是对地方各级人民检察院和人民检察院执行监督职能并进行领导，确保国家法律的统一和正确执行。

最高人民检察院的基础部门下的各部门分别负有主要任务。监狱和拘留部门负责指导行政机关执行处罚、减刑，释放、假释、允许医疗保释监狱，通过强制劳动和额外羁押时间的监督确保监狱、拘留中心的负责教育的机关行动的合法性；指导调查审理不法行为案件之前的相关刑罚执行问题，如虐待在监狱或拘留中心的人员，擅自释放被拘留者，疏忽导致被羁押者逃脱、减刑，由于给予偏袒和从事不正规的做法，允许释放、假释和医疗保释；处理下级检察院对疑难案件提出的问题，研究制定关于监狱，看守所检察工作的规章制度。

此外，总部和管理部门负责指导国内民事和经济纠纷的审判以及行政收费和监督案件；按照检察监督程序，针对各级法院对民事、经济和行政已经实施但实际上是错误案件的判决向最高人民检察院提出抗议；在最高人民法院审判期间，最高人民检察院就抗诉的民事、经济和行政案件出庭；研究国内关于民事和经济争议审理问题和行政案件的指控和监督中的非常棘手的问题并提出解决方案；就下级检察机关对民事、行政工作中的疑难问题进行调查；研究制定有关民事行政监督工作的规章制度。

刑事上诉部门负责指导有关刑事上诉和赔偿诉讼机构的工作；处理公民的刑事申诉、服刑的罪犯或其近亲属或合法代理人的上诉；处理检察机关管辖的刑事申诉案件，督促检察机关调查和报告结果；对刑事申诉和赔偿情况进行全面报道；处理刑事上诉和赔偿；研究制定刑事上诉和赔偿工作的规章制度。

铁路运输检察部门负责指导全国铁路的运输检察工作；直接参与或组织或协调对国家有影响和正在由检察机关处理的重大案件的调查；批准对涉及国家的铁路运输的严重案件的逮捕和指控；研究分析铁路运输中的犯罪活动和趋势，并提出应对形势的政策；研究制定铁路运输起诉工作的规章制度。

疏忽职责侵权检察部门负责指导公务员因玩忽职守、滥用职权非法拘禁他人，通过刑讯逼供、诬陷报复、搜查和从事其他侵犯公民的人身权利和民主权利的犯罪活动案件的调查和询问工作；参与对重大责任和侵权行为重大案件的侦查工作；直接查办国家重大责任事故和侵权行为的重大案件；组织、协调、领导重大涉嫌违法事件和涉及多个省份权利案件的调查工作；研究和分析责任和侵权犯罪的规则和特点,并提出相应的处理对策;处理下级检察机关就其工作中出现的严重和困难问题;研究制定有关起诉和侵权纠纷案件的规章制度。

举报和收费检察部门负责为国内检察机关举报和收费工作提供指导;处理公民提出的举报和收费;将有关举报和收费线索提交有关机构,对不清楚由哪个机构可作为处理机构,因此难以转交有关部门的案件举报和收费线索进行初步调查;对举报和收费情况进行全面报告;研究制定举报和收费工作的规章制度。

滥用职权罪的预防部门负责指导检察机关预防利用职务犯罪的工作;研究分析国家工作人员利用职务犯罪的规律和特点,提出反对贿赂、贪污贿赂和疏忽职务的相关政策;开展预防未成年人犯罪工作;在预防利用职务犯罪人员犯罪方面进行法制宣传;处理下级检察院关于预防利用职务犯罪过程中出现的最难的问题;研究制定利用职务犯罪预防工作的规章制度。

调查监督部门负责对国内刑事案件嫌疑人的逮捕和调查工作(包括检察机关直接处理的涉嫌受贿、贪污和玩疏职守的案件)并提供指导,同时对案件的调查情况进行监督;处理涉及最高人民检察院批准逮捕的案件;对下级检察机关就批准逮捕的疑难问题提出的问询作出答复;指导审查和批准逮捕未成年人犯罪;研究制定关于批准逮捕工作的规章制度。

检察部门负责对提起诉讼的审查提出指导意见,向法院提起指控,并就国内刑事判决和有关刑事案件的判决提出抗议(包括检察机关直接调查受贿罪、贪污罪和玩忽职守罪的案件);对人民法院审判活动的监督提供指导;承担最高人民检察院提起法律诉讼或抗诉的案件和履行最高检向最高法提出抗的案件中的法院职责;处理下级检察机关就提起法律诉讼出现的难点问题;为涉及未成年人案件的法律诉讼工作提供指导;研究制定公共收费工作的规章制度。

反贪污贿赂管理机构负责指导国内检察机关处理的涉贿、贪污挪用公款、巨额资金来源不明、隐瞒海外存款、划分国有私人之间的资金或没收的财产的调查询问工作;参与重大贿赂和贪污刑事案件的调查工作;组织、协调、领导重大贪污贿赂案件调查工作;负责协调调查严重贿赂和贪污案件;研究分析国内贪污贿赂罪的规定和特点,并提出处理此类犯罪的政策;解决下级检察机关就反贪污和贿赂工作疑难问题提出的询问;研究制定反贪污和贿赂罪起诉工作的规章制度。

法律和政策研究室负责研究国家有关检察工作的法律,法规和政策的执行情况,并提出相应的建议;负责起草有关检察工作的法律;处理关于司法协助和引渡协议的法律文件的起草和谈判；对起诉适用理论进行研究；当最高人民检察院被质询时，就国家法律和行政法规草案提出建议；对有关起诉的法律问题给予司法解释；研究和规划检察工作法制建设；负责最高人民检察院检察委员会的日常工作；为检察工作基本理论研究提供指导；对检察机关对法律执行情况的检查提供指导和领导；收集起诉工作的书籍和资料；编辑和编制关于起诉工作的法律、法律文件和年鉴；承担最高人民检察院特别咨询委员会的日常工作；并处理最高人民检察院有关台湾地区的工作。

监察局负责指导国内所有检察机关的监督工作；检查各级检察机关及其下属机构对最高人民检察院或上级检察院的法律、法规、决定的执行情况；处理针对检察机关成员违纪行为的指控和举报；处理违反纪律的检察人员及其对纪律处分决定提出的上诉。

外事局负责检察机关的对外交流和国际司法协助，指导国内检察机关开展对外交流；负责全国各地检察机关与港澳地区的联系和协助；负责调查涉外案件；协调和管理最高人民检察院和外国检察机构之间协议的起草和谈判；翻译和汇编相关资料，研究国际司法发展。

规划、财务和设备局负责向国内检察机关提供规划和财务指导；制定国家检察机关财务和设备的长期和中期发展计划并实施这些计划；分配和管理检察机关的工作、设备和基本建设资金；就技术装备、运输、通信、军备和制服的国家起诉制度规划提供指导；审查和管理最高人民检察院各分支机构和附属机构的日常工作、基建和外事活动的资金；处理物资设备的统一采购和配置。

而且，人民检察院参与刑事诉讼。刑事司法程序中包含四个部分：提起诉讼，调查、起诉和刑事审判。在提起案件是人民检察院或者公安机关应当决定立案侦查或审判。人民检察院调查的案件包括贪污贿赂犯罪，国家工作人员渎职犯罪，涉及侵犯公民人身权利和侵犯公民民主权利罪以及国家工作人员利用职务之便犯下的重大罪行。

根据《刑事诉讼法》第111条的规定，公安机关应当立案侦查的案件而不立案侦查的，人民检察院应当要求公安机关说明不予立案的理由。人民检察院认为公安机关不予立案的理由不成立的，应当通知公安机关立案，公安机关接到通知后，应当立案。

在侦查阶段，对犯罪嫌疑人的讯问必须由人民检察院或公安机关的侦查人员进行。人民检察院认为有必要核实公安机关进行调查研究的，可以要求后者进行勘验或者检查，并可以派检察员参加。在人民检察院直接受理的案件调查中，犯罪嫌疑人的逮捕或者拘留由人民检察院决定，由公安机关执行。

对犯罪嫌疑人的讯问必须在拘留或逮捕后 24 小时内进行,如果发现该人不应被拘留或逮捕,必须立即释放。公安机关对犯罪嫌疑人进行逮捕时,应当连同案件档案和证据提出逮捕批准的书面请求,由同级人民检察院审查批准。人民检察院认为有必要在被直接受理的案件中逮捕被拘留人的,应当在 14 日内作出决定。

对于公安机关移送审查起诉的案件或者人民检察院自行审查起诉的案件进行全面审查后,根据审查结果,人民检察院认为应向法院起诉的,认为应当向法院提起公诉。对于公安机关移送起诉和人民检察院自行审查起诉的案件,经过全面审查,根据审查结果,发现嫌疑人不得依法追究刑事责任,或者案件较轻,违法者不需依法追究刑事责任或者需要依法免除责任或者补充侦查两次后不符合起诉条件的情形,检察院应当决定不将案件移交人民法院审判。审查需要补充侦查的案件,人民检察院可以将案件归还公安机关进行补充侦查或者自行进行侦查。公安机关认为不起诉的决定有错误的,可以要求复议;如果被拒绝,可以将其提交上一级人民检察院提请复核。

在刑事审判中,人民法院审理人民检察院提起公诉的案件。人民检察院派员出庭支持公诉。各国公民有权在法庭诉讼中使用本国的口头和书面语言。诉讼中,人民法院和人民检察院应当向不熟悉当地通用的语言文字的法院诉讼当事人提供翻译。根据 2012 年《中华人民共和国刑事诉讼法》第 64 条的规定,人民法院、人民检察院和公安机关可以根据案件情况对犯罪嫌疑人、被告人可以拘传、取保候审或监视居住。人民检察院对指定住所监视居的住决定和执行的合法性进行监督。

人民检察院发现人民法院处理案件时违反法律规定的诉讼程序的,有权向人民法院提出建议。最高人民检察院发现各级人民法院已经发生法律效率的判决或者裁定中确有错误的,或者上级人民检察院发现下级人民法院已经发生法律效力的判决、裁定存在明显错误的,有权根据审判监督程序,向作出判决、裁定的同级人民法院提出抗诉。

人民法院决定执行死刑前,应当通知同级人民检察院派员监督执行。人民检察院认为人民法院裁定减刑或者假释令不当的,应当自收到书面命令副本之日起 20 日内,提交书面申请向人民法院提出改正建议。人民法院应当自收到建议之日起 1 个月内重新组成合议庭处理案件,并作出最终裁定。人民检察院通过执行机关对刑事处罚进行监督,查明执行是否符合法律规定。一旦发现违法行为的,应当通知执行机关纠正。

七、结 论

在两个有不同法律制度的国家,虽然检察官有不同的权力,但他们殊途同归——那就是维护法治。中国的检察官可以自行调查案件,但这不是对警察职责的干涉。这会使得权利在重大案件中更为有力。

如果警察不履行完成职责,两个国家的检察官都不会将案件进行下去或要求警方完全履行其所有职责。如果法院的临时命令或最终命令不符合法律规定,则必须向上级法院提出上诉或重审。在法院审理程序中,如果法官或律师的行为不符合法律规定,他们要求记录在案并通知上级法院。

中国检察官只是刑事案件和民事案件的法定监督人,中国检察官比缅甸检察官权力更大。缅甸检察官在涉及政府的刑事、民事案件、提出法律建议和其他职能方面有许多责任和义务。因此,为了提高缅甸检察官的技能,每位检察官都必须了解现行法律、国际法、商法和立法起草及其他法律知识。目前,在联邦总检察长办公室,经常有与国际组织合作的为法律干事举办的讲习班、培训和研讨会。一些法律官员被派往国外学习并获得硕士学位和博士学位。尊重人权和法治要求联邦总检察长办公室以公正和功能独立的方式调查和起诉刑事犯罪。在联邦总检察长办公室内部,检察官必须有权以独立、公正和客观的方式诚信履行职责,并保护公共利益。

检察官必须有崇尚正义的精神,他们必须没有恐惧和偏爱的做出决定。联邦总检察长办公室需要更多的合格和公正的检察官。他们不仅可以保护无罪的人民和国家,还可以用他们的法律知识打击犯罪分子。国家将从他们的责任中高效率地获得更多利益。

参考文献

- Attorney General of the Union Act,1948.
- 缅甸联邦社会主义共和国宪法,1974 年。
- The Attorney General Law,1988.
- The Attorney General Law,2001.
- The Attorney General Law,2010.
- The Attorney-General of the Union Law,22/2010.
- 缅甸联邦共和国宪法,2008 年。
- The Attorney-General of the Union Rules,2016.

- 中华人民共和国人民检察院组织法。
- 中华人民共和国宪法,1982 年。
- 中华人民共和国检察官法。
- 刑事诉讼法(缅甸)。
- 中华人民共和国刑事诉讼法,2012 年。

General Principles of Civil Procedure Code in Myanmar

Khin Htar Win[*]

Abstract：As the One Belt And One Road initiative continues to advance，China-Myanmar cooperation in the fields of science，technology，culture and economy has deepened. China has become the largest investor in Myanmar，so it is necessary for us to understand the basic principles of Myanmar's civil procedure law. The civil procedure law of Myanmar was originally derived from Indian law and was influenced by British practices and procedures. Therefore，the legal system is antagonistic. This paper analyzes in detail the basic principles of jurisdiction，prosecution，judgment，decree，execution and trial supervision in the civil procedure law of Myanmar. At the same time，however，the existing civil procedure law of Myanmar also has the problem of being unable to adapt to the status quo. The supreme federal law will review and revise the civil procedure law.

Keywords：Jurisdiction，Prosecution，Decree，Execution Appeal

The Code of Civil Procedure（CPC），1908 is prescribed in Myanmar by English Language；the original Code of Civil Procedure is an India Act. It contains 153 Sections and 53 Orders. The Code of Civil Procedure Code shall be exercised with Sections，Orders and Rules. The Code of Civil Procedure is the procedure law which is consists of the provisions from institution to execution of civil suits，appeals from original decree，reference，review and

---

　＊ Khin Htar Win，Doctoral Student of School of International Law of SWUPL/Assistant Lecturer，Department of Law， University of Myitkyina，Myitkyina ，Kachin State，Myanmar，E-mail：khinkhinhtar. khw@gmail. com.

revision etc. The Myanmar's legal system is as an adversarial system. Cases are heard before the court; before a judge or bench of judges and argued by advocates or pleaders. The Code of Civil Procedure provides the main source of Myanmar's procedural rules relating to civil litigation or civil suits. Advocates or pleaders also refer to the Courts Manual of 1960 and the Evidence Act of 1872.

The practices and procedures of Myanmar, courts were significantly influenced by English practices and procedures. Myanmar does not have a developed disputes resolution mechanism, though courts do conduct arbitration. In general, Myanmar courts have jurisdiction to try all civil suits, except certain cases barred by law. The appropriate court in which to commence proceedings in Myanmar is dependent upon the type and value of the claim and the location of the parties or the place of the business is in or act in question was carried out.

Suits in general are detailed by the Civil Procedure Code. The Court shall have jurisdiction to try all suits of civil nature excepting suits of which their cognizance is either expressly or implied barred. (Section 9)

No Court shall proceed with the trial of any suit in which the matter in issue is also directly and substantially in a previously instituted suit. But these suits must between the same parties or parties under whom they or any of them claim, litigating under the same title, and where such suit is pending in the same Court or any other Court having jurisdiction. (Section 10)

No Court shall try any suitor issue in which the matter directly and substantially in issue has been directly in issue in a former suit between the same parties, litigating same title in the Court such issue has been heard and finally decided. (Section 11)

Where a plaintiff is precluded by rules from instituting a further suit in respect of any particular cause of action, he shall not be entitled to institute a suit for such cause of action. (Section 12)

Jurisdiction in general

Jurisdiction is the extent of the power of the Court to entertain suits, appeals and applications. The jurisdiction of the Court may be original or appellate suits. In the exercise of its original jurisdiction a Court entertains the original suits. In the exercise of its appellate jurisdiction, it hears appeals from decree passed by the subordinate Courts. In the other way, jurisdiction means the extent of the authority of a Court to administer justice not only with reference to the subject-matter of the suit but also to the local and pecuniary limits of its jurisdiction.

Generally, according to the Code of Civil Procedure, four kinds of jurisdiction:

1) Territorial Jurisdiction
2) Pecuniary Jurisdiction
3) Personal Jurisdiction, and
4) Subject-matter Jurisdiction

Powers and jurisdiction of Courts

Regarding to the administration of justice, the Supreme Court of the Union has vested increased the judicial powers to the Courts of the Self-Administered Division, Courts of the Self-Administered Zone, District Courts and Township Courts in disposal of the civil regular cases.

Under the Union Judiciary Law, the Supreme Court has also original civil jurisdiction in matters arising out of bilateral treaties concluded by the Union, other disputes between the Union of Government and the Region or State Government, among the states, between the Region and the State and between the Union Territory and the Region or the State except the Constitutional problems.

Inoriginal civil suit, relating to pecuniary jurisdiction, the Supreme Court and the High Courts of the Region or the State have not limited pecuniary jurisdiction. The other Courts of judges have jurisdiction as follows:

• District Judge- pecuniary jurisdiction to try an original civil suit for a maximum value of 500 million kyats (approximately USD 500,000);

• Deputy District Judge- pecuniary jurisdiction to try an original civil suit for a maximum value of 100 million kyats (approximately USD 100,000);

　• Township Judge- pecuniary jurisdiction to try an original civil suit for a maximum value of ten million kyats (approximately USD 10,000);

　• Additional Township Judge- pecuniary jurisdiction to try an original civil suit for a maximum value of seven million kyats (approximately USD 7,000);

　• Deputy Township Judge- pecuniary jurisdiction to try an original civil suit for a maximum value of three million kyats (approximately USD 3,000).

　In other words, there are many suits that are the very difficult to fix the value in order to make jurisdiction, for instance, the case that the desire to be good relationship between husband and wife and to remove a trustee. These kinds of suit, the value of suit is described by the plaintiff should be accepted as jurisdiction. If the value of the suit cannot be fixed accurately when the plaint is presented, the Court can pass a decree more than own jurisdiction.

　However, the object upon the jurisdiction of the Court that examines a suit in respect of showing money value either more or less should not be accepted or considered by an Appellate Court if a defendant does not object when it is time to give issue or before giving issue.

　According to the Code of Civil Procedure, relating to place of suing, every civil suit shall be commenced with the presentation of a plaint. Moreover, the plaint must be presented to a Court having jurisdiction. But, other suits to be instituted where defendants reside or cause of action arise. And also every suit shall be instituted in the Court of the lowest grade competent to try the suits. (Section 15)

　Conversely, where a suit which ought to have been instituted in a Court of higher grade is institute in a Court of lower grade, such Court shall return the plaint to the plaintiff to be presented to the Court of higher grade.

　In suits for reacquisition of immoveable property; for the partition of immoveable property; for foreclosure, sale or redemption in the case of a mortgage of or charge upon immoveable property; for the determination of any other right to or interest in immoveable property; for compensation for destroying immoveable property; for reacquisition of immoveable property actually under restraint or attachment must be instituted in the court within the local limits of whose jurisdiction the property is located. However, where relief can be entirely obtained through the defendant's compliance, a suit may be instituted either in the court within the local limits of whose jurisdiction the property is situated or in the court within the local limits of whose jurisdiction the defendant actually resides or carries on business or works. (Section 16)

And also according to Order 7, Rule 3, where the subject-matter of the suit is immoveable property, the plaint shall prescribe the description of the property sufficient to identify it, specifying the boundaries numbers.

Therefore, Courts have no power to decide on rights and interests in property lying outside their local jurisdiction. Provided that the court can give the relief I suits respecting immoveable property situate abroad by enforcing their judgments by process in *personam*, i. e., by arrest of the person of the defendant or by attachment of his personal property. But, in order to do this it is essential that the defendant must either reside or curry on business or personally work for gain within the local limit of the Court's jurisdiction.

Process for Institution of suits under the Civil Procedure Code

Civil suit is one kind of a case dealing with money suit or personal damage. It concerns with, there are relevant to civil suit, failure of the promise, debt, to recover of properties, compensation, to serve according to the order, etc. When the suit is instituted, the plaintiff who wants to get relief shall serve a court-fee for his suing.

Relating to the institution of suit, serve the sufficient Court-fees and litigation within the time of limitation. So, subject-matter of the suit must be valued for Court-fees and sufficiently stamped. The Court-fees Act provides fixed Court-fees and court-fees payable in suit value. All fees referred or chargeable under the Act shall be collected by stamps. (The Court-fees Act, Section 25)

Every suit shall be instituted by the presenting of a plaint or in such other manner as may be prescribed by any existing law. Plaint is the statement of a claim, in writing and filed by the plaintiff, in which he sets out his cases of action with all necessary particulars. (Section 26)

Every plaint, as far as applicable, shall comply with the rules contains in Orders 6 and 7 of the Civil Procedure Code (Order 4 Rule 1). And also the essentials of a suit are four in number. There are as follows:

1) The opposing parties

2) The cause of action

3) The subject-matter, and

4) The relief claimed

Under the provisions of Sections 15 to 20 of the Code of Civil Procedure, the plaint is to be presented the Court of the lowest grade competent to try the matter or to its authorized officer. Although the plaint may be validly received on a Court holiday or at the judge's club or at his residence, the Court is not bound to accept it in such manners.

One of the important things is that the suit is not barred to further suit by any law. The following suits are expressly precluded to further suit by the Code of Civil Procedure:

- Res judicata. (section 11)
- The suit shall include the whole of the claim which the plaintiff is entitled to make in respect of the cause of action. If he relinquishes any portion of his claim withoutpermission of the Court, he could not sue further suit relating to the same cause of action. (Order 2, Rule 2)
- The plaintiff does not come to the Court on the day of hearing suit. At that time, the Court can make an order that the suit to be dismissed. (Order 9, Rule 8)
- Suit to be terminated or dismissed in accordance with Order 22, Rule 8 of the Code of Civil Procedure. (Order 22, Rule 9)
- Suit to be withdrawn without permission of the Court, for such suit, a plaintiff cannot sue again. (Order 23, Rule 1)

Moreover, the most important fact is to be correct of the form of suit in the civil suit. It is necessary to be correct form of suit in title and claiming in plaint. The form of suit is based on the cause of action.

When the suit is instituted under CPC, the following facts should be careful, the suit:

- must be civil nature.
- must not the Res judicata (it should not be a final decision).
- should not be barred by any law.
- should be instituted in a Court having jurisdiction.
- should be instituted only in a place where the properties situate for

immoveable properties.

    • should be instituted in a place where a defendant actually or voluntarily resides.

    • should be instituted giving court-fee in respective Court and within the period prescribed by the law of Limitations.

    • should be careful need or not to give notice prescribed by the law.

The Court shall cause the particulars of every suit to be entered in a book to be kept for the purpose of and called the register of civil suits. Ifthe plaintiff submits the two plaints at the same day, the first entry in a book must be the first suit.

Kinds of civil action

The following kinds of suit are may be determined or considered as civil action:

    • Entitles relating to immoveable and moveable property

    • Entitles concerning money

    • Claims relating to specific action

    • Claims relating to abolish, administer and suit for accounts concerned with firms, companies and organizations

    • Claims relating to mortgage

    • Claims relating to social relation, and

    • Claims for compensation

Regarding to the frame of suit, every suit shall be framed as to afford ground for final decision upon the subjects in dispute and to prevent further litigation concerning them.

The suit must be framed as much as possible in order not to have the further litigation dealing with the same cause of action. This kind of suit, the cause of action and parties to suit can be jointly instituted in the suit.

Power of Transfer or withdrawal of Cases

Where a suit is instituted in any one of two or more courts, any defendant, after notice to the other parties, can apply to have the suit transferred to another court at the earliest possible opportunity. The court to which such an application is made will determine in which court the suit will proceed. (Section 22)

In suits that including claiming compensation for a wrong act to the person or to moveable property, where such an act was done within the local limits of the jurisdiction of one court, and the defendant resides, or carries on business or works within the local limits of the jurisdiction of another court, the suit may be instituted at the option of the plaintiff in either of the relevant courts.

When the several courts having jurisdiction are subordinate to the same appellate court, an application shall be made to the appellate court. Where such courts are subordinate to different appellate courts, the application shall be made to the High Court. (Section 23)

The Supreme Court, or the State or Divisional Court (High Court) may at any stage transfer any suit, appeal, or other pending proceeding to any court subordinate to it to try or dispose of the case.

Also, the Supreme Court, or the State or Divisional Court (High Court) may withdraw any suit, appeal, or other pending proceeding in any court subordinate toit and try or dispose of the case itself, or transfer the case for trial or disposal to any court subordinate to it to try or dispose the case. It may also retransfer the same case for trial or disposal to the court from which it was withdrawn. (Section 24)

Judgment

Judgment is the statement given by the judge of the grounds of a decree or order. After the case has been heard the Court may pronounce the judgment at once in open Court or it may reserve its judgment and deliver the same on any future date, of which due notice shall be given to the parties or their pleaders. (Order 20, Rule 1)

And also a judge who is the new presiding judge (successor judge) of the Court may pronounce the judgment written but not pronounced by his predecessor.

The judgment shall be dated and signed by the judge in open Court at the time of pronouncing it and, when once signed, shall not afterwards be altered of added to , save as provided by section 152 or on reviews.

Decree

Decree is the formal expression of an adjudication which, so far as regards the Court expressing it, conclusively determines the rights of the parties with regard to all or any of the maters in controversy in the suit and may be either preliminary or final decree. After the judgment is pronounced the successful party applies to the Court for the drawing up for the decree, which is drawn up by an officer of the Court.

The decree shall consistent with the judgment, and also it shall:

1) contain the number of the suit, the names and description of the parties, and particular of the claims, and shall specify clearly the relief granted or other determination of the suit.

2) state the amount of costs incurred in the suit, and by whom or out of what property and in what proportion such costs are to be paid.

3) direct that the costs payable to one party by the other shall be set off against any sum which is admitted or found to be due from the former to the latter.

The decree shall bear date the day on which the judgment was pronounced, and, when the judge has satisfied himself that the decree has been drawn up in accordance with the judgment, he shall sign the decree. (Order 20, Rule 7)

If where a judge has vacated office after pronouncing judgment but without signing the decree, a decree drawn up in accordance with such judgment may be signed by his successor or, if the Court has ceased to exist, by the judge or any Court to which such Court was subordinate.

So, a decree is to be differed from a judgment. A decree is a thing to be executed and a judgment is a mere a record of the reasons on which the decree is based. There are two types of decree: one is preliminary decree and another is final decree.

Execution of Decrees

Execution is the enforcement of decrees and orders by process of the Court, so as to the judgment-creditor to recover the suits of the judgment. The decree to be executed is the decree of the Court of first instance if no appeal is preferred. If an appeal is preferred, it is the decree of the last Appellate Court.

Decree may be executed either by the Court which passed it, or be the Court to which it is sent for execution. Where the immoveable property forms one estate or tenure situate within the local limits of the jurisdiction of two or more Courts, any one of such Court may attach and sell the entire or tenure. (Section 38)

Relating to application for execution where the holder of a decree desires to execute, he shall apply to the Court which passed the decree or to the officer (if any) appointed in this behalf, or if the decree has been sect under to another Court, then to such Court or to the proper officer thereof.

At the time of presenting the application for execution of at the time of admission thereof the decree-holder may deposit in Court the fees requisite for all necessary proceedings in the execution.

If no application is made by the holder of a decree within six months of the date of the receipt of the papers, the Court shall return them to the Court which passed the decree with certificates stating the circumstances as prescribe by section 41.

The Court to which a decree is sent for execution shall certify to the Court which passed it the fact of such execution, or where the former Court fails to execute the same circumstances attending such failure.

According to Order 21, Rule 11 the Civil Procedure Code, application for execution of decree may be made by two ways:

i. oral application, and

ii. written application

Execution is the final stage goes to the suit. It is the means employed in due process of law to make a decree or order of a Court effective. The successful party makes an application in writing to the executing Court when proceedings in execution are commenced.

The execution of decrees shall, so far as they are applicable, be deemed to apply to the execution of orders. A decree may be executed either by the court which passed it or by the court to which it is sent for execution. The court which passed a decree may, on the application of the decree-holder, send it for execution to another court. The court executing a decree sent to it shall have the same power in executing such decree as if it had been passed itself. All persons disobeying or obstructing the execution of the decree shall be punishable by such court in the same manner as if it had passed the decree. And its order in executing such decree shall be subject to the same rules in respect of appeal.

The court may order to execute the decree in the following manners, subject to the rules and regulations as may be prescribed:

- by delivery of any property especially decrees;
- by sale with attachment or without attachment of any property;
- by arrest and detention in prison;
- by appointing a receiver or;
- in other manners as the nature of its relief may require.

However, where the decree is for the payment of money, execution by detention in prison cannot be ordered without giving the judgment-debtor an opportunity of showing cause why he should not be committed to prison.

According to the provisions of the Civil Procedure Code, relating to execution of decree shall, so far as they are applicable, be deemed to apply to the execution of orders.

Appeals

Subject to the conditions and limitations as may be prescribed, an Appellate Court shall have the power:

- to remand a case;
- to frame issues and refer them for trial;
- to take additional evidence or to require such evidence to be taken.

It also has the same powers and performs the same duties imposed on courts of original jurisdiction in respect of suits instituted therein.

Relating to appeals from original decree or order shall, so far as may be, apply to appeal:

- from appellate decree, and
- from orders made under the Civil Procedure Code or under any special or local law in which a different procedure is not provided.

An appeal can be made from every decree passed by any court exercising original jurisdiction to the court authorized to hear appeals from the decision of such court passed *ex parte*. No appeal shall lie from a decree passed by the court with the consent of parties. (Section 96)

An appeal shall lie with the Supreme Court from every decree passed in appeal by the State or Divisional Court (High Court), on any of the following grounds:

• the decision being contrary to law or to some usage having the binding force of law;

• the decision having failed to determine some important issue of law or usage having the binding force of law;

• a substantial error or defect in the procedure provided by law, which may possibly have produced error or defect in the decision of the case;

• in a suit where the amount of claim or value of the subject-matter of the original suit exceeds two million kyats (approximately USD 2,000);

Every appeal shall be preferred in the form of a memorandum signed by the appellant or his pleader and presented to the Court or to such office as it appoints in this behalf. The memorandum shall be accompanied by a copy of at the decree appealed from and (unless the Appellate Court dispenses therewith) of the judgment on which is founded. (Order 41)

The memorandum shall set forth, concisely and under distinct head's the grounds of objection to the decree appealed from without any argument or narrative; and such grounds shall be numbered consecutively. When Myanmar dates are given the corresponding English dates shall be added. The memorandum shall also contain:

• the full names and addresses of all parties;

• particulars (class, number, year and Court) of the original proceeding; and

• the value of the appeal (i) for court-fees, and (ii) for jurisdiction.

Where a memorandum of appeal is admitted, the Appellate Court or the proper officer of that Court shall endorse thereon the date of the presentation, and shall register and record in book of the Register of Appeals. (Order 41, Rule 9)

Relating to second appeal to the Supreme Court, a Court of first appeal is competent to enter into question of fact, and decide whether the findings of facts, by the lower grade Court are or are not erroneous. But a Court of second appeal is not competent to entertain questions as to the soundness of a finding of fact by the Court of subordinate. A second appeal can only lie on one of the grounds specified in section 100.

According to section 100, save where otherwise expressly provide in the body of the Civil Procedure Code or by any other law for the time being in force, and appeal shall lie to a High Court from every decree passed in appeal by any Court Subordinate to the High Court of the Regions or the Divisions, on any of the following grounds, namely:

1) the decision being contrary to law or to some material issue of law or usage having the force of law;

2) the decision having failed to determine some material issue of law or usage having the force of law;

3) a substantial error or defect in the procedure provide by this Code or by any other la for the time being in force, which may possible have produce error or defect in the decision of the case upon the merits;

4) in a suit where the amount or value of the subject-matter of the original suit exceeds 1,000,000 kyats, any ground which would be a good ground of appeal if the decree had been passed in an original suit whenever the decree of the Appellate Court varies or reverses, otherwise than as to costs, the decree of the original Court.

And also an appeal may lie under section 100 from an appellate decree passed *ex parte*.

An appeal can also arise from made under rules from which appeal is expressly allowed by rules. (Section 104)

An appeal shall lie from the following orders, and save as otherwise expressly provided in the body of this Code or by any law for the time being in force, from no other orders:

• an order was passed under section 35 (A) and section 95;

• an order was passed under any provisions of this Code imposing a fine or directing the arrest or detention in the civil prison of any person expect where such arrest or detention is in execution of a decree;

Provided that no appeal shall lie against any order specified in section 104 (a) save on the ground that no order, or an order for the payment of a less amount, ought to have been made.

Where an appeal from any order in allowed it shall lie to the Court to which an appeal would lie from the decree in the suit in which such order was made, or where such order is made by the Court of the Self-Administered Division or the Court of Self- Administered Zone or the District Court, or the High Court of the Regions or the High Court of the states in the exercise of appellate jurisdiction, then to the immediate higher Court. (Section 106)

An appeal can be made to the Supreme Court from any decree or final order passed by the High Court or by any other court of final appellate jurisdiction; from any decree or final order passed by the High Court in the exercise of its original civil jurisdiction; and from any decree or order when the case is certified to be fit for appeal to the Supreme Court. An appeal to the Supreme Court, against a decree or final order which has been affirmed by a lower court, must involve a substantial legal question. (Sections 109 and 110)

No appeal can lie in the Supreme Court from the decree or order of one judge or of two or more judges of the High Court or any other courts constituted by more than two judges, where such judges are equally divided in opinion and do not amount in number to a majority of the whole of the judges. Also, no appeal can lie in the Supreme Court from any decree from which no second appeal is allowed by law. (Section 111)

Processes for Review

The Supreme Court of the Union, or the High Court of the Regions or the High Court of the State, or the Court of the Self-Administered Division or the Court of the Self-Administered Zone, or the District Court may call for the record of any case which has been decided by any Court subordinate to the e Court of the Union, or the High Court of the Regions or the High Court of the State, or the Court of Self-Administered Division or the Court of the Self-Administered Zone, or the District Court and in which no appealis pending, and if such subordinate Court appear:

- to have exercised a jurisdiction not vested in it by law；or
- to have failed to exercise jurisdiction so vested；or
- to have acted in the exercise of its jurisdiction illegally or with material angularity.

The Supreme Court of the Union，or the High Court of the Regions or the High Court of the State，or the Court of Self-Administered Division or the Court of the Self-Administered Zone，or the District Court may make such order in the case at it thinks fit. However，this rule is inapplicable to the record of any case which has been decided by any court in the exercise of its revision power or appellate jurisdiction.（Section 115）

Any court can state and refer a case to the Supreme Court to get an opinion. Any person considering himself aggrieved can apply for a review of judgment to the court which passed the decree or made the order. Moreover，these requirements do not affect the power of the Supreme Court in the exercise of its revision power.（Sections 113 and 114）

Conclusion

In Myanmar，Myanmar Codes（Volume 1 to 13）codified the laws have to be exercising in Myanmar. There is no comprehensive Civil Code which covers all types of civil suits in Myanmar. The Civil Procedure Code consists of two parts；one is sections and another is orders. The sections are substantive nature which laid down the general principles and the rules furnished machinery for applying those sections. The present Civil Code of Procedure is the Code which was adopted in 1909. Until now，in Myanmar，this CPC is continued to be in force and operation although some provisions were amended in 2000，2008 and 2014. Some laws which were exercising in Myanmar are inconsistence with the present day. So，the Supreme Court of the Union is going to review the laws（includes the Code of Civil Procedure）to be consistence with the current situation of the State.

References

Laws
1. The Civil Procedure Code，1908，The Myanmar Code，Vol-XII.

2. The Law Amendingthe Code of Civil Procedure, 2000 and 2008.

3. Courts Manual, 1970.

4. The Court Fees Act.

5. The Limitation Act.

6. The Supreme Court of the Union Notification No. 100/2011 and 101/2011.

Books

1. Alec Christie,The Rule of Law and Commercial Litigation in Myanmar, 2000.

2. Dinshah Fardunji Mulla, Sir, The Code of Civil Procedure Act V of 1908, Third Edition and Ninth Edition, Culcutta, 1954.

3. BaKyaing, U, Civil Court Practice and Procedure, First Edition, June, 2008.

4. Htin Zaw, U, Notes of Civil Practice Applies, Vol-I, III and XIV.

5. Mya, U, The Code of Civil Procedure, Vol-I, II and III, First Edition, 1990.

6. Myint Lwin, U, Practical Court Civil Pleas, First Edition, 2008.

7. ThanShwe, U, Danuphyu, Notes of Civil Procedure, First Edition, October, 2010.

8. TinShwe, U, Monywa, The Code of Civil Procedure, Vol-I, First Edition, December, 1989.

Websites

1. www. burmalibrary. org.

2. www. unionsupremecourt. gov. mm.

3. www. icnl. org.

4. www. kora. lib. keio. ac. jp.

缅甸民事诉讼法的基本原则

Khin Htar Win[*]

编译　郭雅菲[**]

摘要:随着"一带一路"倡议不断推进,中缅在科技,文化,经济等领域的合作不断深化。中国已成为缅甸最大的投资者,因此,我们有必要了解缅甸民事诉讼法的基本原则。缅甸民事诉讼法最初源于印度法律,受到英国惯例和程序的影响。因此,其法律制度具有对抗性。本文详细分析了缅甸民事诉讼法中的管辖权,起诉,判决,法令,执行和审判监督的基本原则。但与此同时,缅甸现行的民事诉讼法也存在无法适应现状的问题。最高联邦法律将审查和修订民事诉讼法。

关键词:管辖权,检察官,法令,执行上诉

1908 年在缅甸颁行时《民事诉讼法》(CPC) 为英语版本,最初法典源自印度法。《民事诉讼法》包含 153 个法律章节和 53 个法令,其实施依赖法律章节、法令和规则。《民事诉讼法》是程序法,由民事诉讼的产生到执行、原判决的上诉、参考、审查、修订等组成。缅甸的法律制度是对抗式的。法庭上审理案件,在法官或法官席前,律师或答辩人辩论。《民事诉讼法》是缅甸民事诉讼程序规则的主要来源。律师或答辩人也会查找 1960 年的法院指引和 1872 年的证据法。

缅甸的法律实践和程序受到了英国惯例和程序的很大影响。尽管法院确实进行仲裁,但是缅甸没有成熟的争端解决机制。一般来说,缅甸法院有权审判所有的民事诉讼,除了法律禁止的某些案件。在缅甸进行诉讼的管辖法院取决于诉讼请求的类型和诉讼标的额,以及当事人所在地或业务所在地或涉

---

*　西南政法大学国际法学院博士生/缅甸密支那大学法学院助教。

**　西南政法大学 2014 级本科法学专业涉外人才实验班。

案行为发生地。

诉讼一般由民事诉讼法详细规定。法院有权审理所有民事诉讼案件,除了案件管辖权受到明示或暗示的禁止。(第9节)

任何法院都不应审理以下案件,直接的实质上地涉及同一争议的已经开始的诉讼。但是,此类诉讼必须是在相同当事人或以他们名义提起诉讼,以相同权利起诉,并在同一法院或其他有管辖权的法院提起诉讼。(第10节)

任何法院都不应审理以下案件,直接的实质性地涉及该争议的诉讼,在同一当事人之间的在法庭上以相同权利起诉过的前诉中直接涉及该争议,并已经得到法院最终裁判。(第11节)

如果原告被禁止关于特定诉讼理由提起诉讼,他无权为此诉讼理由提起诉讼。(第12节)

一般管辖

司法管辖权是法院受理诉讼、上诉和申请的权力范围。法院管辖权可以是一审的或上诉的诉讼。在行使其原有管辖权时,法院对一审诉讼进行审理。在行使上诉管辖权时,法院审理其下级法院依法交接的上诉。司法管辖权指的是法院的司法权限,它不仅涉及诉讼标的,而且涉及其管辖权的地域和标的额限制。

一般来说,根据民事诉讼法的规定有四种管辖权:

1)地域管辖权;

2)标的额管辖权;

3)个人管辖权和;

4)诉讼标的管辖权。

法院的权力与管辖

在司法管理方面,联邦最高法院将司法权力赋予自治地法院、自治区法院、地方法院和乡镇法院处理民事案件。

根据联邦司法法律,最高法院对下列案件拥有初始管辖权,联邦认定依据双边条约引起的,在联邦政府、地区或州政府之间,各州之间,地区和州之间,联邦领土与地区或者州之间除了宪法问题的其他纠纷。

在一审民事诉讼中,对于标的管辖权,最高法院和该地区或州的高等法院的司法管辖权没有金额限制。其他法院法官的管辖权规定如下：

· 地区法官——一审民事诉讼管辖权标的额最多为 5 亿缅币(约 500000 美元)；

· 地区副职法官——一审民事诉讼管辖权标的额最多为 1 亿缅币(约 100000 美元)；

· 乡法官——一审民事诉讼管辖权标的额最多为一千万缅币(约 10000 美元)；

· 乡额外法官——一审民事诉讼管辖权标的额最多为七百万缅币(约 7000 美元)；

· 乡副职法官——一审民事诉讼管辖权标的额最多为三百万缅币(约 3000 美元)。

换言之,有很多的诉讼标的是很难确定价值的。比如,夫妻关系复合、解除受托人。这类诉讼,原告主张的诉讼标的额应为管辖权所认可。如果原告陈述的诉讼标的额不能准确地确定,法院可以裁判超过自己的标的额限制的案件。

然而,如果被告未在规定时间,在审理争议或者在审理争议前提出法院标的额高于或低于法定金额的管辖权异议,上诉法院不予认可或者支持。

根据《民事诉讼法》,关于起诉,每一民事诉讼都应以原告陈述的方式开始,必须向有管辖权的法院提出。但是,在其他诉讼中,应在被告居住的地方或者争议发生地起诉。并且都应在符合法律规定的最低等级的法院提起诉讼。(第 15 节)

相反,本应向高等法院提起诉讼的案件,原告向下级法院提起诉讼的,下级法院应将诉状返还原告,并告之向高等法院起诉。

下列诉讼:重新获得不动产;分割不动产;因不动产抵押或索价而丧失抵押品赎回权、出售或赎回权;确定不动产的其他权利或权益;损害不动产的赔偿;重新获得受到限制或扣押的不动产,必须在地方管辖范围内的不动产所在地法院诉讼。然而,如果被告同意,可以在地方管辖范围内的不动产所在地法院诉讼也可以在地方管辖范围内的被告住所地、经营业务所在地、工作地法院诉讼。(第 16 节)

根据法令第 7 条,第 3 规则,诉讼标的为不可移动的财产时,起诉书中对该财产的描述应足以认定该财产,并指明边界位置数字。

因此,法院无权决定在其地域管辖范围之外的财产的权利和利益。如果法院能通过对个人的程序对位于国外不动产执行,即以逮捕被告人或扣押其个人财产的方式。但是,为此,必须满足被告住所地、经营业务所在地或者工作地必须在法庭的管辖范围内。

《民事诉讼法》中的起诉程序

民事诉讼处理金钱诉讼或个人损害案件。与民事诉讼有关的,包括承诺、债务、财产追回、赔偿、依法令送达等。提起诉讼时,希望得到救济的原告应向法院支付诉讼费用。

提起诉讼,需要缴纳足够的诉讼费用在诉讼时效期间提起诉讼。因此,以诉讼标的为标准确定诉讼费用并缴纳足够的税费。《法院费用法》规定了固定的法院费用和诉讼费用给付标准。依据《法院费用法》所涉及或应收取的所有费用,均须以印花税收集。(《法院费用法》第25节)

诉讼应以起诉状形式提起或以任何现行法律所规定的方式提出。起诉状是由原告以书写和书面形式提出的请求陈述,原告在起诉状中列举了所有必要的详情。(第26节)

符合要求的起诉状,应遵守《民事诉讼法》法令第6条和第7条的规定(法令第4条,第1规则),基本要件有如下四点:

1)对立的双方当事人;

2)诉讼理由;

3)诉讼标的;

4)诉讼请求。

根据《民事诉讼法》第15节至第20节的规定,将向有管辖权的最低一级法院提交审理该案件或向获授权官员提交。虽然在法庭假日或法官俱乐部或其住所可以有效地收到起诉状,但法院并无义务接受以这种方式提交的起诉状。

重要的是,更进一步的诉讼没有被任何法律禁止。以下诉讼明确排除了民事诉讼程序的进一步诉讼:

· 已决案件。(第11节)

· 索赔诉讼应包括全部原告根据诉讼理由有权作出的主张。如果他在没有得到法院许可的情况下放弃他的部分主张,他就不能依据同样的诉讼理由进行有关的进一步诉讼。(法令第2条,第2规则)

· 原告在审理时未出庭。法院可以缺席裁定驳回诉讼。(法令第9条,第8规则)

·根据《民事诉讼法》法令第 22 条第 8 规则被终止或被驳回诉讼。(法令第 22 条,第 9 规则)

·未经法院许可撤回起诉,原告不能再次起诉。(法令第 23 条,第 1 规则)

此外,最重要的是正确的民事诉讼形式。正确的诉讼形式对于所主张的权利十分必要,并应体现在起诉状里。诉讼形式是基于诉讼理由而确定的。

提起诉讼时,应注意以下事实:

· 必须为民事性质的案件。

· 必须不是已决案件(不应最终裁判)。

· 不应被任何法律禁止。

· 应该在有管辖权法院。

· 应该只在不动产所在地。

· 应该在被告实际或自愿所在地。

· 应该在法律规定的期限内缴纳诉讼费用。

· 应确保起诉需要或者未受到法律限制。

法院应将每一诉讼详情书面备存,即制作民事诉讼登记册。如果原告在同一天提交了这两份起诉状,那么登记册中的第一项内容必须是第一份起诉。

民事诉讼种类

下列各项诉讼可以确定或视为民事诉讼:

· 不动产和动产权利;

· 金钱权利;

· 侵权行为索赔;

· 有关废除、执行的主张和关于公司、企业和组织的账目诉讼;

· 抵押贷款相关的主张;

· 社会关系相关的主张;

· 申请赔偿。

关于诉讼范围,每一诉讼都应被框定为对争议的主体作出最终裁决,并防止对其进行进一步的诉讼。

该诉讼必须尽可能解决全部争议,以避免同样的诉讼理由产生进一步的诉讼。诉讼理由和当事人可以共同构成这种诉讼。

案件的转移和撤销权力

案件同时在几个有管辖权的法院起诉的,被告在通知其他当事人后,可以尽早申请将诉讼转移到另一个法院。接收申请的法院决定诉讼将在哪个法庭进行。(第22节)

对人或动产侵权的赔偿诉讼符合受理案件法院管辖范围,被告住所地、经营业务所在地、工作地法院满足管辖条件,原告可以选择其中的一个法院。

有管辖权的几个法院属于同一个上诉法院的,应当向上诉法院提出申请。法院属于不同的上诉法院的,应当向高等法院申请。(第23节)

最高法院、州或地方法院(高等法院)可以在任何阶段将任何诉讼、上诉或其他未决诉讼移交给下级法院审理或处理案件。

最高法院、州或地方法院(高等法院)可能撤回任何其下属法院的未决诉讼,自己审理案件,或者将案件转移至某下属法院审理此案,也可以将同样的被撤回案件再次移交法院审理或处理。(第24节)

判　决

判决是法官根据法律或法令作出的。经过审理后,法官可当庭宣判或者通知当事人或其请求人定期判决。(法令第20条,第1规则)

此外,法官是法院的新主审法官(继任法官),他可能会宣布他的前任所写且尚未宣布的判决。

判决应在宣布时由法官在公开法庭上注明日期和签署,一旦签署后,除了在第152节或评论的情况,不得修改、增加。

令　状

令状是一项裁决的正式文件,法院决定当事各方在诉讼中有争议的所有或任何一名当事人的权利,可能是初步的或最终的令状。判决宣布后,胜诉方向法院申请起草该令状,该令状由法院的一名官员起草。

令状应当与判决相一致,并且应当:

1)包含案号、当事人的姓名和介绍,以及具体的索赔要求,并明确该诉讼的救济或其他决定。

2)说明在诉讼中所发生的费用,以及由谁或从什么财产中支付,以及在何种比例下支付。

3)直接向另一方支付的费用,计算时应与被承认或被发现由前者支付给后者的任何款项相抵销。

令状应在判决宣布之日载明日期,当法官认为令状已根据判决起草,他将签署该令状。(法令第 20 条,第 7 规则)

法官在宣告判决后辞去职务,但未签署令状的,依照该判决而制定的令状,可以由其继任人签署或者法院被撤销的,由法官或者其所下属的法院签署。

因此,令状与判决不同。令状是要执行的,而判决仅仅是令状所依据理由的记录。令状有两种:一个是初步的令状,另一个是最终的令状。

令状的执行

执行是通过法院的程序执行令状和命令,从而使败诉方依据判决恢复原状。如果当事人未上诉,被执行的令状是第一审法院的令状。如果上诉是首选,被执行的是最后上诉法院的令状。

令状可以由审理法院执行,也可以由被移送执行的法院执行。不动产物权在两个以上法院管辖范围内的,任一法院可以附加和出售所有权或者使用权。(第 38 节)

令状的持有者希望获得有关申请执行,他应当向通过令状的法院或受任命的官员(如果有的话)申请,如果该令状被移送到另一个法院,那么向该法院或者适当的官员申请。

在提出执行申请时,令状持有人可在法庭上缴所有必要的执行程序所需的费用。

在收到文件之日起 6 个月内,如果没有人提出申请,法院应将令状和符合第 41 节规定的情形的证明交还给通过该令状的法院。

执行命令的法院应当向通过该判决的法院证明其执行的事实,或者前法院与此相同的情况下未能执行的事实。

根据《民事诉讼法》法令第 21 条、规则第 11 条的规定,执行命令的申请可以通过以下两种方式进行:

i.口头申请;

ii.书面申请。

执行是民事诉讼的最后阶段。在法律程序中使用合法手段使法院的令状或命令生效。胜诉方向执行法院提出书面申请使执行程序开始。

令状的执行规则适用于执行命令。一项令状可以由原法院或由被送交执行的法院执行。通过一项令状的法院可以对令状持有人的申请,将其送交另一法院执行。执行该令状的法院在执行该令状时应与通过判决的法院有同等的权力。所有不服从或妨碍执行该令状的人,应受到法庭的惩罚。执行该令状的命令须遵守同样的上诉规则。

法院在遵守相关法律规定的情况下可以通过下列方式执行该令状:

- 移转任何特别是令状规定的财产;
- 出售存在附属物或无附属物的任何财产;
- 逮捕和监禁;
- 指定接受者;
- 符合救济性质所要求的其他方式。

但是,金钱支付令状的执行,如果不给被执行人一个机会,表明他不应该被关进监狱的理由,法院不能命令执行监禁。

根据《民事诉讼法》的规定,有关执行在适用范围内法令的规定,适用于执行命令。

上 诉

根据可能涉及的条件和限制规则,上诉法院具有下列权力:

- 案件发回;
- 梳理争议焦点进行审理;
- 调取证据或者要求当事人提供证据。

它也有与原管辖法院同样的权力和义务。

下列与原令状或命令有关的诉讼,应适用于上诉:

- 上诉令状;
- 根据《民事诉讼法》或者未规定其他救济方式的特别地方法律作出的命令。

上诉可以针对所有原审法院的令状,上诉法院通过单方审查程序决定上诉程序的进行。未经当事人同意,法院通过的法令不得上诉。(第96节)

最高法院受理针对州或地方法院(高等法院)通过的令状提出的上诉,具体情况如下:

- 违反法律或者有法律约束力的惯例的决定;
- 没有解决法律或者有法律约束力的惯例涉及的重要争议点的决定;
- 在法定程序上有重大错误或者缺陷,可能使案件判决产生错误或者缺陷的;
- 诉讼索赔或诉讼标的价值超过二百万缅币(约 2000 美元)的诉讼。

上诉应以上诉人或其代理人签署上诉状的形式,向法院或代表机构的办公室提出。该上诉状应附有原令状的副本,除非上诉法院免于提供,其还应提供关于该令状所依据的判决。(法令第 41 条)

上诉状应提出明确的理由,即反对该令状的全部理由或叙述,并且应连续编号。标注缅甸日期的情况应添加相应的英语日期。上诉状还应包含:

- 当事各方的全名和地址;
- 原审法院程序事项(包括法院层级、案号和受理法院);
- 上诉价值、诉讼费用、司法管辖权。

上诉被受理时,上诉法院或该法庭的适当官员应在上诉状上签署开庭审理日期,并在上诉登记簿上登记和记录。(法令第 41 条,第 9 规则)

最高法院审理的第二次上诉,第一次上诉法庭可以审理事实问题,并决定下级法院的事实调查结果是否错误。但第二上诉法庭不能审理下级法院对事实的裁决是否合理。第二次上诉只能依据第 100 节的规定。

根据第 100 节的规定,除了《民事诉讼法》另有规定或者其他法律强制规定的,高等法院审理其管理范围内下属法院通过的令状,具体情况如下:

1) 违反法律或者法律的部分实质问题或者有法律约束力的惯例;

2) 没有解决法律的部分实质问题或者有法律约束力的惯例的适用;

3) 程序中出现的违反《民事诉讼法》或者其他法律强制规定的重大错误或缺陷,可能会在该案件的判决程序中产生错误或缺陷;

4) 诉讼索赔或诉讼标的价值超过二百万缅币(约 2000 美元)的一审诉讼,无论这个数额是否在上诉法院发生变更。

此外,根据第 100 节的规定,上诉法院可能单方通过上诉。

根据明确允许上诉的规则,也可以提出上诉。(第 104 节)

除非《民事诉讼法》另有规定或者其他法律强制规定,下列命令才能上诉:

- 根据第 35 节(A)和第 95 节通过的命令;
- 依据征收罚款或逮捕或拘留的民事监禁规定作出的命令,除非这样的逮捕或拘留是执行令状。

不符合第 104 节第(a)款规定的命令不得上诉,除了不作出命令或者命令规定的支付金额少于实际的情况下应当上诉。

允许上诉的命令是依据法院令状或者上述命令,由自治地法院或者自治区法院或地区法院或地区高等法院或者州高等法院在上诉管辖范围作出,应移送更高等级法院审理。(第 106 节)

向最高法院提出的上诉,来自高等法院或由其上诉管辖的其他法院作出令状或者最终命令;由高等法院在行使其原有民事管辖权时所通过的任何令状或最终命令;案件被证明适合上诉至最高法院的任何令状或命令。对下级法院作出的令状或最终命令,若要将其上诉至最高法院,必须涉及实质性的法律问题。(第 109 节和第 110 节)

在审理中出现意见分歧时,一个或多个高等法院法官或者其他法院的多个法官代表少数意见做出的令状或者命令,最高法院不受理对其的上诉。此外,最高法院不受理法律规定不得二次上诉的案件。(第 111 节)

审查程序

在当事人未上诉时,如果其下属法院出现下列情况,联邦最高法院、地区或州高等法院、自治地法院、自治区法院或者地区法院可能要求其下属法院提供审判记录:

- 超越法律管辖权规定审理案件;
- 未能行使法律赋予的管辖权;
- 在行使管辖权的过程中,不合法或者实质不合理的。

联邦最高法院、地区或州高等法院、自治地法院、自治区法院或地方法院可以对此作出合适的命令。但是,本规则不适用于法院在其地区管辖权或上诉管辖权范围内审理案件的情况。(第 115 节)

任何法院都可以对于某问题或者案件寻求最高法院的意见。任何为自己愤愤不平的人可以向通过令状或作出命令的法院申请复审。此外,这些要求不影响最高法院行使其修正的权力。(第 113 节和第 114 节)

结 论

在缅甸,缅甸法典(第 1 卷至第 13 卷)编纂了缅甸的现行法律。缅甸没有涵盖所有类型民事诉讼的综合民法典。民事诉讼法由两部分组成:一个是法律章节;另一个是法令。法律章节的部分具有实质性,规定了适用的一般原则和规则的构成机制。现行的民事诉讼法是 1909 年通过的。到目前为止,在缅甸,这部《民事诉讼法》仍在有效运行,部分条款在 2000 年、2008 年和 2014 年进行了修订。在缅甸实行的一些法律无法适应时代发展的要求,因此,联邦最高法院将审查法律(包括民事诉讼法典)以符合国家的现状。

Review of Labor Law in Myanmar

Khwar Nyo Oo [*]

Abstract: In order to protect the rights of workers, establish a good employment relationship, and promote the formation of independent labor organizations, the Legislature of the Republic of the Union of Myanmar promulgated the Labor Law in accordance with Article 24 of the Constitution. At the same time, some labor laws and regulations were amended, and new laws and regulations were formulated in accordance with international standards. In addition, workers registered or unregistered in the Ministry of Labor are seeking overseas employment opportunities due to poverty, unemployment and lack of employment opportunities. In this regard, this article will outline some important labor laws and regulations. At present, there are many labor problems in Myanmar, especially the minimum wage and migrant workers; in the labor market, in addition to the increased demand for skilled workers, the demand for laws and regulations regulating the labor market has also arisen.

Keywords: Labor, Protection, Labor Law, Contract of labor, Dispute settlement, Overseas employment

The legal system of Myanmar is rooted in common law because Myanmar was colonized by the British Empire in 1885 after the third Anglo-

---

* Khwar Nyo Oo, Doctoral Student of School of International Law of SWUPL/Assistant Lecturer, Department of Law, University of Myitkyina, E-mail: khwarnyo1986@gmail.com.

Myanmar War. It is unique combination of the common law legal system and civil law legal system. Most of the labor laws from colonial period have survived and been effective. Some of the relevant Labor Laws are as follows:

—Workmen's Compensation Act (1923) as amended 2005

—Leave and Holiday Act (1951) as amended 2014

—Factories Act (1951) as amended 2016

—Oilfields (Labor and Welfare) Act 1951

—Income Tax Law (1974) as amended by Union Tax Law 2016

—Law Relating to Overseas Employment (1999)

—Labor Organization Law (2011)

—Social Security Law (2012)

—Settlement of Labor Disputes Law (2012) as amended 2014

—Employment and Skill Development Law (2013)

—Minimum Wage Law (2013)

—Payment of Wages Law (2016)

—Shop and Establishment Law (2016)

—Various sector-specific lawswhich contain labor regulations and rules.

Labor Laws apply to all persons who are working within the Myanmar. According to the Minimum Wage Law, the following workers and staff do not include the term "worker":

(a) Wife, husband, children, parents and blood brothers and sisters who are the members of employer and doing the worker of employer by depending upon and living with the employer;

(b) Civil service personnel;

(c) Seafarers. [1]

Citizens shall enjoy equal opportunity in carrying out the following functions:

—Public employment;

—Occupation;

---

[1] Section 2(a), the Minimum Wage Law, 2013.

—Trade;

—Business;

—Technical know-how and vocation;

—Exploration of art, science and technology. ①

The Union prohibits forced labor except hard labor as a punishment for crime duly convicted and duties assigned by the Union in accord with the law in the interest of the public. ② On March 16, 2012, Myanmar and the ILO signed a Memorandum of Understanding on Strategy for elimination of forced labor in Myanmar by 2015. In the MOU under the paragraph jointly agreed and prioritized, time-bound action plan designed to stop forced labor practices in the whole nation. Under this strategy, an action plan has been implemented by the working group comprised of concerned ministries. ③

One of the problems of Myanmar is Child labors who are widespread in Myanmar. It is difficult to know the number of working children in Myanmar exactly. Children face numerous challenges to their survival. Myanmar has been a state party to the Convention on the Right of the Child (CRC) since 1991. According to the Child Law (1993), every child has the right to engage in work in accordance with law and of his own volition. ④ A person who has not attained the age of 16 years can be determined as a child. ⑤ The definition of underage with regards to labor under Myanmar labor laws varies.

1.1　Minimum age for the worker

According to Myanmar Labor Laws, in order to do work the minimum age is 14. Under the Factories Act, 1951 as amended in 2016, child means a person who has completed his fourteenth year. Such child shall posses the

---

① Section 349, the Constitution of the Republic of the Union of Myanmar, 2008.

② Section 359, the Constitution of the Republic of the Union of Myanmar, 2008.

③ http//www. commerce. gov. mm/... second.

④ Section 24(a)(i) of Child Law, 1993.

⑤ Section 2(a) of Child Law, 1993.

age permissible to do work (certified) by the medical practitioner. [1] Under this Law, a child who is under the age of 14 is not permitted to do work. [2] Child may work for a maximum of four hours a day and shall not be permitted to work at 6 pm to 6 am. [3] The period of work for all children shall be limited to two shifts which shall not overlap, and only one factory. [4]

According to the shop and Establishment Act, 1951 as amended in 2016, the child that is under the age of 14 years shall not be permitted to work in any shop, commercial establishment. [5] A child who is the ages of 14 but not attained the age of 16 may work with the permission of the medical practitioner. However, they must not be permitted to work between the hours of 6pm and 6 am. Any worker who does not complete the age of 18 shall not be allowed to work in hazardous conditions of work which are specially identified. [6] The Ministry of Labor shall protect and safeguard in accordance with law to ensure safety of children workers at the work place and prevention of infringement and loss of their rights. National Committee on the Right of the Child has to protect and safeguard to the Childs' rights. [7] Moreover, Child Law prohibits employing or permitting a child to perform work which is hazardous to the life of the child or which may cause disease to the child or which is harmful to the child's moral character. [8]

The Factories and General Labor Laws Inspection Department (FGLLID) has empower to extend its coverage of effective labor inspection. FGLLID has been given the important task of providing the necessary protection of working children and to ensuring that businesses and

---

[1] section 2(a) of the factories Act, 1951 as amended 2016.

[2] section 75 of the factories Act, 1951 as amended 2016.

[3] Section 79(a) and (b) of the Factories Act, 1951 as amended 2016.

[4] Section 79(2) of the factories Act, 1951 as amended 2016.

[5] Section 13(a) of Shop and Establishment Law, 2016.

[6] Section 14 of the Shop and Establishment Law, 2016.

[7] Section 5(a) of the Child Law, 1993.

[8] Section 65(a) of the Child Law, 1993.

workplaces comply with the Factories Act and Shops and Establishment Act. [1]

1.2 Minimum Wage

Wage means the fee, wage or salary entitled to be obtained by the worker for carrying out hourly work, daily work, weekly work, monthly work or other part-time work of the employer. And also includes bonuses and overtime but it does not apply to allowances for travel, pension and gratuity payments, social security cash benefits, accommodation, meals, electricity charges, water service charges and duties, taxes, medical treatment and recreational purposes and severance payments and any other fees stipulated by the Ministry of Labor and approved by the Union Government. [2] The particulars to be based in determining the minimum wage are as follows:

(a) the needs of workers and their families;

(b) Existing salaries;

(c) Social security benefits;

(d) Living cost and changes of such living costs;

(e) Compatible living standard;

(f) Employment opportunities in conformity with the needs for State's economy and development of production;

(g) Gross domestic production value of the State and per capita income;

(h) Hazardous to health and harmful to work, nature of the work;

(i) Other facts stipulated by the Ministry with the approval of the Union Government. [3]

The other fundamental facts relating to fix the minimum wage provides in the Minimum Wages Rules. The National Minimum Wage committee set out the minimum wage of MMK 3600 on June 2015 for all employees

---

[1] http://www.commerce.gov.mm/.../second.

[2] Section 2(e) of the Minimum Wage Law, 2013.

[3] Section 7 of the Minimum Wage Law, 2013.

without discrimination against employment. The minimum wage rate is 450 kyat per hour and 3600 kyat for eight hour working day. The Payment of Wages Law provides the mandatory payment way. Employer must pay wages that are not exceeding one month. [①] An employee has the right to enjoy the minimum wage stipulated under this Law, if the minimum wage contained in the employment agreement is less than the minimum wage stipulate under this Law. [②] If necessary, the relevant factory, workshop, departments under this law shall be paid for not less than 50% of the remuneration within the three months, 75% of the remuneration for probation period respectively. [③] The terms of probation does not exceed three months. This Law provides that both man and women should receive the minimum wage without discrimination. [④]

The employer shall not have the right to deduct any other wage except the wage for which it has the right to deduct stipulated in the notification issued under this Law. According to the Payment of Wages Law (2016), the employer can deduct from wages on the following situations:

—For absences except when such absence is during a public holiday or entitled leave, according to the law.

—Accommodation charges, meal allowances, charges for water and electricity, taxes and errors in payment.

—Pre-issued, expensed and saved or contributed amount according to the law upon the employee contract.

—Judgment of the Court of Arbitration Jury Council, direct damage which is either intentional or due to negligence or due to the failure of the employee concerned with company property to take proper care.

—A breach of the employment contract or breech of any rules for which a fine had been previously set. [⑤]

---

① Section 4(b) of the Payment of Wages Law, 2016.
② Section 14(c) of the Minimum Wage Law, 2013.
③ Section 43(i) of the Minimum Wages Rules, 2013.
④ Section 14(h) of the Minimum Wages Rules, 2013.
⑤ Section 7 and 11 of the Payment of Wages Law, 2016.

For the worker who is under 16 years old can't be deducted under this Law. [1] The total amount of other deductions shall not be more than 50% of the employee's wages other than the employee fails to perform their duties. [2] In the case of family or parents funeral affairs, his entitled remuneration should not be deducted and shall be arranged to enjoy according to Leave and Holiday Act. [3] If worker does not obtain all wages or other benefits entitled to be obtained, or obtains less than the stipulated minimum wage, may submit to the relevant Union Committee, Region or State Committee and Department within one year from the day he is entitled to obtain such benefits. Moreover, he has the right to institute civil proceeding. [4] Any employer who fails to pay a worker the stipulated rate of minimum wages shall be punished with imprisonment for a term not exceeding one year or with fine not exceeding 5 lakhs or with both. [5]

Businesses within the Myanmar's Special Economic Zones will not be subject to this stipulated rate of minimum wage. The relevant Special Economic Zone Management Committees are responsible to set the rate of minimum wage for the workers of such zones under the guidance of the National Committee for Minimum Wage, subject to the approval of the Union Government. [6] In fixing the minimum wage for the joint venture business with the foreigner or for the foreign investment business or the citizen employees who are working in the said businesses shall be entitled to enjoy the minimum wage similar to the foreign employees depending on the skill. [7] The directorate will advertise the minimum wage in the gazette and newspaper or inform the notification to the relevant organizations, employer and employees. [8] The person who does not satisfy the amount of minimum

---

[1] Section 10(e) of the Payment of Wages Law, 2016.
[2] Section 9 of the Payment of Wages Law, 2016.
[3] Section 44(d) of the Minimum Wages Rules, 2013.
[4] Section 15 of the Minimum Wage Law, 2013.
[5] Section 23 of the Minimum Wage Law, 2013.
[6] Section 9 of the Minimum Wage Law, 2013.
[7] Section 41(c) of the Minimum Wages Rules, 2013.
[8] Section 34(b) of the Minimum Wages Rules, 2013.

wage can object in accordance with the Law. After announcing the notification, relating to the wage, salary or the remuneration or leave, holiday, any benefit entitled to enjoy for the employees shall not affected. [1]

According to the Minimum Wage Law 2013, employers must inform their workers of the rate of minimum wage relating to the business among the rates of minimum wage stipulated under this law payable to them. [2] If he fails to inform to the employees, he will be punished with imprisonment for a term not exceeding six months or with fine not exceeding kyat 3 lakhs or with both. [3] The National Committee for Minimum Wage may revise the rate of minimum wage by way of a new notification at least once every two years. [4]

The National Minimum Wage committee expects to fix the minimum wage at 4400 instead of 3600 according to the Minimum Wages Law. [5] Moreover, in determining the minimum wage there is necessary to consider the employers' cost in production and employees' productivity.

1.3 Employment Contract

In 2015 the Ministry of Labor, Employment and Social Security (which is now called the Ministry of Labor, Immigration and Population) announced in its Notification 1/2015 that employers must use the official template contract published by the Ministry.

An employer must enter into written employment contracts with its employees within 30 days of employment according to section 5 (a) Employment and Skill Development Law (2013). However, it shall not apply to permanent workers of government department and organizations. Subject to the Employment and Skills Development Law, every employee

---

① Section 41(d) of the Minimum Wages Rules, 2013.

② Section 13 of the Minimum Wage Law, 2013.

③ Section 25 of the Minimum Wage Law, 2013.

④ Section 7 of the Minimum Wages Rules, 2013.

⑤ The Myawady Daily, Vol VII, No. 90.

shall be employed under a written employment contract. Section 5(b) of the Employment and Skill Development Law sets out the terms required to be included in the employment contract. This law further provides, that the employment contract shall be submitted to the respective township labor office for review, approval and registration. [1] Any amendment must be approved by the relevant township labor office.

Under section 38 of the Employment and Skill Development Law 2013, an employer who fails to sign an employment agreement with its employee can be punished with imprisonment for up to six months, a fine, or both. Moreover, employment contract may be declared void that it is not registered with the labor department.

1.3.1 Working Hours

Business hours and working times are stipulated in various laws. The Shops and Establishments Law (2016) stipulates working hours which are normally provide eight hours a day or 44 hours a week. Weekly working hours must not exceed 48 hours. [2] Subject to the law, at least one day per a week shall be granted as paid rest day. The employee can be enjoyed wage without deduct for such day. [3] An employee shall not be worked without a break of at least half an hour after four continuous hours of work. [4] Moreover overtime payments need to be paid for worked beyond the prescribed time. In the Factories Act (1951) provides worker shall not be allowed to work in a factory for more than forty-four hours in a week. Provided that an adult male worker in a factory engaged in work which for technical reasons must be continuous throughout the day may work forty-eight hours in a week. [5]

---

[1] http//www. luther-lawfirm. com>Myanmar.

[2] Section 11(a) of the Shop and Establishment Law 2016.

[3] Section 15 of the Shop and Establishment Law 2016.

[4] Section 12(a)of the Shop and Establishment Law 2016.

[5] Section 59 of the Factories Act, 1951as amended 2016.

1.3.2　Public Holidays

Every employee shall be granted by his employer the public holidays with full wages. Minimum Wages Rules provides salary earner, wages earner, piece rate employees are entitled to enjoy allowed public holidays. If any public holiday falls on any weekly day of rest or on any other holiday, an alternative holiday shall not be allowed, but that weekly day of rest or holiday on which the public holiday incidentally falls shall be regarded as a public holiday.[①] Myanmar Law recognizes all public holidays. Every employee shall be granted paid public holiday as announced by the Government in the Myanmar Gazette.

1.3.3　Overtime

Overtime may be termed by agreement between the employer and employee in accordance with the provisions of law. Every work in excess of eight hours per day or 48 hours per week is considered overtime. Overtime pay shall be calculated as double on the basic wage.[②] Subject to the Shops and Establishments Law, overtime is limited to a maximum of 12 hours per week, or 16 hours in cases of special needs.[③] For work on the weekly rest day, the employee may further be enjoyed a substitute rest day.[④] Worker has the right to enjoy a holiday per week with pay in the salary-paid work. If he is employed in such holiday, he shall have the right to obtain over-time fee in accord with the existing law.[⑤]

1.3.4　Leaves

Myanmar law recognizes various types of leave. Leaves are governed by the Leave and Holiday Act (1951) as amended in 2014, but additional rules

---

① Section 3 of the Leave and Holiday Act, 1951 as amended 2014.

② Section 73 of the Factories Act, 1951 as amended 2016.

③ Section 11(b) of the Shop and Establishment Law 2016.

④ http//www. luther-lawfirm. com>Myanmar.

⑤ Section 14(f) of Minimum Wage Law, 2013.

cover in accordance with other laws, such as the Social Security Law 2012 for employees contributing to the Social Security Fund. [1]

(a)Casual Leave

Employee is entitled to six days of casual leave with wages or pay in a year of employment. Casual leave will be cancelled if it does not take within a year. It may not be granted for more than three consecutive days at any one time. Moreover it can't be combined with any other type of leave. [2]

(b) Earned Leave

An employee has completed twelve consecutive months of service and then he may be granted earned leave by his employer for a period of ten consecutive days (in the case over 15-year employee) and for a period of 14 consecutive days (in the case of under 15-year employee) during the subsequent period of 12 month. [3]

(c) Medical Leave

Under the Leave and Holiday Act and Social Security Law, employee is entitled to 30 days in a year of medical leave with wage if 6 months service has been completed. If 6 months service does not complete, leave without pay will enjoyed. If it does not take within a year, it is void. [4] Medical leave can be joined with earned leave. [5] Employees covered by the Social Security Law (2012) are also entitled to 30 days of medical leave (if they completed six months of service) and may enjoy additional leave in case of certain work injuries and illnesses. They may receive part of their salary from the Social Security Fund. [6]

(d) Maternity Leave

Woman workers are entitled to 14 weeks of paid maternity leave to be taken six weeks before confinement and a minimum of eight weeks after con-

---

① http//www. luther-lawfirm. com＞Myanmar.

② Section 5 of the Leave and Holiday Act, 1951 as amended 2014.

③ Section 4 of the Leave and Holiday Act, 1951 as amended 2014.

④ Section 6 of the Leave and Holiday Act, 1951 as amended 2014.

⑤ Section 7 of the Leave and Holiday Act, 1951 as amended 2014.

⑥ http//www. luther-services. com.

finement with wage. Maternity leave may be joined medical leave. [1] Employees covered by the Social Security Law(2012) are entitled to similar 14 weeks of maternity leave, but may further enjoy additional four weeks in case of twins or up to six weeks in case of a miscarriage (exception: criminal abortion). [2] In addition, the employee should be able to receive maternity expenses equivalent to an amount representing the following percentages of her average wage per month:

—50 percent for single delivery;or

—75 percent for twins;or

—100 percent for triplets and above. [3]

An insured man has the right to enjoy 15 days of paternity leave after confinement of his wife, 70 percent of average wage of previous one year as maternity benefit for the leave period if his wife is an insured person and half of maternity grant if his wife is not an insured person. [4]

1.3.5 Termination, Resignation and Dismissal

Subject to the template contract of the Ministry of Labor, an employee may be terminated in line with the employment contract or work rules. The employer and employee may negotiate to terminate the employment contract. To terminate a fixed-term contract, the employer must give one month prior notice and pay a severance payment. Even during the probation period, termination would require one month notice and strong reasons. [5] The Ministry of Labor, Employment, and Social Security (Ministry of Labor, Immigration and Population) published Notification No. 84/2015 on severance payment rates which shall be paid by employer to the terminated employee. Subject to the template contract of the Ministry of Labor, employees may resign by giving one month notice or seven days' notice

---

[1] Section 7(a) of Leave and Holiday Act, 1951 as amended 2014.

[2] Section 25(c)&(d) of the Social Security Law, 2012.

[3] Section 27 of the Social Security Law, 2012.

[4] Section 28 of the Social Security Law, 2012.

[5] http//www. luther-sevices. com.

during the probation period. Severance payment is not required. ①

An employee who violates the terms of employment contract or the work rules will be given the three time warning (verbal, written and bond). If the employee commits further violation after these three warnings, the employee can be dismissed without severance payment. ② The Ministry of Labor, Immigration and Population has issued severance payment rates depending on the service period by the notification No. 84/2015, as follows:

(a) Six months to one year of service: one-half of monthly salary

(b) One to two years of service: one month's salary

(c) Two to three years of service: one and a half's month salary

(d) Three to four years of service: three months' salary

(e) Four to six years of service: four months' salary

(f) Six to eight years of service: five months' salary

(g) Eight to ten years of service: six months' salary

(h) Ten to 20 years of service: eight months' salary

(i) 20 to 25 years of service salary: ten months' salary

(j) Over 25 years: 13 months' salary.

1.4　Social Welfare

In 2012, the Government of the Union of Myanmar enacted a new Social Security Law, 2012. The Ministry of Labor, Employment and Social Security (now Ministry of Labor, Immigration and Population) has established 77 Labor Exchange Office in districts and townships throughout the country and measures are being taken for Myanmar nationals at working age to enjoy opportunities in local and abroad. ③ This new law provides for an extended social security scheme:

—More branches of social security are covered (family benefit, old age pensions, disability and survivors' pensions, unemployment insurance and

---

① www. luther-services. com.

② http//www. uk. practicallaw. thomsonreuters. com.

③ http//www. social. protection. org/gimi/gess.

housing benefits).

—The cash benefits existing under the Social Security Act, 1954, (sickness, maternity and work injury) have higher levels under the new law.

—The medical care scheme opens the possibility to contract medical facilities outside of the SSB owned facilities.

—The mandatory registration could be extended progressively to smaller enterprises and a voluntary registration is made possible for the sectors that are not covered by mandatory registration.

A social security fund is derived from contributions of employer and employee. Employees contribute 2% of their wages and the employer contributes 3% of the employees' wages to the fund. [1]. Additionally, the new Social Security Law, 2012, provides for the creation of a housing fund in which workers would be able to place savings and then would access rights to buy housing at subsidized rate and with subsidized loan. [2]

Furthermore, the unemployment insurance system is introduced in the new law. The requirements for enjoyment of unemployment benefit under the existing Social Security Law are that an insured person must fulfill 36 months of contribution and must be covered under the facts as follow:

(a) Being unemployed not for voluntary resignation but for being removed from work or job terminated because of permanent close-down of work;

(b) Those who are dismissed as a punishment in relation to work, not for those who are dismissed due to abuse, breaking civil servant regulation and falling to obey workplace disciplines;

(c) Those who are in good health and capable to work and willing to work;

(d) Those who are registered as the unemployed at the concerned Township Labor Exchange Offices in line with the specifications and report

---

[1]　www. uk. practicallaw. thomsonreuters. com.

[2]　http://www. staging. ilo. org /public/libdoc/ilo/2015.

to the Township Labor Exchange Offices and township social security offices once a month as the employed. ①

The Social Security Law, 2012, contains provisions on the right to appeal. Establishments have the right to appeal if they are not satisfied with the decisions of the Board. Similarly, Insured workers who are not satisfied with the decisions of the Board have the right to appeal to the Appeal Tribunal.

1.5   Forming the Labor Organization

The Republic of the Union of Myanmar recognizes the labor organization and collective bargaining play in ensuring protection for workers. Labor Organizations are allowed to form freely and independently in accord with Section 24 of the Constitution of the Republic of the Union of Myanmar, to protect the rights of the workers, to have good relations among the workers or between the employer and the worker. Every citizen shall be at liberty in exercising their rights to form associations and organizations under section 354 of the Constitution of the Republic of the Union of Myanmar. Organization shall have the right to carry out its activities under its own name and common seal and perpetual succession and the right to sue and be sued. ② The worker who carries out work in a trade or activity and have working age stipulated in existing law desirous to participate in a worker organization formed according to their category of trade or activity voluntarily. A worker can participate in a worker organization and resign from it. ③

Basic Labor Organizations may be formed by a minimum number of 30 workers working in the relevant trade or activity according to the category of trade oractivity. If it is a trade or activity having less than 30 workers, it

---

① www. social-protection. org/gimi/gess/ResourceDownload. action.

② Section 5 of the Labor Organization rules, 2012.

③ Section 3 of the Labor Organization rules, 2012.

may form so jointly with any other trade of the same nature. [1] The labor organizations have the right to participate in solving the collective bargains of the workers in accord with the labor laws. [2] The employer shall recognize the labor organizations of his trade as the organizations representing the workers. [3] The Law also allows for employers to organize in parallel structure.

The law allows strikes for labor organization but requires permission of labor federation (14 days for public utility service and 3 days for others). [4] The law also allows employers' lock out with the permission of the relevant conciliation body. [5] However, illegal lock-out or illegal strike may be prohibited in accord with the existing Law. [6] Concerning illegal lock-out and illegal strike provides in section 41 of the Labor Organization Law. If a dispute arises between the employer and worker, these organizations have the right to send representatives to the Conciliation Body in settling a dispute to reach the mutual agreement. [7]

1.6 Dispute settlement

If the employer or worker fails to comply with the Employment Contract and dispute relates to other labor affairs, the Workplace Coordinating Committee shall settle the dispute at the workplace under the Settlement of Labor Dispute Law. If the disputes could not be settled, it shall be settled by the Conciliation Body. The Conciliation Body shall refer the dispute which does not reach settlement to the relevant Arbitration Body. If the dispute cannot be settled even in this stage, the Arbitration Council shall settle the dispute. Party has the right to institute criminal or

[1] Section 4(a)(i) of the Labor Organization Law.
[2] Section 21 of the Labor Organization Law.
[3] Section 29 of the Labor Organization Law.
[4] Section 38(a) and 39 of the Labor Organization Law.
[5] Section 40(a) of the Labor Organization Law.
[6] Section42 of the Labor Organization Law.
[7] Section 19 of the Labor Organization Law.

civil proceedings in respect of such dispute during conciliation or arbitration. [1]

The Myanmar government has focused more attention on the effective resolution of labor disputes to avoid a repeat of the disruptive strikes that occurred in the Shwe Pyi Thar Industrial Zone in February and March 2015. The Settlement of Labor Dispute Law (2012), which mandates parties to consider using negotiation, conciliation, and arbitration as a first step before resorting to lock-outs and strikes. But most of them have ignored the rules and regulations that are in place to promote the peaceful resolution of disputes. In response to this, the government has recently set out to remedy the problem and promote dispute resolution. In a progressive move, the Ministry of Labor has established a Dispute Settlement Arbitration Council, a quasi-judicial body for resolving labor disputes, to save time and expenses. [2]

1.7 Overseas Employment

Concerning the overseas employment, the Ministry of Labor Immigrationand Population is taking the activities in accordance with the Law Relating to Overseas Employment promulgated in 1999.

Overseas employment seeker shall register themselves as oversea employment seekers at the Department of Labor. If a person registered obtains overseas employment, he shall be registered as a worker with the Department. [3] A person who has been in any overseas employment, prior to coming into operation of this law, after temporarily returning home, continues with the overseas employment, shall be registered as a worker in accordance with the stipulations. [4] Before going abroad, worker must undergo a medical examination as directed by the Supervisory Committee,

---

[1]　Section 52 of the Settlement of Labor Dispute Law 2012.

[2]　http//www. lexology. com＞library＞detail.

[3]　Section 9 of the Law relating to Overseas Employment, 1999.

[4]　Section 11 of the Law relating to Overseas Employment, 1999.

and obtain a health certificate. Moreover, he shall have obtained a certificate of registration issued by the Department as supporting evidence. ① A registered worker who has gone abroad and has been working there shall report any unusual condition of work to the Service Agent in accordance with the stipulations. If it is not a case of working there after communicating with the Service Agent he shall report to the Myanmar Embassy or to the Consular Office in accordance with the stipulations. If there are no such offices he shall report to the Department. ②

Concerning the right of the overseas worker, they have the right to claim through the Service Agent full compensation or damages to which he is entitled for injury sustained at a foreign work site. Furthermore, they possess the right to take civil or criminal action for loss of his rights and privileges relating to such employment. ③

Workers have gained access to new labor markets, especially within the Association of Southeast Asian Nations (ASEAN) community. Thailand has been the largest recipient of Myanmar labor. Many Myanmar live and work in Thailand, most of them are unregistered. ④ Myanmar worker enter Thailand through unofficial routes to avoid the expenses of crossing legally at border town. Thai government enacted the Decree Concerning the Management of Foreign Workers' Employment on June 23, 2017, registered workers and unregistered migrant workers from Myanmar, Cambodia, Laos and Vietnam have fled Thailand as the new law imposes disproportionate criminal penalties on migrants who work without a permit, mandating up to five years in prison and fines. ⑤ This situation led difficulty to stay and work in Thailand for the Myanmar migrant workers. Myanmar Government issued the notification No. 2/2017 for Myanmar migrant workers who are

---

① Section 20 of the Law relating to Overseas Employment, 1999.
② Section 21 of the Law relating to Overseas Employment, 1999
③ Section 24 of the Law relating to Overseas Employment, 1999.
④ http//www. migrationpolicy. org.
⑤ http//www. hrw. org＞news＞2017/07/07.

working in the Thailand. [1]

In Myanmar, the Special Economic Zone Law enacted in 2014. There are currently three SEZs in development: Kyauk Phpy in Rakhine State, Dawei in the Thanintharyi Region and the Thilawa in Yangon. Government promulgated the Myanmar Investment Law 2016, which effectively combines the Myanmar Citizens Investment Law (2013) and the Foreign Investment Law (2012). As a result, new Myanmar Investment Law include reformulation of tax incentives with incentives being given to investment in rural areas, the introduction of a fast-track approval process for simple investment projects and express provisions requiring the Government to treat foreign investors no less favourably than their domestic counterparts. [2] Practically, migrant workers face many difficulty in abroad particularly language and skill. This is a chance to engage work opportunities for person who wants to do work within the nation.

1.8   Occupational Safety and Health

The object of the Factories Act is to ensure adequate safety measures and to promote health and welfare of the workers employed in factories. The Factories and General Labor Laws Inspection Department (FGLLID) is responsible for enforcing occupational health and safety rules, mainly through factory inspections and training. [3]

Under the Workmen's Compensation Act (1923), employer is also responsible for providing compensation for injuries or occupational disease with the exception. [4] Employers by making contribution to the social security plan are exempt from the provisions of the Workmen's Compensation Act of 1923.

Employers have the responsibility to protect workers from occupational hazards arising out of physical facilities, harmful substances and

---

[1]   http//www. mol. gov. mm/mm/Announce-2-17.

[2]   www. lexology. com.

[3]   http//www. internationalsosfoundation. org.

[4]   Section 3 of the workmen's compensation Act, 1923 as amended 2005.

environmental factors at the workplace under the Social Security Law (2012). [1] Thus, employer should arrange for safety to protect from natural disasters, force majeure and manage and educate the employees regarding occupational health and safety.

In addition, employers must comply with occupational health and safety rules in accordance with the relevant laws and by the relevant labor departments. The Occupational Safety and Health Law is currently being drafted.

The Draft Workplace Safety and Health Law will complement the Factories Act and other prevailing laws, rules and regulations covering workplace safety and health. [2]

---

[1]　http//www. internationalsosfoundation. org.

[2]　http//www. luther-lawfirm. com/…/newsletter/Myanmar.

缅甸劳动法评论

Khwar Nyo Oo[*]

编译 马逸璇[**]

摘要:为了保护劳动者的权利,建立良好的雇佣关系,并促进组建独立的劳动组织,立法机关根据《缅甸联邦共和国宪法》第 24 条颁布《劳动法》。同时,对部分劳动法律规定予以修改,并按照国际标准制定了新的法律法规。此外,在劳动部注册或未注册的劳动者由于贫穷、失业和缺乏就业机会,纷纷寻求海外就业机会。对此,本文将概述一些重要的劳动法律法规。目前,缅甸存在诸多劳动问题,尤其是最低工资和流动劳动者问题;在劳动力市场方面,除了投资增加产生的对熟练工人的需求,同时也产生了规范劳动力市场的法律法规的需求。

关键词:劳动保护,劳动法,劳动合同,争端解决,海外就业

为了保护劳动者的权利,建立良好的雇佣关系,并促进组建独立的劳动组织,缅甸立法机关根据宪法第 24 条颁布劳动法。同时,对部分劳动法律规定予以修订,并按照国际标准制定了新的法律法规。此外,在劳动部注册或未注册的劳动者由于贫穷、失业和缺乏就业机会,纷纷寻求海外就业机会。对此,本文将概述一些重要的劳动法律法规。目前,缅甸存在诸多劳动问题,尤其是最低工资和流动劳动者问题;在劳动力市场方面,除了投资增加产生的对熟练工人的需求,同时也产生了规范劳动力市场的法律法规的需求。

---

[*] 西南政法大学国际法学院博士生/缅甸密支那大学法学院助教。

[**] 西南政法大学 2014 级本科法学专业学术人才实验班。

引　言

　　近年来,缅甸进行了重大的法律改革。新劳动法受缅甸劳动部旧法律法规的约束。为推行新劳动法,与其相关的法律法规需进行相应修订。现行劳动法下,所有的劳动者都拥有相同的权利,包括临时工、派遣工、兼职人员,但没有一条具体法律规范对在缅工作的外籍人员予以规范。对此,缅甸劳动、移民及人力部将向联邦总检察长办公室提交关于在缅工作的外籍人员工作许可的法律草案,并由其审查。可以说,劳动法标准化改革对持续性吸引外资具有重要意义。

　　自第三次英缅战争到 1885 年期间,缅甸一直在英国的殖民统治之下,因此其法律体系植根于普通法系。它是英美法系和大陆法系的独特结合。殖民时代流传下来的大多数劳动法至今有效。部分相关劳动法如下:

　　(1)《工人赔偿法》(1923),2005 年修订;

　　(2)《休假法》(1951),2014 年修订;

　　(3)《工厂法》(1951),2016 年修订;

　　(4)《油田(劳工及福利)法》(1951);

　　(5)《所得税法》(1974),2016 年修订为《联邦税法》;

　　(6)《海外就业法》(1999);

　　(7)《劳动组织法》(2011);

　　(8)《社会保障法》(2012);

　　(9)《劳动争议解决法》(2012),2014 年修订;

　　(10)《就业与技能发展法》(2013);

　　(11)《最低工资法》(2013);

　　(12)《工资支付法》(2016);

　　(13)《零售店铺及商业机构法》(2016);

　　(14)各部门具体法律,包括劳动法规和规章。

　　劳动法适用于所有在缅甸工作的人。根据《最低工资法》的规定,下列人员不属于"劳动者":

　　(1)雇佣夫妻、子女、父母、有血缘关系的兄弟姐妹,依靠并与雇主共同生活的人;

　　(2)公务人员;

（3）船员。①

下列工作，公民应当享有平等的机会：

（1）公职；

（2）就业；

（3）贸易；

（4）商业；

（5）职业技术；

（6）艺术与科技的探索。②

缅甸联邦禁止强迫劳动，除非强迫劳动是对犯罪的惩罚，并符合公众利益。③ 2012 年 3 月 16 日，缅甸与国际劳工组织签署了一份缅甸在 2015 年前消除强迫劳动战略的谅解备忘录。在该谅解备忘录中，双方共同商定并确定了一项有时限的行动计划，旨在消除全国范围内强迫劳动的行为。在这一战略下，这一行动计划是由有关部门组成的工作组执行。④

缅甸一大问题是国内童工现象普遍，童工具体数量难以统计，孩子们面临众多的生存。自 1991 年以来，缅甸一直是《儿童权利公约》的缔约国。根据 1993 年《儿童法》的规定，每个儿童都有权依照法律和个人意愿从事工作。⑤ 儿童的年龄界定为未满 16 周岁。⑥ 在缅甸劳动法部门法下，未成年人的定义并不相同。

一、劳动者最低工作年龄

根据缅甸劳动法的规定，劳动者最低年龄为 14 周岁。根据 2016 年修订的《工厂法》（1951）的规定，儿童为未满 14 周岁的人。这类儿童在其年龄下工作，仅能从事执业医师所允许的工作或由职业医师提供证明。⑦ 根据该法，未

---

① 《最低工资法》第 2 条第 1 款。

② 缅甸联邦共和国宪法（2008）第 349 条。

③ 缅甸联邦共和国宪法（2008）第 359 条。

④ http//www. commerce. gov. mm/... second.

⑤ 《儿童法》（1993），第 24 条第 1 款第 9 项。

⑥ 《儿童法》（1993），第 2 条第 1 款。

⑦ 《工厂法》（1951），修订于 2016 年，第 2 条第 1 款。

满 14 周岁的儿童禁止劳动。① 儿童每天至多工作 4 小时,且禁止在下午 6 点到早晨 6 点之间工作。② 所有儿童的工作需分两班,不得重叠,且仅能在一个工厂工作。③

根据 2016 年修订的《零售店铺及商业机构法》(1951)的规定,未满 14 周岁的儿童不得在零售店铺、商业机构工作。④ 已满 14 周岁未满 16 周岁的儿童可以在执业医师允许下工作。然而,其不得在下午 6 点到早晨 6 点之间工作。未满 18 周岁的劳动者,不得在危险劳动条件下工作。劳动部依法保护和保障劳动者在工作场所的安全,防止劳动者受到侵犯和丧失劳动权利。⑤ 国家儿童权利委员会必须保护和维护儿童的权利。⑥ 另外,《儿童法》禁止雇用或允许儿童从事危害其生命,或使儿童罹患疾病,或对儿童的道德品行有害的工作。⑦

工厂和一般劳工法检查部门(FGLLID)已被授权,扩大其对有效劳工的检查范围。工厂和一般劳工法检查部门有一项重要任务,即为工作的儿童提供必要的保护,并确保企业和工作场所遵守《工厂法》和《零售店铺及商业机构法》。⑧

二、最低工资

工资是指劳动者在每小时工作、每日工作、每周工作、每月工作或其他兼职工作中获得薪水和收入。另外还有奖金和加班工资,但其不适用于旅游津贴、养老金、小费、社会保障现金福利、住宿费、伙食费、电费、供水服务税费、税收、医疗和娱乐目的费用、遣散费,以及由劳动部规定和联邦政府批准的其他费用。⑨ 最低工资参考因素如下:

(1)劳动者及其家庭需求;

---

① 《工厂法》(1951),修订于 2016 年,第 75 条。
② 《工厂法》(1951),修订于 2016 年,第 79 条第 1 款、第 2 款。
③ 《工厂法》(1951),修订于 2016 年,第 79 条第 2 款。
④ 《零售店铺及商业机构法》(2016),第 13 条第 1 款。
⑤ 《零售店铺及商业机构法》(2016),第 14 条。
⑥ 《儿童法》(1993),第 5 条第 1 款。
⑦ 《儿童法》(1993),第 65 条第 1 款。
⑧ http://www.commerce.gov.mm/.../second.
⑨ 《最低工资法》(2013),第 2 条第 5 款。

(2)现有报酬；

(3)社会保障福利；

(4)生活成本及生活成本的变动；

(5)基本生活标准；

(6)符合国家经济发展和生产需要的就业机会；

(7)国内生产总值和人均收入；

(8)对健康有危害性质的工作；

(9)联邦政府批准、部委规定的其他因素。[①]

《最低工资细则》提供其他影响最低工资有关的其他因素。2015 年 6 月，国内最低工资委员会发布劳动者最低工资标准为 3600 缅元，所有劳动者不受就业歧视。每小时最低工资 450 缅元，8 小时工作日最低工资 3600 缅元。《工资支付法》规定了强制性的支付方式。用人单位必须支付不超过 1 个月的工资。[②] 如果劳动合同中规定的工资标准低于最低工资，则劳动者有权依据法律规定享有最低工资待遇。[③] 必要时，本法规定的有关工厂、车间、部门应当在 3 个月内相应地支付不少于 50% 的报酬，75% 的试用期报酬。[④] 试用期不得超过 3 个月。该法规定，男女平等享有最低工资待遇，不得歧视。[⑤]

用人单位无权扣减工资，法律另有规定的除外。根据 2016 年《工资支付法》，用人单位在如下情况下可扣减工资：

(1)缺勤，根据法律规定在法定假日期间或允许请假期间请假除外；

(2)住宿费、伙食费、水电费、税费和错误付费；

(3)根据劳动合同的规定，提前发放、支付、保存或缴纳金额；

(4)仲裁委员会的认定直接损害是由于故意或过失造成的，或者是由于公司雇员未能妥善保管公司财物；

(5)违反先前规定罚款的劳动合同或任何规则。[⑥]

根据该法，未满 16 周岁的劳动者不能被扣减工资。[⑦] 除员工未履行职责

---

① 《最低工资法》(2013)，第 7 条。

② 《工资支付法》(2016)，第 4 条第 2 款。

③ 《最低工资法》(2013)，第 14 条第 3 款。

④ 《最低工资法》(2013)，第 43 条第 9 款。

⑤ 《最低工资法》(2013)，第 14 条第 8 款。

⑥ 《工资支付法》(2016)，第 7 条、第 11 条。

⑦ 《工资支付法》(2016)，第 10 条第 5 款。

外,其他扣除额不得超过职工工资的 50%。① 如遇家属或父母丧事,用人单位不得扣减劳动者报酬,且劳动者有权根据《休假法》的规定享受相关待遇。如劳动者未取得全部工资或者其他应获利益,或者取得低于最低工资标准的工资,其可以自有权获得该等福利之日起 1 年内,向有关的工会委员会、地区、各联邦委员会和部门提出。② 此外,其还有权提起民事诉讼。③ 用人单位未按规定的最低工资标准支付劳动者工资的,处 1 年以下有期徒刑或者拘役,单处或并处不超过 50 万缅元的罚金。④

缅甸经济特区内的企业不受本规定关于最低工资标准的限制。有关的经济特区管理委员会负责在全国最低工资委员会的指导下,经工会政府批准,为该地区的劳动者制定最低工资标准。⑤ 在确定与外国人合资的企业、外商投资企业的缅甸劳动者最低工资时,缅甸劳动者有权依据其自身技能享受与外籍员工类似的最低工资。⑥ 董事会会在公报和报纸上宣传最低工资或者通知有关组织、用人单位和劳动者。⑦ 不符合最低工资标准的人可以依法反对。在发布通知后,有关工资报酬、休假、法定假日、员工福利,均不受影响。⑧

根据 2013 年《最低工资法》的规定,用人单位必须告知劳动者其支付的工资与最低工资标准之间的差额。⑨ 用人单位未按规定告知劳动者的,处 6 个月以下有期徒刑,单处或并处不超过 30 万缅元的罚金。⑩ 全国最低工资委员会至少每两年发布一次新的通知修改最低工资标准。⑪

根据《最低工资法》,全国最低工资委员会要求将最低工资标准定为 4400 缅元,而不是 3600 缅元。⑫ 此外,在确定最低工资时,需要考虑用人单位的生产成本和劳动者的生产力。

---

① 《工资支付法》(2016),第 9 条。
② 《最低工资法》(2013),第 44 条第 4 款。
③ 《最低工资法》(2013),第 15 条。
④ 《最低工资法》(2013),第 23 条。
⑤ 《最低工资法》(2013),第 9 条。
⑥ 《最低工资法》(2013),第 41 条第 3 款。
⑦ 《最低工资法》(2013),第 34 条第 2 款。
⑧ 《最低工资法》(2013),第 41 条第 4 款。
⑨ 《最低工资法》(2013),第 13 条。
⑩ 《最低工资法》(2013),第 25 条。
⑪ 《最低工资细则》(2013),第 7 条。
⑫ The Myawady Daily, Vol Ⅷ, No. 90.

三、劳动合同

2015 年,劳动、就业和社会保障部(现称"劳动、移民和人口部")在通知中宣布,用人单位必须使用部门发布的官方模板合同。

用人单位必须根据《就业与技能发展法》(2013)第 5 条第 1 款的规定,在 30 天内与雇员签订书面劳动合同。然而,该条不适用于政府部门和政府组织的长期工作人员。根据《就业与技能发展法》的规定,每一名劳动者都应根据书面的劳动合同受聘。《就业与技能发展法》第 5 条第 2 款列明劳动合同应包括的条款。本法进一步规定,劳动合同应当提交各自的乡镇劳动部门审查、批准和登记。任何修改必须经有关乡镇劳动局批准。①

根据 2013 年《就业与技能发展法》第 38 条的规定,未与劳动者签订劳动合同的,处 6 个月以下有期徒刑,单处或并处罚金。此外,劳动合同未在劳动部门登记注册的,可以宣告无效。

(一)工作时间

商务时段和工作时间规定在各种法律之中。

工作时间由各种法律规定。《零售店铺及商业机构法》(2016)规定了通常每周工作 8 小时或每周工作 44 小时的工作时间。周工作时长不得超过 48 小时。② 根据该法,至少每周一天为带薪休息日,即劳动者在这一天也可享受工资。③ 劳动者连续工作 4 小时后至少有半小时的休息时间。④ 此外,工作超过规定的时间需要支付加班费。《工厂法》(1951)规定,劳动者一周不得超过 44 小时的工作时间。如果工厂中的成年男性工作者由于技术原因必须连续工作一周,则可以在一周内工作 48 小时。⑤

(二)法定节假日

所有劳动者在法定节假日期间均带薪休假。《最低工资细则》规定,工资

---

① http//www. luther-lawfirm. com＞Myanmar.

② 《零售店铺及商业机构法》(2016),第 11 条第 1 款。

③ 《零售店铺及商业机构法》(2016),第 15 条。

④ 《零售店铺及商业机构法》(2016),第 12 条第 1 款。

⑤ 《工厂法》(1951),修订于 2016 年,第 59 条。

收入者、计件工人有权享受法定节假日。如果法定节假日与每周休息日重合，并不允许有替代假日，该重合的休息日视为法定节假日。[①] 缅甸法律承认所有的法定节假日。所有带薪的法定节假日均由政府在缅甸公报上公布。

(三)加班

劳动者可以按照其和用人单位之间的劳动合同依法加班。每天工作超过 8 小时或每周工作超过 48 小时视为加班。加班工资应以基础工资的双倍计算。[②] 根据《零售店铺及商业机构法》的规定，每周加班至多 12 小时，特殊需求下至多加班 16 小时。[③] 如劳动者在每周休息日工作，其可另外享受休息日。[④] 劳动者有权每周享受带薪工作的假期。在休假期间工作的，其有权依照现行法律领取加班工资。[⑤]

(四)休假

缅甸法律承认各种类型的休假。休假适用 2014 年新修订《休假法》(1951)的规定，同时适用其他法律如 2012 年《社会保障法》关于员工缴纳社保基金等规则。[⑥]

(1)事假

劳动者每年享有 6 天的带薪休假。如果一年内未适用，则将取消。一次性请假三天以上可能不获批。此外，事假不能与其他休假种类混合。[⑦]

(2)赚取的假期

劳动者连续工作 12 个月，则其在接下来的 12 个月内享有连续 10 日的假期(不足 15 年工龄的劳动者)或享有连续 14 日的假期(已有 15 年工龄的劳动者)。[⑧]

(3)病假

根据《休假法》和《社会保障法》的规定，劳动者连续工作满 6 个月后，每年

---

① 《休假法》(1951)，2014 年修订，第 3 条。
② 《工厂法》(1951)，修订于 2016 年，第 73 条。
③ 《零售店铺及商业机构法》(2016)，第 11 条第 2 款。
④ http//www. luther-lawfirm. com＞Myanmar.
⑤ 《最低工资法》(2013)，第 14 条第 6 款。
⑥ http//www. luther-lawfirm. com＞Myanmar.
⑦ 《休假法》(1951)，2014 年修订，第 5 条。
⑧ 《休假法》(1951)，2014 年修订，第 4 条。

有权享有 30 日的带薪病假。如果工作未满 6 个月,病假期间无工资。如果 1 年内未适用,则将取消。[①] 病假不能计入赚取的假期。[②] 根据 2012 年《社会保障法》的规定,劳动者享有 30 日的带薪病假(前提是劳动者工作已满 6 个月),并且可以享有由于特定工伤或生病导致的额外假期。部分薪金有社会保障基金提供。[③]

（4）产假

女职工有资格享受 14 周的带薪产假,包括分娩前 6 周和分娩后的至少 8 周。产假可并入病假。[④]《社会保障法》(2012)所涵盖的劳动者有权享受 14 周产假,但如果是双胞胎,则可享受额外 4 周的产假;如果是流产(如流产),则可享受 6 周以上的产假。[⑤] 此外,职工能获得其每月平均工资以下百分比的产妇费用:

①一胎,月均工资的 50%;

②双胞胎,月均工资的 75%;

③三胞胎及以上,月均工资的 100%。[⑥]

如果被保险人是丈夫,其有权在妻子分娩后享受 15 日陪产假;如果妻子是被保险人,则在产假期间享有前一年平均工资的 70% 作为分娩津贴;如果妻子不是被保险人,妻子享有一半的分娩津贴。[⑦]

(五)终止、辞职和辞退

根据劳动部门的模板合同,劳动者可以按照劳动合同或者劳动细则的规定终止合同。劳动者与用人单位也可以通过协商终止劳动合同。如终止定期劳动关系,用人单位需要提前 1 个月通知劳动者并支付遣散费。即使在试用期内,终止劳动关系也需要提前 1 个月通知并充分告知理由。[⑧] 劳动、就业和社会保障部发布第 84/2015 号关于用人单位向结束劳动关系的劳动者支付遣

---

① 《休假法》(1951),2014 年修订,第 6 条。

② 《休假法》(1951),2014 年修订,第 7 条。

③ http//www. luther-services. com.

④ 《休假法》(1951),2014 年修订,第 7 条第 1 款。

⑤ 《最低工资法》(2013),第 25 条第 3 款、第 4 款。

⑥ 《最低工资法》(2013),第 27 条。

⑦ 《最低工资法》(2013),第 28 条。

⑧ http//www. luther-sevices. com.

散费率的通知。根据劳动、就业和社会保障部的模板合同，劳动者可在试用期内提前1个月或7日通知辞职。此时，用人单位不必支付遣散费。[①]

违反劳动合同或工作规则的劳动者将被给予3次警告（口头、书面和保证书）。如果劳动者在这3次警告之后有进一步的违规行为，用人单位可以在不支付遣散费的情况下将其解雇。[②] 劳动、移民和人口部根据第84/2015号通知规定的工作期限发放遣散费，具体如下：

(1)工作6个月至1年：半个月的工资；

(2)工作1年至2年：1个月工资；

(3)工作2年至3年：1个半月工资；

(4)工作3年至4年：3个月工资；

(5)工作4年至6年：4个月工资；

(6)工作6年至8年：5个月工资；

(7)工作8年至10年：6个月工资；

(8)工作10年至20年：8个月工资；

(9)工作20年至25年：10个月工资；

(10)工作超过25年：13个月工资。

四、社会福利

2012年，缅甸联邦政府发布了新的《社会保障法》。劳动、就业和社会保障部在全国各地设立了77个地区和乡镇的劳动交流办公室，并正在采取措施，为适龄的缅甸公民提供国内外的就业机会。[③] 这项新法规定了扩大的社会保障计划：

(1)更多的社会保障部门被覆盖（家庭福利、养老金、残疾和幸存者的保障金、失业保险和住房福利）。

(2)根据1954年《社会保障法》的规定，现金福利如疾病、生育和工伤在新法律下水平更高。

(3)医疗保健计划为在SSB自有设施之外获取医疗设施提供了可能。

---

① www. luther-services. com.

② http//www. uk. practicallaw. thomsonreuters. com.

③ http//www. social. protection. org/gimi/gess.

（4）强制注册逐步扩展到小型企业，并为那些没有被强制注册的部门提供自愿登记。

社会保障基金来源于用人单位和劳动者的贡献。劳动者从其工资中拿出2％，雇主从其发放给劳动者的工资中拿出3％到社会保障基金。[1]此外，2012年新出台的《社会保障法》规定，设立住房公积金，工人可以在该基金中储蓄，随后获得以补贴利率和补贴贷款购买住房的权利。[2]

此外，新法规定了失业保险制度。现行的《社会保险法》规定，对享受失业救济的要求是，被保险人必须工作满 36 个月，并且必须符合以下事实：

（1）失业不是自愿辞职导致的，而是因为工作单位永久关闭而被解雇；

（2）工作原因被辞退，而非由于滥用职权、违反公务员规章制度、违反工作纪律被辞退；

（3）身体健康，有能力、有意愿继续工作；

（4）按规定登记为有关乡镇劳动交流办公室失业人员，每月需向乡镇劳动交流办公室、乡社会保障办公室报告。[3]

2012 年《社会保障法》包含上诉权利的条款。如果商业机构对董事会的决定不满意，亦有权上诉。类似的，被保险的劳动者不满意董事会决定，也有权向上诉法庭上诉。

五、劳工组织的组建

缅甸联邦共和国承认劳工组织和集体谈判，以确保工人得到保护。劳工组织可以自由、独立地按照《缅甸联邦共和国宪法》第 24 条的规定，保护劳动者的权利，在劳动者之间或用工单位与劳动者之间建立良好的关系。每一个公民都可自由行使其在《缅甸联邦共和国宪法》第 354 条规定下组成协会和组织的权利。组织有权以自己的名义、印章、永久继承权、诉讼权开展活动。[4]从事贸易或者活动的劳动者，在现有法律规定的劳动年龄中，可以自愿参加由他们的贸易或者活动类别组成的职工组织。劳动者可以参加劳工组织，也可

① www. uk. practicallaw. thomsonreuters. com.
② http://www. staging. ilo. org /public/libdoc/ilo/2015.
③ www. social-protection. org/gimi/gess/ResourceDownload. action.
④ 《最低工资法》(2013)，第 5 条。

以从中退出。①

基本劳工组织可由从事相关贸易或活动的至少 30 名工人组成。如果该贸易或活动少于 30 位劳动者,其可与相同性质的其他贸易活动共同组成劳工组织。② 劳工组织有权依照劳动法律,参与解决集体劳动的问题。③ 用人单位应当承认其行业的劳工组织可以代表劳动者。④ 该法同样允许用人单位组建类似的组织。

法律允许劳工组织罢工,但需要劳工联合会的许可(公共事业服务 14 日,其他 3 日)。⑤ 法律还允许用人单位在相关的调解机构允许的情况下限制劳动者进厂。⑥ 然而,非法的限制入厂或非法的罢工是为现行法所禁止的。⑦《劳工组织法》第 41 条规定了非法限制入厂和非法罢工。如果用人单位与劳动者之间发生争议,这些组织有权派代表参加调解、解决纠纷,以达成双方协议。⑧

六、争端解决

如果劳动者或用人单位没有遵守劳动合同,工作场所协调委员会应根据《劳动争议解决法》解决劳动争议。如果争议没有解决,则将由调解机构处理。调解机构将处理尚未提交给有关仲裁机构的纠纷。如果争端在该阶段仍未解决,仲裁委员会将解决争端。在调解或仲裁期间,当事人有权就该争议提起刑事诉讼或民事诉讼。⑨

缅甸政府将更多的注意力放在有效解决劳资纠纷上,以避免 2015 年 2 月和 3 月 Shwe Pyi Thar 工业区发生的破坏性罢工事件重演。《劳动争议解决法》(2012)规定,各方应首先考虑谈判、调解和仲裁,然后再考虑限制入厂或采取罢工行动。但是,他们中的大多数人忽视了促进和平解决争端的规则和条

---

① 《最低工资细则》(2013),第 3 条。
② 《最低工资细则》(2013),第 4 条第 1 款第 1 项。
③ 《最低工资细则》(2013),第 21 条。
④ 《最低工资细则》(2013),第 29 条。
⑤ 《最低工资细则》(2013),第 38 条第 1 款、第 39 条。
⑥ 《最低工资细则》(2013),第 40 条第 1 款。
⑦ 《最低工资细则》(2013),第 42 条。
⑧ 《最低工资细则》(2013),第 19 条。
⑨ 《劳动争议解决法》(2012),第 52 条。

例。为此,政府最近在着手解决这一问题并促进争端的解决。争端解决发展过程中,劳动部建立了一个争端解决仲裁委员会,这是一个解决劳资纠纷的准司法机构,旨在节省时间和费用。①

七、海外就业

关于海外就业,劳动、移民和人口部根据 1999 年颁布的有关海外就业的法律进行活动。

海外求职者应在劳动部注册为海外求职者。如果海外求职者在海外成功就职,其应在该部门注册为劳动者。② 在本法实施之前从事过海外工作的人在暂时回国后继续在海外就业的,应当按照规定注册为劳动者。③ 出国前,劳动者必须按照监督委员会的指示接受体检,并取得健康证明。此外,其还应获得该部门颁发的注册证书作为支撑证据。④ 已出国在境外工作的注册工作人员,应当按照规定向服务代理机构报告异常工作情况。在与服务代理人沟通后,劳动者如不在那儿工作,应按照规定向缅甸大使馆或领事厅报告。如该处无缅甸大使馆或领事厅,其应向劳动部报告。⑤

关于海外工作者的权利,海外工作者有权通过服务代理向外国工作单位请求全部补偿损害赔偿金。此外,对于其被侵害的有关劳动的权利和特权,劳动者有权提起民事或刑事诉讼。⑥

劳动者可以寻求新的劳动力市场,尤其是在东南亚国家联盟(东盟 ASEAN)内。泰国是缅甸劳动力的最大输入国。许多缅甸人在泰国生活、工作,但绝大部分没有注册。⑦ 缅甸劳动者通过非官方途径进入泰国,主要是为了避免在国外居住合法跨境的花费。泰国政府于 2017 年 6 月 23 日颁布关于外国人就业管理的法律后,来自缅甸、柬埔寨、老挝和越南的注册和未注册的移民劳动者逃离泰国,因为新法律对没有工作的移民进行不恰当的刑事处罚,

---

① http//www.lexology.com＞library＞detail.
② 《海外就业法》(1999),第 9 条。
③ 《海外就业法》(1999),第 11 条。
④ 《海外就业法》(1999),第 20 条。
⑤ 《海外就业法》(1999),第 21 条。
⑥ 《海外就业法》(1999),第 24 条。
⑦ http//www.migration policy.org.

对于没有工作许可证的移民,强制五年以下的监禁和罚款。① 这种状况(情况)导致在泰国的缅甸移民工作者(劳动者)难以在泰国继续生活与工作。缅甸政府发布第 2/2017 号关于工作在泰国缅甸移民工作者的通知。②

2014 年缅甸颁布经济特区法律。目前有三个经济特区正在开发中:若开邦的 Kyauk Phpy、Thanintharyi 地区的 Dawei 和仰光的 Thilawa。政府颁布了 2016 年缅甸投资法,该法将《缅甸公民投资法》(2013)和《外商投资法》(2012)有效结合起来。因此,《新缅甸投资法》包括重新制定税收优惠政策,鼓励对农村地区进行投资,对简单投资项目实行快速审批程序,并明确要求政府给予外国投资者的待遇不差于外国投资者的国内同行。③ 实际上,移民工作者人口在国外面临着许多困难,特别是语言和技能。这为希望在国内工作的人提供了工作机会。

八、职业安全与健康

《工厂法》旨在确保采取适当的安全措施,促进工厂工人的健康和福利。工厂和普通劳动法检查部门主要通过进行工厂检查和开民菜培训来负责执行职业健康和安全规定。④

根据《工人赔偿法》(1923),用人单位应对职工受伤或患职业病进行赔偿,但存在例外情况。⑤《工人赔偿法》(1923)规定对社会保障计划作出贡献的用人单位为前述例外。

根据《社会保障法》(2012 年),用人单位负有保护职工免受工作场所的设施、有害物质和环境因素引起的职业危害的义务。⑥ 因此,用人单位应作出相应安排,保护职工免受自然灾害、不可抗力危害,并对职工进行职业健康与安全教育。

此外,用人单位必须遵守相关法律和有关劳动部门的职业安全与健康规则。《职业安全与健康法》正在修订。

---

① http//www. hrw. org＞news＞2017/07/07.
② http//www. mol. gov. mm/mm/Announce-2-17.
③ www. lexology. com.
④ http//www. internationalsosfoundation. org.
⑤ (2)《工人赔偿法》(1923),2005 年修订,第 3 条。
⑥ http//www. internationalsosfoundation. org.

　　《工作场所安全与健康法（草案）》将补充《工厂法》以及其他涵盖工作场所安全与健康的现行法律、法规和条例。①

结　语

　　伴随着劳动法的完善，工作机会将增多。用人单位、劳动者及其各自组织都应遵守相关法律法规。政府方面应向所有利益相关者推广劳动法律意识，尤其是职业安全与健康。一方面，对于危险工厂或行业，企业要受到惩罚，而非仅对其进行罚款；另一外面，对违法的工人亦应予以有效惩罚。通过两个方面，有效减少工作场所伤亡事故的发生。为建立起良好的雇佣关系，三方会议、研讨会和专题讨论应该定期举行。缅甸劳动法律必须不断促使劳动关系双方在对创造就业环境和经济发展的需求方面达成平衡。

---

　　①　http://www.luther-lawfirm.com/…/newsletter/Myanmar.

Formation of Contracts under the Contract Act of Myanmar

May Thu*

Abstract:A contract is an agreement between two or more persons that can be enforced by law. Every person in one way or other, as all of us enter into a number of contracts everyday. Each contract creates some rights and duties on the contracting parties. A variety of business activities depend on the use of contracts. The Law of Contract is in the nature of Civil Law and it covers the legal rinciples concerning commercial or trade transaction and also many civil matters. The Contract Act 1872 is the foundation for all contracts under the law of Myanmar: it is the general law.

Keywords:Cojntract, Contract Law, Myanmar

Introduction

The Law of Contract deals with the law relating to the general principles of contract.

In Myanmar, the "Contract Act" was enacted in 1872 and is still a subsisting law of Myanmar. The Contract Act consists of two parts: (i). General principles of the Law of Contract, (ii). Special kinds of contracts. The general principles of the Law of Contract are contained in Sections 1 to

---

* May Thu, Doctoral Student of School of International Law of SWUPL/Lecturer, Department of Law, University of Myitkyina, Myitkyina , Kachin State, Myanmar, E-mail:maythu. on7@gmail. com.

75 of the Contract Act. These principles apply to all kinds of contracts irrespective of their nature. Special contracts are contained in Section 124 to 238 of the Contract Act. These special contracts are Indemnity, Guarantee, Bailment, Pledge and Agency.

A study of the contract law of any country begins with the study of the basic requirements of formation of contract. In formation of contract, the necessary factors must be constituted. First, offer and acceptance and that offer and acceptance must be communicated each other. Secondly, there must have a consideration. The third is free consent of the parties and fourthly, the capacity of the parties to contract. Finally, there is a formality which shows how to make contract legally.

Definition of Contract

The term contract is defined in Section 2(h) of the Contract Act as, an agreement enforceable by law is a contract. This definition shows that a contract must have the two elements: (i). An agreement and (ii). The agreement must be enforceable by law. Thus, a contract is a combination of an agreement and its enforceability. Agreement is defined in Section. 2(e) of the Contract Act, "every promise and every set of promises, forming the consideration for each other, is an agreement".

The term promise is defined in Section. 2(b) of the Contract Act, a proposal, when accepted, becomes a promise. This above two mentioned provisions shows that an agreement is an accepted proposal (offer). Thus, every agreement consists of an offer from one party and its acceptance by the other. But every agreement is not a contract. When an agreement creates some legal obligations and is enforceable by law, it is regarded as a contract. The conditions of enforceability are laid down in Section. 10 of the Contract Act as all agreements are contracts if they are made by the free consent of parties competent to contract, for a lawful consideration and with a lawful object and are not hereby expressly declared to be void.

This Section. 10 is one of the most important in the Contract Act, as it defines, the fundamentals of every contract are:

1. The agreement must be made by the free consent[①] of the parties. Thus, the consent is not free, when it is obtained by coercion,[②] undue influence,[③] fraud,[④] misrepresentation[⑤] of facts etc. If the consent of the parties is not free, then no valid contract comes into existence.

2. The agreement must be made by the parties who are competent to contract. A person who is major,[⑥] of sound mind,[⑦] and is not disqualified from contracting by law, is competent to enter into a valid contract. For the purpose of entering into contract, the age of majority is eighteen years. [⑧] Where a guardian of a minor's person or property has been appointed under the Guardian and Wards Act 1890; such a person attains majority on completion of 21 years.

3. The agreement must be made for a lawful consideration and with a lawful object. The lawful consideration and lawful object is that which is not fraudulent, defeat the provisions of any law, forbidden by law, immoral or opposed to public policy. [⑨]

4. The agreement must not be expressly declared to be void. In order to be a valid contract, the agreements must not have been expressly declared to be void by any law in force in the country.

These basic requirements of every contract are considered in detail by the succeeding sections (secs.), e.g. (1) by secs. 13-22, (2) by secs. 11-12, (3) by secs. 24, and (4) by secs. 25- 30.

---

① The Contract Act 1872, s. 14.
② Ibid. s. 15.
③ Ibid. s. 16.
④ Ibid. s. 17.
⑤ Ibid. s. 18.
⑥ Ibid. s. 11.
⑦ Ibid. s. 12.
⑧ The Majority Act 1875, s. 3.
⑨ The Contract Act 1872, s. 23.

Basic requirements for a valid contract

In order to form a valid contract, an agreement must have the following essential elements:

(1) Proposal or offer;

(2) Acceptance of such proposal or offer;

(3) The contracting parties must be competent to contract;

(4) Free consent of the contracting parties;

(5) Lawful consideration and lawful object;

(6) The agreement must not be expressly declared to be void; and

(7) In writing if so to create required by law.

(1) Proposal or offer

Offer and acceptance are necessary ingredients in the formation of a contract in Myanmar. To form a contract; the first essential element is a proposal which is made by one person and accepted by another. An offer is the proposal by one person to another to enter into a legally binding agreement with him. [1]

An offer is defined in Section 2 (a) of the Contract Act 1872, as a proposal is an act when one person signifies to another his willingness to do or to abstain from doing anything, with a view to obtaining the assent of that other to such act or abstinence.

Every proposal made by a person is not legally regarded as an offer. A legal offer must consist of the following two parts: (i) Expression of one person's willingness to do or to abstain from doing something. (ii) Such expression should be made with a view to obtain the assent of the other person to the proposed act or abstinence.

A proposal (offer) is not a mere declaration or intention to make an

---

[1] P. P. S. Gogna, "A Textbook of Business and Industrial Law", 1st ed. 2007, S. Chand & Company Ltd. , New Delhi. p. 9.

offer. There must be request to accept his offer. It must be made with an intention to create legal relation. The terms of a proposal must be certain. It may be general or specific. It is to be distinguished from an invitation to make offer. Every statement that seems to be an offer is not an offer, and does not always create legal obligations. Very offer such statements are merely invitation to offer.

(2)Acceptance of an offer

To form a contract; the second essential element is an acceptance by which the person to whom the proposal is made signifies his assent to such proposal. An offer is the starting point in the making of an agreement. However, an offer in itself does not create any legal relationship. The legal relationship results only when an offer is accepted. The acceptance of an offer is necessary to create legal relationship. [1]

Section-2(b) of this Act defines "acceptance as that when the person to whom the proposal is made signifies his assent thereto, the proposal is said to be accepted. A proposal, when accepted, becomes a promise".

So, an acceptance is the consent given to the offer, and a binding contract between the offeror and the offeree comes into existence on the acceptance of the proposal. [2]

Inorder to convert a proposal into a promise, the acceptance must be absolute and unqualified. [3] It means that the acceptance should be an unqualified acceptance of all terms of the offer and without any condition. It must conform to the proposal. If the offer is accepted with some condition then also the acceptance is invalid and without any legal effect.

In order to constitute a promise, a proposal must be accepted absolutely according to section 7 of the Contract Act. If there is an amendment or

---

① P. P. S. GoGNA, "A Textbook of Business and Industrial Law", 1st ed. 2007, S. Chand & Company Ltd. ,New Delhi. p. 9.

② Ibid. p. 13.

③ The Contract Act 1872,s. 7(a).

different statement in acceptance, it is only counter proposal. [1]

The acceptance must be in the prescribed manner. If the proposor does not prescribe any specific method, the acceptor has to follow usual and reasonable mode. [2] Usual and reasonable manner includes the ordinary practice followed in a particular trade or business or place. A personal message through the acceptor's agent was deemed to be under this expression.

Performance of the conditions of a proposal, or the acceptance of any consideration for reciprocal promise which may be offered with a proposal, is an acceptance of the proposal. [3] In case of general offer, any person who fulfills the conditions of an offer shall be deemed to have accepted or acted on the offer, and the proposor shall be bound on the contract.

The acceptance cannot be presumed from silence. The proposor cannot impose upon the acceptor the penalty that in event of his silence, he would be deemed to have accepted.

Communication of offer and acceptance

In order to become an agreement, there must be communication of offer and acceptance. Communication of offer means that an offer must be communicated to the offeree before it can be accepted. The offeree can't accept an offer unless he knows of it. According to Section. 4 of the Contract Act of Myanmar, an offer becomes complete only when it comes to the knowledge of the offeree.

Communication of acceptance means that in general rule, the acceptance must be communicated to the offeror.

The communication of the acceptance is complete, _ as against the proposer, when it is put in a course of transmission to him, so as to be out of the power of the acceptor; as against the acceptor, when it comes to the

---

[1] Sasoon Ezekial Salom vs. Myanmar Wharf and Warehouse Co. Ltd B. L. R 364.

[2] The Contract Act 1872, s. 7(b).

[3] Ibid. s. 8.

knowledge of the proposer. [1]

Therefore, under the Contract Law of Myanmar, the communication of an acceptance is complete at different times for the offeror and the acceptor. For the offeror, the communication of an acceptance is complete when it is put in a course of transmission to him. For the acceptor, the communication of an acceptance is complete when it comes to the knowledge of the offeror. [2]

Revocation of offer and acceptance

Section. 5 of this Act states that a proposal may be revoked at any time before the communication of the acceptance is complete as against the proposer, but not afterwards.

For example, if "A" has offered his house for sale to "B" to agree to pay a certain sum for it, "A" may revoke this proposal if the communication of its acceptance by another is not yet complete. The Contract Act allows unaccepted proposals to be revoked.

And Section 6 explains how the revocation is done: A proposal may be revoked in any one of four ways:

(1) by the communication of notice of revocation by the proposer to the other party;

(2) by the lapse of the time prescribed in such proposal for its acceptance, or, if no time is so prescribed, by the lapse of a reasonable time, without communication of the acceptance;

(3) by the failure of the acceptor to fulfill a condition precedent to the acceptance; or

(4) by the death or insanity of the proposer, if the fact of his death or insanity comes to the knowledge of the acceptor before acceptance.

An acceptance may be revoked at any time before the communication of

---

[1] The Contract Act 1872. s. 4, second para.

[2] P. P. S. Gogna, "A Textbook of Business and Industrial Law", 1st ed. 2007, S. Chand & Company Ltd. ,New Delhi. p. 16.

the acceptance is complete as against the acceptor, but not afterwards. ①

(3)Competency to contract

An agreement cannot be enforceable as a contract if one or both of the parties lacked capacity to make the contract. Section 10 of the Myanmar Contract Act specifically requires that the parties must be competent to contract.

According to Section 11, every person is competent to contract (i) who is of the age of majority, according to the law to which he is subject, and (ii) who is sound mind, and (iii) is not disqualified from contracting by any law to which he is subject.

This section deals with the capacity of the parties in three parts. Each party to a contract must have attained the age of majority. The age of majority is explained in the Section 3 of the Majority Act that, every person shall be deemed to have attained majority when he shall have completed the age of eighteen years and not before.

Persons of unsound mind are incapable of entering into a valid contract. The term "sound mind" for the purpose of contracting, is defined in Section 12 of the Contract Act, a person is said to be of sound mind for the purpose of making a contract if, at the time he makes it, he is capable of understanding it and of forming a rational judgment as to its effects upon his interests.

A person who is usually of unsound mind, but occasionally of sound mind, may make a contract when he is of sound mind.

A person who is usually of sound mind, but occasionally of unsound mind, may not make a contract when he is of unsound mind.

Section 12 is that a person is of sound mind if she has a general ability to understand the main effect of a contract, and that a party who seeks to argue that she was not of sound mind, and therefore not bound by a contract, will have to persuade the court that she was incapable of

---

① The Contract Act 1872, s. 5, second para.

understanding anything at all. [1]

The third requirement of "competency to contract" is that the person should not be disqualified from entering into a contract by any law which is properly applicable to him.

The disqualificationmay arise from corporate bodies or political status. For example

1. A statutory company cannot enter into a contract out of its memorandum.

The original rule was that if a company makes an agreement which is beyond the legal powers of the company, as theseare defined by the Companies Act 1914 and other legislation, and by the Memorandum and Articles of Association, the agreement will be void. [2]

2. An alien enemy is incompetent to contract.

(4)Free consent of contracting parties

The Contract Act provided that, in order to be a valid contract, the agreement must have been made with free consent of the parties. Consent is the foundation of a contract. When two parties enter into a contract they should give their consent. Consent is defined by Section 13 of the Myanmar Contract Act, "two or more persons are said to consent when they agree upon the same thing in the same sense".

The consent of both parties entering into contract must also be free. It is the essential requirement of a valid contract. According to the Section 14 of the Contract Act, consent is said to be free when it is not caused by (i) coercion, (ii) undue influence, (iii) fraud, (iv) misrepresentation and (v) mistake.

Consent is said to be so caused when it would not have been given but for the existence of such coercion, undue influence, fraud, misrepresentation or mistake.

This section shows that when consent of either party is obtained by one

---

[1] Adrian Briggs QC (Hon) and Andrew Burrows QC (Hon), "The Law of Contract in Myanmar". p. 54.

[2] Ibid. p. 55.

of the above mentioned elements, it will not be free.

If the consent is obtained by coercion, undue influence, fraud, misrepresentation, the effect to the agreement voidable at the option of the party whose consent was so obtained.

If it is induced by mistake (which must be of mutual and one of fact material to the agreement) it is void.

(ⅰ)**Coercion**

If there is a sufficient case of coercion, it would not be right to hold the coerced party to the contract. Consent give under coercion is not free consent; and consent caused by coercion allows the coerced party, the victim, to rescind the contract. [1]

An agreement, in which consent is caused by coercion, is voidable at the option of the party whose consent was so obtained. [2] Moreover, such party is also entitled to take back the money or the goods etc., paid or delivered under the contract. [3]

The meaning of coercion is provided in Section 15 of the Myanmar Contract Act, "Coercion is the committing or threatening to commit, any act forbidden by the Penal Code, or the unlawful detaining, or threatening to detain, any property, to the prejudice of any person whatever, with the intention of causing any person to enter into an agreement. "

The consent is said to be caused by coercion when it is obtained by either of the following acts:

(1)an act or threat to commit an act forbidden by the Penal Code (or)

(2)an unlawful detention (or)

(3)threat to unlawfully detain any property.

It is obvious that if any of the things mentioned in Section 15 is done, any consent which is caused by that thing is not a free consent, and the

---

[1]   Adrian Briggs QC (Hon) and Andrew Burrows QC (Hon), "The Law of Contract in Myanmar". p. 98.

[2]   The Contract Act 1872, s. 19.

[3]   Ibid. s. 72.

victim cannot be held to the contract against his will. [1]

All acts mentioned as crimes in the Penal Codeare unlawful act. Torture is an act forbidden by the Penal Code. A threat to commit such an act would come within the purview of Section 15 of the Contract Act. [2]

(ii)Undue Influence

Holland has defined it as "undue influence" is the unconscientious use of power over another person, such power being obtained by virtue of a present or previously existing dominating control, arising out of relationship between the parties.

The contract will be voidable at the option of the party whose consent was obtained by undue influence.

Sec. 16(1) of the Contract Act defines "undue influence" as follows: "a contract is said to be induced by undue influence where the relations subsisting between the parties are such that one of the parties is in a position to dominate the will of the other and uses that position to obtain an unfair advantage over the other.

All the three conditions laid down by the sec. 16 (1) must be fulfilled before a contract can be set aside on the ground of undue influence. Firstly, the relationship must be such that one party is in a position to dominate the will of the other. Secondly, such party must have used that dominant position, thirdly, he must have, by such use, obtained an unfair advantage over the other. If any one of the three elements is absent, the transaction cannot be set aside on the ground of undue influence. [3]

The effect of undue influence is that when consent to an agreement is caused by undue influence, the agreement is a contract voidable at the option of the party whose consent was so caused. [4]

Sec. 16(2) of this Act defines when a person is presumed to be in a

---

① Adrian Briggs QC (Hon) and Andrew Burrows QC (Hon), "The Law of Contract in Myanmar". p. 98.

② Ma Ain Yu vs. Dr. Miss A. G. D. Netto and others, 1952 B. L. R (S. C) 65.

③ Ranjitlal Harilal Pandia, "Principles of Mercantile Law" 3rd ed. 1955, p. 21.

④ The Contract Act 1872, s. 19 A.

position to dominate. It is so "(i) where he holds a real or apparent authority over the other, or(ii) where he stands in a fiduciary relation to the other; or (iii) where he makes a contract with a person whose mental capacity is temporarily or permanently affected by reason of age, illness, or mental or bodily distress."

The relationships referred to in Section 16(2), are those in which one party is weak (whether by reasons of young age[①] or old age,[②] or sickness or illness) where another is strong, or in which one party is in a position of dependence (such as may be true of a client, patient, or novice) on another who has power over her (such as her lawyer, her doctor, or the head of her religious institution). [③]

Undue influence is ordinarily presumed in relationship, such as—

(a) parent and child

(b) guardian and ward

(c) trustee and beneficiary

(d) solicitor and client

(e) doctor and patient

(f) spiritual adviser and disciple.

Sec. 16(3) lays down a rule of evidence. It say "where a person, who is in a position to dominate the will of another, enters into a contract with him, and the transaction appears, on the face of it or on the evidence adduced, to be unconscionable, the burden of proving that such contract was not induced by undue shall lie upon the person in a position to dominate the will of the other".

This Sec. 16(3) throws the burden of proving that the burden is shifted to the stronger party to prove that the consent of the other party is freely given, and the contract is not induced by any undue influence.

(ⅲ) **Fraud**

---

① See The Contract Act 1872, Illustration (a) to Section 16.

② Ibid. Illustration (b) to Section 16.

③ Adrian Briggs QC (Hon) and Andrew Burrows QC (Hon), "The Law of Contract in Myanmar". p. 101.

The definition of fraud is given in Section 17 of the Contract Act，"Fraud" means and includes any of the following acts committed by a party to a contract，or with his connivance，or by his agent，with intent to deceive another party thereto or his agent，or to induce him to enter into the contract：

(4)the suggestion，as a fact，of that which is not true，by one who does not believe it to be true；

(5)the active concealment of a fact by one having knowledge or belief of the fact；

(6)a promise made without any intention of performing it；

(7)any other act fitted to deceive；

(8)any such act or omission as the law specially declares to be fraudulent.

The most important requirement of a fraud is that the misstatement of facts must be made by one party with an intention to deceive the other. This Section. 17 shows that any act which falls in the above-mentioned five categories，amounts to fraud. Mere silence is not fraud unless there is a duty to speak or unless it is equivalent to speech. [1] When consent to an agreement was caused by fraud，the agreement is a contract voidable at the option of the party whose consent was so caused. [2]

(ⅳ)**Misrepresentation**

"Misrepresentation" means and includes_

(9)the positive assertion，in a manner not warranted by the information of the person making it，of that which is not true，though he believes it to be true；

(10)any breach of duty which，without an intent to deceive，gains an advantage to the person committing it，or any one claiming under him，by misleading another to his prejudice or to the prejudice of any one claiming under him；

---

① The Contract Act 1872，Explanation of Section 17.

② Ibid. s. 19.

(11) causing, however innocently, a party to an agreement to make a mistake as to the substance of the thing which is the subject of the agreement.[1]

Section 18 of the Contract Act provides three categories of act which constitute misrepresentation. It includes (a) an unwarranted positive assertion of what is not true, even though he might believe it to be true; or (b) committing a breach of duty which misleads another to his prejudice or to the prejudice of any one claiming under him; or (c) causing a party to the contract to make a mistake as to the subject matter of the agreement.

The most important requirement of misrepresentation is that the false statement of facts is made by a party without any intention to deceive the other party.[2] The contract is voidable at the option of the party whose consent is obtained by misrepresentation.

(Ⅴ) Mistake

Section 20 of the Contract Act provides that where both the parties to an agreement are under a mistake as to a matter of fact essential to the agreement, the agreement is void.

For example, "A" agrees to sell to "B" a specific cargo of goods supposed to be on its way from England to Yangon. It turns out that, before the day of the bargain, the ship conveying the cargo had been cast away and the goods lost. Neither party was aware of the facts. The agreement is void[3].

In order to render a contract void the ground of mistake, there should exist the following three conditions:

(1) the mistake must be of both the parties; (i. e. mutual mistake)

(2) it must be a mistake of fact and not of law;

(3) it must be about a fact essential to the agreement.

(a) Contract caused by a mistake of fact

---

[1] Ibid. s. 18.

[2] P. P. S. GoGNA, "A Textbook of Business and Industrial Law", 1st ed. 2007, S. Chand & Company Ltd. , New Delhi. p. 60.

[3] The Contract Act 1872, Illustration (a) to Section 20.

Mistake of fact may be classified into the following two types：

(1)Bilateral mistake and (2) Unilateral mistake.

An agreement will be rendered void when both parties made a mistake as to a matter of fact essential to the agreement. [①]The bilateral mistake of essential facts renders the agreements void.

A contract is not voidable merely because it was caused by one of the parties to it being under a mistake as to a matter of fact. [②] The unilateral mistake does not affect the validity of the agreement. In other words，it is only a bilateral mistake which can avoid a contract.

(b)Contract caused by a mistake of law

Section 21 lays down that a contract is not voidable because it was caused by a mistake as to any law in force in the Union of Myanmar；but a mistake as to a law not in force in the Union of Myanmar has the same effect as a mistake of fact.

The mistake of the Myanmar Law does not render the agreement void. Everyone is supposed to known the laws of the State whose subject he is. He cannot get any relief on the ground that he done a particular act in the ignorance of the law. Thus，the mistake of the Myanmar Law does not affect the validity of the agreement.

On the other hand，one cannot be expected to know the laws of a foreign State. A mistake of such law，therefore，is regarded as a mistake of fact. [③]

In Myanmar we have got a case[④]，there was a contract to inherit the property of the deceased，by common mistake on Chinese Customary Law and it was held to be void according to Section 20 and 21.

[①]　Ibid. s. 20.

[②]　Ibid. s. 22.

[③]　Ranjitlal Harilal Pandia，"Principles of Mercantile Law" 3rd ed. 1955，p. 31.

[④]　Daw Saw Hla (a) Mrs. Chan Chin Leong vs. Mrs. Maung Sein and eight other，1963 B. L. R (C. C) 773.

(5) Lawful consideration and lawful object

The factor which converts the promise or promises into an agreement is consideration. A promise, standing alone, is not by itself enforceable; the common law, and the Contract Act, requires the promise to be supported by consideration before it may become a contract. [1]

Consideration is one of the important elements in the formation of a contract. Section 25 of Contract Act specifically states that "an agreement made without consideration is void." Thus, the general rule is that an agreement is void if there is no consideration to it. However, certain exceptions to this rule are also provided in Section 25 itself.

The term "consideration" is defined in Section 2 (d) of the Contract Act, which are as follows; "when at the desire of the promisor, the promisee or any other person has done or abstained from doing, or does or abstains from doing, or promises to do or to abstain from doing, something, such act or abstinence or promise is called a consideration for the promise."

The essential parts of the consideration are _

1. The consideration is an act (i. e. doing of something), or an abstinence (i. e. abstinence from doing something).

2. Such act or abstinence should be done at the desire of the promisor.

3. Such act or abstinence may be done by the promisee or any other person.

4. Such act or abstinence is either already executed, or is in the process of execution or may be still executory. It means that the consideration may be past, present or future.

One of the conditions of a valid contract is that its consideration and object must be lawful. And if the consideration or object of an agreement is unlawful, such an agreement is void.

According to Section 23 of the Contract Act, the consideration or object

---

[1] Adrian Briggs QC (Hon) and Andrew Burrows QC (Hon), "The Law of Contract in Myanmar". p. 32.

of an agreement is lawful, unless- it is forbidden by law; or is of such a nature that, if permitted, it would defeat the provisions of any law; or is fraudulent; or involves or implies injury to the person or property of another; or the Court regards it as immoral, or opposed to public policy.

In each of these cases, the consideration or object of an agreement is said to be unlawful. Every agreement of which the object or consideration is unlawful is void.

When consideration or object of an agreement will be regarded as unlawful is laid down by Section. 23 of the Contract Act. The object or consideration of an agreement is unlawful in the following cases:

(ⅰ)**forbidden by law**

The object or consideration of an agreement is forbidden by law. The agreement, with such an object or consideration, is unlawful and void. No action can be brought upon a contract which is prohibited by law as being an illegal contract.

A court cannot enforce an agreement to do an act which is itself forbidden by law, and cannot enforce an agreement for which the consideration said to support the promise is itself unlawful. [1]

(ⅱ)**defeat the provisions of any law**

Sometimes, the object or consideration of an agreement is no express prohibited by the law. But the nature of the contract is such that it would defeat the provision of any law. In such cases, the object or consideration is unlawful.

(ⅲ)**fraudulent**

Fraudulent consideration or object of an agreement is said to be unlawful and void.

(ⅳ)**Injury to the person or property of another**

Agreement involves or implies injury to the person or property of another is void.

---

① Adrian Briggs QC (Hon) and Andrew Burrows QC (Hon), "The Law of Contract in Myanmar". p. 66.

(Ⅴ) Immoral or opposed to public policy

All agreement in violation of morality and founded upon consideration contrary to public policy are void.

Section 23 dealt with cases in which consideration is wholly void or illegal. Section 24 provides that if any part of a single consideration for one or more objects, or any one or any part of any one of several considerations for a single object is unlawful, the agreement is void.

Section 24 refers to agreements in which a part of the consideration or object being illegal, it cannot be separated from the other part which is valid and effective. In such a case, the whole agreement is void. [1]

(Ⅵ) Agreement Expressly Declared to be Void

One of the conditions of valid as defined by sec. 10 is that it must not be one which is declared to be void by the Act. There are fourteen kinds of a- greement which the Contract Act has expressly declared to be void. They are;

1. Agreements made by incompetent persons: [2]

2. Agreements made under mutual mistake as to a matter of fact or law: [3]

3. Agreements of which consideration or object is unlawful: [4]

4. Agreements of which consideration or object is unlawful in part: [5]

5. Agreements without consideration: [6]

6. Agreements in restraint of marriage: [7]

7. Agreements in restraint of trade: [8]

---

[1] Ranjitlal Harilal Pandia, "Principles of Mercantile Law" 3rd ed. 1955, p. 38.

[2] The Contract Act 1872, s. 11.

[3] Ibid. s. 20, s. 21.

[4] Ibid. s. 23.

[5] Ibid. s. 24.

[6] Ibid. s. 25.

[7] Ibid. s. 26.

[8] Ibid. s. 27.

8. Agreements in restraint of legal proceedings: [1]

9. Agreements the meaning of which is uncertain or not capable of being made certain: [2]

10. Agreements by way of wager: [3]

11. Agreements contingent on an event happening, and the event becomes impossible. [4]

12. Where the agreement is to do an act which subsequently becomes impossible or unlawful: [5]

13. Contracts to do act afterwards becoming impossible or unlawful: [6]

14. Reciprocal promise to do things legal and also other things illegal. [7]

(Ⅶ) **In writing if so to create required by law.**

Ordinarily, writing is not necessary to make a contract, but writing or attestation or registration is necessary, if so required by any law. The agreement must comply with the provision of any law requiring it to be in writing or attested or registered.

Section 10 of the Contract Act confirms the rather obvious point that if other legislation requires a contract to be made in writing, or to be witnessed, or a registration to take place, that legislation continues to bind the parties and operate on the contract, contracts do not generally need to be made in writing. [8]

---

① Ibid. s. 28.

② Ibid. s. 29.

③ Ibid. s. 30.

④ 54 The Contract Act 1872, s. 32, 36.

⑤ Ibid. s. 56 first para.

⑥ Ibid. s. 56 second para.

⑦ Ibid. s. 57.

⑧ Adrian Briggs QC (Hon) and Andrew Burrows QC (Hon), "The Law of Contract in Myanmar". p. 10.

Conclusion

Formation of contract under Contract Act of Myanmar differs from contract formation law in other civil law countries. Under the Contract Act of Myanmar, the first ingredients of the basic requirements of making a contract are offer and acceptance. The second ingredient there is free consent of the contracting parties; free in sense that it should not be caused by:

(1) coercion, (2) undue influence, (3) fraud, (4) misrepresentation and (5) mistake. The third ingredient of the formation of contract is called capacity; there have to consider the three factors: (1) capacity of age, (2)of sound mind (3) disqualification. In respect to the fourth ingredient, provides that under section 20 regarding lawful consideration and lawful objects. The fifth ingredient is that the agreement must not be expressly declared to be void. Finally, as for the sixth ingredients, whenever the law says that such agreement should be in writing or if it mentions the number of attesting witness or if such agreement should be registered, it should be done in accordance with such provision, so that it will be enforceable by law. Contract formation law in other civil law countries, consideration is not required before a contract become legally binding and mutual exchange of consideration is not required. In Myanmar, Consideration is an important element in the formation of a contract. The Contract Act of Myanmar can simply be found and understood by reading the Contract Act 1872 must be dispelled. Although that Act has many virtues, it was never comprehensive. Legal framework for contract should be upgraded to be in line with the development of contract law and global practice.

References

Contract Act 1872; Myanmar Code Vol. IX.

The Majority Act 1875; Myanmar Code Vol. XI.

Adrian Briggs QC (Hon) and Andrew Burrows QC (Hon), "The Law of Contract in Myanmar" 2017, Ashford Colour Press.

Ranjitlal Harilal Pandia, "Principles of Mercantile Law" 3rd ed. 1955,

N. M. Tripathi Private Ltd，Bombay.

P. P. S. Gogna，"A Textbook of Business and Industrial Law"，1st ed. 2007，S. Chand & Company Ltd. ，New Delhi.

Cases

Daw Saw Hla（a）Mrs. Chan Chin Leong vs. Mrs. Maung Sein and eight other，1963 B. L. R（C. C）773.

Ma Ain Yu vs. Dr. Miss A. G. D. Netto and others，1952 B. L. R（S. C）65 Sasoon Ezekial Salom vs. Myanmar Wharf and Warehouse Co. Ltd B. L. R 364.

合同构成要素研究
——以《缅甸合同法》为研究对象

May Thu*

编译　林　俊**

摘要：合同是两个或两个以上的当事人签订的有强制执行力的协议。我们每个人每天可能会以某种方式签订合同。每份合同都为缔约方创设了一些权利和义务。各种商业活动的进行取决于合同的运用。《缅甸合同法》（以下简称《合同法》）属于民法范畴，涵盖商业或贸易交易中涉及到的法律原则以及许多民事关系。1872 年《缅甸合同法》是一部普遍适用的法，因此其是缅甸法律中所有合同构成的基础。

关键词：合同，合同法，缅甸

一、介　绍

《合同法》规定了有关合同的基本原则。在缅甸，《合同法》于 1872 年颁布，现仍在施行。合同法由两部分组成：第一是合同法的一般原则；第二是特殊合同。《合同法》的一般原则载于《合同法》第 1 条至第 75 条。这些原则适用于各种合同而不论其性质如何。《合同法》第 124 条至第 238 条载有特殊合同，这些特殊合同指的是赔偿、担保、保释、质押和代理。

对任何国家合同法的研究都是从对合同形成的基本要求的研究开始的。在签订合同时，必须具备其必要的要素。首先，邀约和承诺必须相互传达；其次，必须有一个对价；再次是各方的意思自治；又次，是各方缔约合同的能力；最后，必须存在合同合法有效的形式要件（形式上签订的合同合法有效）。

＊　西南政法大学国际法学院博士生/缅甸密支那大学法学院讲师。

＊＊　西南政法大学 2017 级国际法硕士研究生。

二、合同的定义

《合同法》第 2(h)部分将合同定义为"有强制执行力的协议"。这个定义表明，合同必须具备两个要素：(i)协议；(ii)协议必须由法律强制执行。因此，合同是协议与其可执行性的组合。协议规定于《合同法》第 2(e)条，"每一个承诺和每一套承诺所形成彼此的对价，都是一项协议"。

"承诺"定义于《合同法》第 2(b)条中，"当一项提案在被接受时成为承诺"。上述两项条款表明协议是一项被接受的提议（要约）。因此，每个协议都包含一方的要约和另一方的承诺。但是并非每个协议都是合同。当协议产生一些法律责任并且可以依法执行时，它被视为合同。"可执行性的条件"规定于《合同法》第 10 条规定："如果协议是有权签订合同的各方根据自由意思同意，具备合法对价和合法标的，且并未明确声明无效，那么所有协议均构成合同。"

这是《合同法》中最重要的部分之一，因为它定义了每个合同的基本原则是：

1. 该协议必须通过双方的自由协商[1]。因此，当通过胁迫[2]、不当影响[3]、欺诈[4]、对事实的歪曲[5]等获得的同意不是自由。如果当事人的同意不是自愿的，那么就不存在有效的合同。

2. 协议必须由有能力的当事方订立。一个成年的[6]、精神健全的[7]，并且没有丧失订立法律合同资格的人有权签署有效的合同。为达成合同，成年年限为 18 周岁。根据 1890 年《监护人和被监护人法》任命未成年人的人身或财产的监护人。[8] 这样的人在过了 21 岁后达到成年。

3. 该协议必须以合法的对价和合法的目的作出。合法的对价和合法的客

---

[1] 1872 年合同法第 14 条。

[2] 1872 年合同法第 15 条。

[3] 1872 年合同法第 16 条。

[4] 1872 年合同法第 17 条。

[5] 1872 年合同法第 18 条。

[6] 1872 年合同法第 11 条。

[7] 1872 年合同法第 12 条。

[8] 1875 年成年法案，第 3 条。

体是不欺诈、不违反法律所禁止、不道德的或反对公共政策的规定①。

4. 协议不得明确宣布为无效。为使合同有效,协议不得被国家现行法律明确宣布为无效。

每个合同的这些基本要求在后续章节中详细考虑,如(1)第13～22章;(2)第11～12章;(3)第24章;(4)第25～30章。

三、有效合同的基本要求

为了形成有效的合同,协议必须具备以下基本要素:

1. 要约邀请或要约;

2. 承诺或要约;

3. 缔约方必须有缔结合同的能力;

4. 缔约双方的意思自治;

5. 合法对价和合法标的;

6. 法律不得明确协议为无效;以及

7. 根据法律要求提供书面形式。

(一)要约

要约和承诺是缅甸合同形成的必要组成部分。为了达成合同,第一个基本要素是由一个人提出并被另一个人接受的提案。要约是一个人向另一个人提出与他签订具有法律约束力的协议的提议②。

1872年《合同法》第2(a)部分规定了要约:要约是一个人向另一个人表示愿意做或不做任何事情的行为,以期获得另一方对拟议作为或不作为的同意。

每个人提出的建议在法律上都不被视为要约。合法邀约必须由以下两部分组成:(1)表达一个人作为或不作为的意图。(2)这种表达应该是为了获得另一人对拟议作为或不作为的同意。

要约不仅仅是声明或意图提出要约,必须有接受他的提议的请求,必须有设法律关系的意图。要约的条款必须确定,它可以是一般的或具体的,它与要约邀请不同。从表面陈述上看起来是要约的,并不是真正意义上的要约。并

---

① 1872年《合同法》第3条。

② P. P. S. Gogna,《商业和工业法教科书》,2007年版,S. Chand&Company Ltd., New Delhi,p. 9.

不总是产生法律义务。提供这样的声明只是要约邀请。

(二)承诺要约

为了达成合同,第二个基本要素是受要约人同意要约。要约是制定协议的起点。但是,要约本身并不构成任何法律关系。只有当提议被接受时,法律关系才会产生。承诺是建立法律关系所必需的[1]。

本法第 2(b)节将"承诺"定义为当受要约人表示同意要约时,该要约已被接受。要约在被接受时成为承诺。

因此,承诺是对要约的同意,并且在接受提案时,要约人和受要约人之间存在具有约束力的合同[2]。

为了将要约转化为承诺,接受必须是绝对的和无条件的[3]。这意味着接受应该是无条件地接受提议所有条件。它必须符合要约。如果要约要在特定情况下被接受,那么承诺是无效的,并且没有任何法律效力的。为了构成承诺,必须根据《合同法》第 7 条绝对接受要约。如果受要约方对要约内容提出修改或作不同表述,那么只是仅要约。[4]。

承诺必须以规定的方式进行。如果提出者没有规定任何具体的方法,那么接受者必须遵循通常合理的方式[5]。通常合理的方式包括在特定行业或企业或地区遵循的一般惯例。经受要约者的代理人作出的回应被认为是受要约者作出。

对提案条件的履行,或接受可能与提案一起提出的互惠承诺的任何对价,都是对提案的接受。[6]。对于全面要约,任何满足要约条件的人应为视为已接受或采取行动,与此同时发出要约者应受合同约束。

承诺不能默示推定。要约人不得向承诺人施加如果承诺人对提出的要约沉默,将被视为已经接受的规定。

---

① P. P. S. GoGNA,《商业和工业法教科书》,2007 年版,新德里 S. Chand&Company Ltd. ,p. 9.

② P. P. S. GoGNA,《商业和工业法教科书》,2007 年版,新德里 S. Chand&Company Ltd. ,p. 13.

③ 1872 年《合同法》第 7(a)条。

④ Sasoon Ezekial Salom vs. Myanmar Wharf and Warehouse Co. Ltd B. L. R 364.

⑤ 1872 年《合同法》第 7(b)条。

⑥ 1872 年《合同法》第 18 条。

1. 承诺和要约的传递

为了达成协议,必须有要约和承诺的传递。要约的传达意味着要约必须在可接受之前传达给受要约人。除非受要约人知道,否则受要约人不能接受要约。根据缅甸《合同法》第 4 条的规定,只有在受要约方了解要约的情况下,才能完成要约。

一般来说,承诺的传递意味着承诺必须送达要约人。

承诺的到达是完整的,即对要约者来说,当承诺被传递给他时,承诺就不可撤回;当要约者了解到承诺的内容时,对承诺者来说,承诺的发出才是完整的。[①]。

因此,根据承诺传达的完整性表现在不同时间。对于要约人来说,承诺的发出在被传递给他时才是完整的。对于受要约人来说,要约人了解到承诺的内容时,承诺的到达才是完整的[②]。

2. 要约和承诺的撤回

《合同法》第 5 节规定,对要约人来说,在承诺到达之前的任何时候,要约可能会被撤回,而不是在到达之后。

举个例子,如果 A 提议将他的房屋出售给 B,以同意为其支付一定金额,如果其另一方的承诺的到达尚未完成,则 A 可以撤回该提议,《合同法》允许撤回未接受的要约。

该法第 6 节解释了撤销是如何完成的:一项要约可以通过四种方式中的任何一种被撤回:

(1)通过要约人向另一方发出撤回通知;

(2)超过该要约规定的承诺时间,或者如果没有规定时间,则经过合理的时间,仍未发出承诺;

(3)承诺人未能履行承诺的先决条件;或者

(4)如果要约人的死亡或精神错乱,且该事实在承诺发出之前被承诺人知悉。

对承诺者来说,一项承诺可以在承诺完整到达要约人之前的任何时候被撤回,而不是之后。[③]。

---

① 1872 年《合同法》第 4 条,第 2 段。

② P. P. S. Gogna,《商业和工业法教科书》,2007 年版,S. Chand&Company Ltd.,New Delhi,p. 16.

③ 1872 年《合同法》第 5 条,第 2 节。

(三)合同缔约能力

如果合同双方中的一方或双方缺乏签订合同缔约能力,协议就无法构成合同而强制执行。缅甸《合同法》第 10 条明确规定当事人必须有能力订立合同。

根据第 11 条的规定,根据他所服从的任何法律,(1)成年;(2)头脑健全;(3)没有丧失订立合同的资格的人都有权订立合同。

本节分三部分讨论各方的缔约能力。合同的每一方都必须达到成年年龄。《成年法》第 3 条解释了成年标准,即每个人过了 18 岁后,都应被视为已达到成年。

心智不健全的人不能签订有效的合同。在签订合同时,"智力健全"一词在《合同法》第 12 条中被定义,在订立合同时,一个智力健全的人有能力理解合同(条款),能够对影响其自身利益的因素形成合理的判断。

一个大部分时间心智不健全但偶尔心智健全的人,在心智健全的情况下,可以签订合同。

一个大部分时间心智健全,但偶尔心智不健全的人,在心智不健全时,不能签订合同。

第 12 条指的是如果一个人具有理解合同主要效力的一般能力,那么就表示他心智健全。而一方试图争辩他的思想不健全,由此而不受合同约束时,他必须说服法庭合同相对人根本不能理解任何东西[1]。

"合同缔约能力"的第三个要求是一个人不应因任何适用于他的法律而丧失订立合同的资格。

资格的丧失夺可能由于其法人主体或政治地位。例如:

1.法定公司不能超出章程范围订立合同。

正如根据 1914 年《公司法》和其他立法以及公司章程大纲定义的那样,如果一家公司制定的协议超出了公司的法定权力,该协议将是无效的[2]。

2.对国家有危害的外国人没有签订合同的能力。

(四)缔约双方的自由意志

《合同法》规定,为了形成有效的合同,协议必须经过双方的自由同意。同

---

① Adrian Briggs QC(Hon)and Andrew Burrows QC(Hon),《缅甸合同法》,p.54.

② Adrian Briggs QC(Hon)and Andrew Burrows QC(Hon),《缅甸合同法》,p.55.

意是合同的基础。当双方签订合同时,他们应该表示同意签订该合同。缅甸《合同法》第13条对"同意"进行了定义:"两人或多人在同一意义上就同一事物达成一致意见时,表示同意。"

双方签订合同的同意也必须是自愿作出的。这是合同有效的基本要求。根据《合同法》第14条,同意的"自愿"指的是,签订合同时不存在以下事实:(i)胁迫;(ii)不当影响;(iii)欺诈;(iv)虚假陈述;(v)误解。

除非事先明确约定,除了胁迫、不当影响、欺诈、否则或误解几类情况,则会被认定为同意。

本条规定表明,如果任何一方的同意是通过上述要素之一获得的,则不属于自愿。

如果同意是通过胁迫、不正当影响、欺诈、失实陈述获得的,则对于获得同意的一方而言,该协议的效力是可撤销的。

如果它是由误解引起的(这必须是相互的,而且是协议的事实之一),合同则是是无效的。

1. 胁迫

如果有足够多的胁迫的事实,将被胁迫方置于合同还是不对的。强制下的同意不是自由的;并且由胁迫造成的同意赋予被胁迫方当事人解除合同的权利①。

如果协议的达成中的一方同意是通过胁迫得到的,则该被胁近的当事方有撤销权②。此外,该方也有权收回根据合同支付或交付的金钱或货物等③。

缅甸《合同法》第15条规定了胁迫的含义,"胁迫是指实施或威胁实施刑法所禁止的任何行为,或非法扣留或威胁扣留任何财产侵害他人合法权益,目的在于迫使他人签订合同"。

这种同意是由下列任何一种胁迫行为造成的:

(1)实施刑法禁止的行为或威胁实施刑法禁止的行为(或);

(2)非法拘禁(或);

(3)威胁非法扣留财产。

很明显,如果第15条中提到的事实都已经具备,那么由该事实引起的任

---

① Adrian Briggs QC(Hon)and Andrew Burrows QC(Hon),《缅甸合同法》,p.98.

② 1872年《合同法》第19条。

③ 1872年《合同法》第72条。

何同意不是自愿的同意,受害者也不能违背自身的意愿而签订合同①。

所有在刑法中被称为罪行的行为都是非法行为。酷刑是刑法禁止的行为。威胁实施此类行为属于《合同法》第15条的范围②。

2. 不当影响

荷兰将"不当影响"定义为行为人对另一人的不正当使用权力,这种权力是通过当事人之间的关系产生的,现有或以前存在一方对另一方的主导控制权获得的。

如果合同一方作出的决定是基于不当影响,则合同为可撤销合同。

《合同法》第16(1)条对"不当影响"的定义:如果合同双方之间存在的关系使一方能够控制另一方的意愿,并利用这一立场取得对另一方的不公平优势。

必须满足第16(1)条规定的所有三个条件才能在不当影响的基础上搁置合同。首先,这种关系必须是一方能够支配另一方的意愿。其次,该方必须利用这种支配地位;再次,他必须通过这种利用获得不公平的优势。如果三个要素中的任何一个不存在,交易就不能以不适当的影响为由搁置③。

不当影响的后果是,当对一项协议的同意是由不当影响引起的时候,被不当影响的可以撤销该合同④。

本法第16条第(2)款界定了一个人被推定为具有主宰他人地位的情况。即是(i)他对另一方拥有真实或明显的权力;或者(ii)他处于与另一方的委托关系中;或(iii)他与一个因年龄、疾病、精神或身体不适而暂时或永久影响其精神能力的人签订合同。

第16(2)条中提到的关系是指一方当事人弱势(无论是因年龄较小⑤、年龄较大⑥、患病或生病)而另一方强势,或一方当事人处于依赖地位(如客户、病人或学员)而另一方对他享有权利(如他的律师,他的医生或他的宗教机构的负责人)⑦。

不当影响通常被认为存在于下列关系中,例如:

---

① Adrian Briggs QC (Hon) and Andrew Burrows QC (Hon),《缅甸合同法》,p. 98.
② Ma Ain Yu vs. Dr. Miss A. G. D. Netto and others,1952 B. L. R (S. C) 65.
③ Ranjitlal Harilal Pandia,《商业法原理》,1995年第3版,第21页。
④ 1872年《合同法》第19A条。
⑤ 参见1872年《合同法》,Illustration (a)至第16节。
⑥ 参见1872年《合同法》,Illustration (b)至第16节。
⑦ Adrian Briggs QC (Hon) and Andrew Burrows QC (Hon),《缅甸合同法》,p. 101.

（a）父母和子女；

（b）监护人和被监护人；

（c）受托人和受益人；

（d）律师和客户；

（e）医生和病人；

（f）精神顾问和弟子。

第 16 条第（3）节规定了一个证据规则。该条款规定："一个能够支配另一个人意愿的人与他签订合同，并且交易在表面上或被引证的证据上看是不合情理的，证明这种合同不是由不当引起的证明责任应当归于支配方。"

第 16（3）条将承担举证责任的重任移交给较强势的一方当事人，证明另一方的同意是自愿的，并且合同没有受到任何不当影响。

3. 欺诈

《合同法》第 17 节作出欺诈的定义："欺诈"是指并包括由合同当事方明示或默示或其代理人实施了下列行为，意图欺骗另一方或其代理人，诱使他签订合同。

（1）一个不相信他是真实的一方向另一方提出的实际上是不真实的建议；

（2）知道或相信事实的人积极隐瞒事实；

（3）无意执行意图的承诺；

（4）任何其他满足欺骗的行为；

（5）其他如法律特别声明为欺诈行为的任何此类行为或不作为。

欺诈的最重要的要求是，对事实的错误陈述必须由一方当事人作出，以欺骗另一方。第 17 条规定表明，属于上述五类的任何行为均构成欺诈行为。除非有义务告知或者除非某种沉默等同于告知，否则纯粹的沉默不是欺诈行为[1]。当协议的同意是由欺诈造成的，该协议就是一项可撤销合同，可由受欺诈方选择撤销[2]。

4. 虚假陈述

"虚假陈述"包括并指：

（1）一方当事人以不能保证真实性的方式提出其积极的主张，即使他自己认为这种主张是真实的，但其实它是虚假的；

---

[1] 1872 年《合同法》第 17 条解释。

[2] 1872 年《合同法》第 19 条解释。

（2）一方当事人在没有欺骗意图的情况，通过误导他人或声称代表他的人来侵害他人的合法权益的违反义务的行为，从而被侵害人上获得利益；

（3）无恶意地导致协议当事人对协议标的物的实质内容产生误解①。

《合同法》第18条规定了三类构成虚假陈述的行为。它包括：(a)即使行为人以为它是真实的，但实际不是的且没有保证的；或(b)实施违背义务的行为误导他人或代表他人的人，侵犯他人合法权益；或者(c)导致合同当事人对协议标的事项产生错误认识。

虚假陈述的最重要的要求是虚假的事实陈述是由一方当事人作出的，并且无欺骗另一方当事人的意图②。由于一方的虚假陈述而给予同意的另一方当事方可以选择撤销合同。

5. 误解

《合同法》第20条规定，如果协议的双方对协议的实质内容都存在误解，协议无效。

例如，A同意向B出售从英国到仰光途中的特定货物。事实证明，在讨价还价之前，运送货物的船已经被抛弃并且货物丢失了。双方都没有意识到这一事实。该协议无效③。

误解引起的合同无效应该存在以下三个条件：

（1）这个误解必须是双方的误解（即相互误解）；

（2）它必定是对事实的误解而不是对法律的误解；

（3）它必须是协议必不可少的事实。

（a）合同是基于对事实的误解而签订的。

事实错误可以分为以下两种类型：双方误解、单方误解。

当双方当事人对协议的实质内容存在误解时，协议将失效④。对重要事实的双方误解导致协议失效。

合同仅仅因为其中一方当事人在事实上有错误认识的情况下引起时，是不可撤销的⑤。单方的误解并不影响协议的有效性。换句话说，只有合同双

---

① 1872年《合同法》第18条解释。

② P. P. S. GoGNA，《商业和工业法教科书》，2007年版，S. Chand & Company Ltd.，New Delhi，p. 60.

③ 1872年《合同法》，Illustration (a)至第20条。

④ 1872年《合同法》第20条解释。

⑤ 1872年《合同法》第22条解释。

方当事人的误解才能使一个合同无效。

（b）基于法律上的误解的合同

第 21 条规定,由于对缅甸对联邦现行法律的错误认识签订的合同不是无效的;但对缅甸联邦未实施的法律产生误解与事实误解具有相同的效力。

缅甸法律的错误认识并不意味着协议无效。每个人都应该知道他服从的国家的法律。在不知晓法律的情况下实施的特定行为得不到任何救济。因此,对缅甸法律的错误并不影响协议的有效性。

不能期望人们知道外国的法律。因此,对这种法律的错误认识被认为是事实认识错误[1]。

在缅甸有一个案子[2],基于人们对中国习惯法的普遍认识错误,认为有一种可以继承死者财产的合同,但其实根据第 20 条和第 21 条规定,这种合同被认定无效。

(五)合法的对价和合法的标的

将承诺转化为协议的因素是对价。承诺本身,并不是可执行的;普通法和《合同法》要求承诺在可能成为合同之前得到对价的支持[3]。

对价是合同形成的重要因素之一。《合同法》第 25 条特别规定:"没有对价的协议是无效的。"因此,一般规则是,如果没有对价,则协议无效。但是,第 25 条本身也提供了该规则的某些例外情况。

《合同法》第 2(d)条规定了"对价"一词,具体如下:"基于承诺人的要求,受约人或任何其他人已经做过或已经弃权不做;正在做或正在弃权不做;承诺会做或将放弃做某事,此类行为或自制或承诺,被称为承诺的对价。"

对价的基本组成部分是:

1.对价是一种行为(如做某事)或自制(即禁止做某事)。

2.这种行为或自制应该按照承诺者的意愿完成。

3.这种行为或自制可以由受约人或任何其他人来完成。

4.这种行为或自制要么已经执行,要么正在执行中,要么可能被执行。这意味着对价可能发生在过去、现在或将来。

---

① Ranjitlal Harilal Pandia,《商业法原理》1955 年第 3 版,p.31.

② Daw Saw Hla (a) Mrs. Chan Chin Leong vs. Mrs. Maung Sein and eight other, 1963 B. L. R (C. C) 773.

③ Adrian Briggs QC (Hon) and Andrew Burrows QC (Hon),《缅甸合同法》p. 32.

有效合同的条件之一是它的对价和标的必须合法。如果协议的标的或对价是非法的，则该协议无效。

根据《合同法》第23条，除非法律禁止，协议的对价或对象是合法的；或者如果允许的话，它具有将违反某些法律的规定的性质；或者是欺诈性的；或牵涉到或暗示他人的人身或财产受到损害；或者法院认为它是不道德的，或者违反公共政策。

在以上每一种情况下，协议的对价或标的都被认为是非法的。任何标的或对价不合法的协议都是无效的。

根据《合同法》第23条的规定，协议的对价或标的将被视为非法。在下列情况下，协议的标的或对价是不合法的：

（1）法律禁止

合同的标的或对价是法律所禁止的。具有这样的标的或对价的协议是非法和无效的。对于法律禁止的合同是非法合同，且不得采取任何行动。

当某一协议中的某项行为被法律所禁止时，法院不能执行该协议，也不能执行具非法对价的协议。①

（2）违反若干法律的规定

有时，法律没有明确禁止协议的标的或对价，但是合同的性质决定了它会违反若干法律的规定。在这种情况下，该标的或对价是非法的。

（3）具欺诈性质的

协议中的欺骗性的对价或标的是非法和无效的。

（4）损害另一人的人身或财产

牵涉到或隐含着对他人的人身或财产的损害的协议是无效的协议。

（5）不道德的或违反公共政策的

所有违反道德的协议都是无效的，具有违背公共政策的代价的协议是无效的。

第23条涉及对价完全无效或非法的情况。第24条规定，如果一个或多个标的的单一对价的任一部分，或单个标的的若干对价中的任一对价或任一部分是非法的，则该协议无效。

第24条是指一部分对价或者标的是非法的协议，不能与其他有效的部分

① Adrian Briggs QC (Hon) and Andrew Burrows QC (Hon)，《缅甸合同法》，p. 66.

分开,在这种情况下,整个协议是无效的①。

(六)明确声明为无效的协议

第 10 条定义的有效条件之一是,它不能被该法声明为无效。《合同法》记录了明确声明为无效的十四种协议。它们是:

1. 无缔约能力人员达成的协议②;

2. 在事实或法律方面基于相互误解达成的协议③;

3. 对价或标的或是不合法的协议④;

4. 部分对价划标的违法的协议⑤;

5. 没有对价的协议⑥;

6. 约束婚姻的协议⑦;

7. 限制贸易的协议⑧;

8. 限制法律程序的协议⑨;

9. 协议的含义不确定或无法确定⑩;

10. 通过赌注达成的协议⑪;

11. 协议目的的实现取决于不可能发生的事件⑫;

12. 协议要做的事后来变得不可能或不合法⑬;

13. 事后做出的合同变得不可能或不合法⑭;

14. 双方恶意串通,以合法形式掩盖非法目的⑮。

---

① Ranjitlal Harilal Pandia,《商业法原理》,1955 年第 3 版,p. 38.

② 1872 年《合同法》第 11 条。

③ 1872 年《合同法》第 20 条、第 21 条。

④ 1872 年《合同法》第 23 条。

⑤ 1872 年《合同法》第 24 条。

⑥ 1872 年《合同法》第 25 条。

⑦ 1872 年《合同法》第 26 条。

⑧ 1872 年《合同法》第 27 条。

⑨ 1872 年《合同法》第 28 条。

⑩ 1872 年《合同法》第 29 条。

⑪ 1872 年《合同法》第 30 条。

⑫ 1872 年《合同法》第 32 条、第 36 条。

⑬ 1872 年《合同法》第 56 条第 1 段。

⑭ 1872 年《合同法》第 56 条第 2 段。

⑮ 1872 年《合同法》第 57 条。

(七)根据法律要求提供书面形式

通常情况下,签订合同不需要书面形式,但如果法律有此要求,则需要书面证明或登记。协议必须符合法律的规定要求的书面形式,证明或登记。

《合同法》第10条确认了一个非常明显的观点,即如果其他立法要求以书面形式订立合同,或者进行证明或进行登记,该立法继续约束当事人并适用于合同,合同通常不需要书面形式[①]。

结　论

缅甸合同法订立的合同与其他大陆法系国家的合同形成法是不同的。根据《缅甸合同法》,合同形成的第一要素是要约和承诺。第二要素是缔约方的自由同意。同意不应该由以下原因引起:

(1)胁迫;(2)不当影响;(3)欺诈;(4)虚假陈述;(5)误解。合同形成的第三要素叫作缔约能力,它必须考虑三个因素:(1)年龄;(2)智力因素;(3)订立合同的资格。关于合同形成的第四个要素,根据第20条规定,合同须有合法的对价和合法标的。第五个要素是法律没有明确声明协议是无效的。关于第六要素,每当法律规定这种协议应该以书面形式提出,或者规定证明证人的数量,或者如果这种协议应该被登记,就应该按照这种规定来做,以便可依法强制执行。根据其他大陆法系国家的合同法构成,在合同具有法律约束力之前是不需要对价的,不需要相互交换对价。在缅甸,对价是形成合同的一个重要因素。通过阅读缅甸《合同法》能很容易被查明和理解并有所修改。虽然该法有很多优点,但一直都不够全面。合同法律框架应进行升级以便适应合同法和国际惯例的发展。

---

① Adrian Briggs QC(Hon)and Andrew Burrows QC(Hon),《缅甸合同法》,p.10.

The Arbitration Law in Myanmar

Thin Thin Oo[*]

Abstract: The Myanmar Federal Parliament enacted the Arbitration Law in 2016, which further clarified the arbitration rules for investment dispute settlement, increased foreign arbitration and its enforcement system, and improved the substantive content and procedural framework of arbitration. The provisions of the free appointment arbitrator and the free choice of the applicable law are of great significance to the parties, and the relationship between the jurisdiction of the court and the jurisdiction of the arbitral tribunal is more explicit, which could help investors to choose the right investment Dispute settlement, but there are still many imperfections in this law, I think the arbitration system should be further improved, such as the establishment of arbitration institutions or arbitration committees to make up for Inadequacies.

Keywords: Arbitration, jurisdiction, arbitration procedure, Applicable law, Recognition and execution

Introduction

With the implementing of the sound national economy in Myanmar, the legal reform process are also highly performing. In the legal reforming process the promulgation of Myanmar Investment Law, Competition law, the arbitration law are also one achivement. To settle domestic commercial disputes and international

---

* Thin Thin Oo,Doctoral Student of School of International Law of SWUPL/fStaff Officer, Union Attorney General's Office,Building 25, Nay Pyi Taw, Myanmar, E-mail: m15123164414@163. com.

commercial disputes in a fair and effective manner; to settle disputes by means of arbitration, and to recognize and enforce the foreign award; and to encourage settlement of disputes by means of arbitration the Pyidaungsu Hluttaw enacted the arbitration law on 5 January 2016. This new law gives effect to the New York Convention on the Recognition and Enforcement of Foreign Arbitral Awards (New York Convention), which Myanmar acceded to in 2013. The new arbitration law is primarily based on the United Nations Commission on International Trade Law (UNCITRAL) rules. UNCITRAL rules provided well-established internatioal standards for arbitral procedures. The objective of this article is to introduce the Myanmar arbitration law, in other words, to mention the basic provisions of arbitration law. The arbitration law is provided that the domestic arbitration, foreign arbitration and enforcement of foreign arbitral awards. In the law specifically provided definitions, organizational and procedural rules, interim measures, composition of arbitral tribunal, jurisdiction, governing law and sustantive law, the award and enforcement.

(a)Background of the Arbitration law in Myanmar

The 1944 Arbitration Act only provided for domestic arbitration and did not provide a framework for the recognition and enforcement of foreign arbitral awards. Under the 1944 Arbitration Act, a Myanmar arbitral award could not generally be enforced abroad and was only enforceable against a foreign party within the country if it had assets in Myanmar. Theoretically, foreign arbitral awards could have been enforced in Myanmar; however, for decades there were no reported cases. Additionally, a foreign award was only enforceable if it was rendered in a country that had signed the Geneva Protocol on Arbitration Clauses 1923 or the Geneva Convention on the Execution of Foreign Arbitral Awards 1927. In reciprocity for the apparent failure of Myanmar to recognize foreign judgments, Myanmar arbitral awards were generally not recognized abroad. [1]

---

[1] Arbitration in Myanmar—The Best Option?, William D. Greenlee, Jr. Published in *International Law News*, Volume 45, Number 3, 2017. © 2017 by the American Bar Association.

(b)Application

In respect of the application, section 2 provided that

(a)Subject to sub- section (b), an Arbitration Agreement whether made in the State or not, shall apply to the provisions of this Law when the legal place of arbitration is in the state.

(b)If the place of arbitration is in any country other than the State, or if the place of arbitration has not been designated or decided upon, section 10,11,30, 31 and Chapter 10, shall be applied.

(c)Where any other existing law of the State which imposes restriction that disputes may not be settled by means of arbitration, the provision of this law shall not prejudice on the said law.

According to above mentioned, this arbitation law can use in domestic arbitration and foreign arbitration. For the application of foreign arbitration the provision of section 10;Referral to Arbitration and Stay of Court Action, section 11; powers of the court to intervence in arbitral proceedings, section 30; requesting assistance from a court in taking evidence and section 31;court execution of intrim award made by arbitral tribunal are also primarily concerned. If the existing law of the state restricted the disputes to apply the settlement mechanism of arbitration, the said disputes cannot be settled by arbitration.

(c)Organization of Tribunal

The disputing parties may determine freely the number of arbitrators and it more than one shall be the odd number. For the number of arbitrator fails, it shall be one. In respect of the appointment of arbitrators mentioned in section 13. It provided that

(a)Unless otherwise agreed by the disputing parties, a citizen of any country may carry out act as an arbitrator

(b)Subject to the provisions contained in sub-section (d), the disputing parties may agree freely to determine a proceedure to appoint an arbitrator or arbitrators,

(c)If the procedure to appoint arbitrators had been agreed by the disputing parties, it shall be parties carried out as the said procedure. In case of failure of one contracting parties, or failure by the two appointed arbitrators to appoint a third arbitrator, or failure of any entrusted third person or organization to perform and where no other method for appointment of arbitrators is specified in the arbitration agreement, a disputing party may request by application to the Chief Justice or any person or organization determined by the Chief Justice, for appointment of arbitrators.

(d) If failing agreement to determine the arbitrators as mentioned in sub-section (b),

(1) in an arbitration with three arbitrators, each party shall appoint one arbitrator, and the two arbitrators thus appointed shall choose the third arbitrator who will act as the presiding arbitrator of the arbitral tribunal. If a party fails to appoint the arbitrator within thirty days of receipt of a request to do so from the other party, or if the two arbitrators fail to agree on the third arbitrator within thirty days of their appointment, the appointment shall be made, upon request of a party, by the Chief Justice or any person/institution selected by the Chief Justice.

(The Chief Justice mentioned in this section refers to the Chief Justice of the High Court of the Region or High Court of the State within their jurisdiction for domestic arbitration and refers to the Chief Justice of the Union for the international arbitration)

(2) in an arbitration with a sole arbitrator, the Chief Justice or any person/institution selected by him shall, upon request of a party, appoint the sole arbitrator if a party fails to appoint the sole arbitrator within thirty days of receipt of a request to do so from the other party.

(e) The Chief Justice or any person/institution selected by him, in appointing an arbitrator, shall have due regard to the qualifications required of the arbitrator by the agreement of the parties and such considerations as being an independent and impartial arbitrator.

(f) The Chief Justice or any person/institution selected by him may perform appropriate functions entrusted to him by subsections (c) and (d) of this section.

(g) In appointing a sole or third arbitrator for international arbitration in which parties are of different nationalities, the Chief Justice or any person/institution selected by him may take into account appointing an arbitrator of a nationality other than those of the parties.

(h) A decision on a matter entrusted to the Chief Justice or any person/

institution selected by him by subsections (c) and (d) of this section shall be subject to no appeal.

In the portion of composition of the tribunal, the challenges of the arbitrator are provided in section 15. It stated that When a person is approached in connection with his possible appointment as an arbitrator, he shall disclose any circumstances likely to give rise to justifiable doubts as to his impartiality or independence.

(b) If an arbitrator did not inform such circumstances to the parties as mentioned in subsection (a), from the time of his appointment and throughout the arbitral proceedings, he shall disclose any such circumstances to the parties without delay.

(c) An arbitrator may be challenged only if:

(1) circumstances exist that give rise to justifiable doubts as to his impartiality or independence, or

(2) he does not possess qualifications agreed to by the parties.

(d) A party may challenge an arbitrator appointed by him, or in whose appointment he has participated, only for reasons of which he becomes aware after the appointment has been made.

And termination of mandate and replacement of an arbitrator are specifically provided in section 16.

(d)The relation between court and arbitration

Arbitration law provided many provisions concerning the role of the court in the arbitration proceedings. Chapter 4 Arbitration Agreement, chapter 7 Conduct of Arbitration, chapter 9 Jurisdiction of the Court related to Domestic Award, chapter 10 Recognition and Enforcement of Foreign Award are mostly concerned. In this part only mentions the provisions in chapter 4.

Sometimes it may arise the complex issue between the court and arbitration proceedings. For this issues section 10 stated that:

(a)a court before which an action is brought in a matter which is the subject of an arbitration agreement shall, if a party so requests not later than when submitting his written statement on the substance of the dispute, refer the parties to arbitration unless it finds that the agreement is null and void, inoperative or incapable of being performed;

(b) where an action referred to in subsection (a) of this article, arbitral proceedings may nevertheless be commenced or continued, and an award may be made, while the issue is pending before the court;

(c) If the court refuses to refer the parties to arbitration, any decision making before filing a suit relating to any matter of the arbitration contained in the arbitration agreement, shall not effect to the suit;

(d) the court shall order to stay the suit before the court, if the court refers the parties to arbitration;

(e) No appeal shall be allowed against the court decision which refers to arbitration under subsection (a);

(f) Appeal shall be allowed relating to the court decision refusing to refer to the arbitration.

Unless otherwise agreed by the parties, if a party requests the court, the court shall have power to make decision as its own jurisdiction for:

(1) taking evidence;

(2) the preservation any evidence;

(3) pass an order related to the property in disputes in arbitration or any property which is related to the subject-matter of the dispute;

(4) inspection, taking photo for evidence, preservation and seizure of the property which is related to the dispute;

(5) samples to be taken from, or any observation to be made of or experiment conducted upon, any property which is or forms part of the subject-matter of the dispute;

(6) allow to enter in the premises owned by or under the control of the parties to disputes for the purpose of above mentions matters;

(7) sale of any property which is the subject-matter of the dispute;

(8) an interim injunction or appointment of a receiver;

(b) If the interim measure is needed urgently in arbitration, the court may pass an order relating to preservation of evidence and related properties upon the application of a party as require.

(c) If the interim measure is not needed urgently, upon the application of a party in arbitration, the court shall deal such matter after delivering a notice to the other parties and arbitral tribunal and with the approval of the arbitration tribunal or with the written consent of the other party.

(d) The court shall only deal with the matters which the authorized person of the parties or arbitral tribunal or arbitral institution or other institution has no authority to do or not able to handle effectively.

(e) The decision of a Court made by this section may be appealed.

(f) An order made by the court shall cease to have effect in whole or in part if the arbitral tribunal makes an order which expressly relates to the order under subsection (a). (section 11)

(e)Jurisdiction

Jurisdiction is one of the important part of the arbitration proceeding. To determine the jurisdiction, section 18 provided that

(a)Unless otherwise agreed by the parties, the arbitral tribunal may rule on its own jurisdiction, including any objections with respect to the existence or validity of the arbitration agreement [Relating with the arbitration agreement, writing agreement under section 3, subsection (b) means: an arbitration agreement shall be deemed in writing if it is signed by the parties; if the information contained in electronic communication is accessible so as to be useable for subsequent reference, such arbitration agreement by means of electronic communication shall be deemed in writing. An arbitration agreement may be in the form of an arbitration clause in a contract or in the form of a separate agreement (section 9)]. In doing so:

(i) an arbitration clause in a contract shall be treated as agreement independent from other terms of the contract;

(ii) a decision by the arbitral tribunal that the contract is null and void shall not entail *ipso jure* the invalidity of the arbitration clause.

(b) A plea that the arbitral tribunal does not have jurisdiction shall be raised not later than the submission of the statement of defence. A party is not precluded from raising such a plea by the fact that he has appointed, or participated in the appointment of, an arbitrator.

(c) A plea that the arbitral tribunal is exceeding the scope of its authority shall be raised as soon as the matter alleged to be beyond the scope of its authority is raised during the arbitral proceedings.

(d) The arbitral tribunal may admit a later plea referred to in subsection (b) and (c) if it considers the delay justified.

(e) The arbitral tribunal may rule on a plea referred to in subsections (b) and (c) as preliminary issue or as an arbitral award. If the arbitral tribunal rules that it has jurisdiction or not, any party aggrieved by the arbitral award, may appeal to the court, subject to section 43, subsection (d) (1)(2) and section 47, subsection (b) (1), within 30 days from the date of receiving of such decision.

(f) Although the application is pending in the court, the arbitral tribunal shall continue the arbitral proceedings and make an award.

(f)Power of arbitral tribunal to order interim orders

Unless otherwise agreed by the parties, an arbitral tribunal shall have powers to make decision, order and instructions to any party for: security for costs; discovery of documents and interrogatories; giving of evidence by affidavit; the preservation, interim custody or sale of any property which is part of the subject-matter of the dispute; samples to be taken from, or any observation to be made of or experiment conducted upon, any property which is or forms part of the subject-matter of the dispute; the preservation and interim custody of any evidence for the purposes of the proceedings; securing the amount in dispute; an interim injunction or any other interim measure. [section 19(a)]

An arbitral tribunal may have power not only to administer oaths to the parties and witnesses but also to adopt inquisitorial procedures as its consider appropriate.

(d) The power of the arbitral tribunal to order a claimant to provide security for costs as referred to in subsection (a)(1) shall not be exercised solely because the claimant is: (i) an individual ordinarily residing outside the Republic of the Union of Myanmar;

(ii)a corporation or an association incorporated or formed under the law of the other country.

All decisions, orders or instruction made by an arbitral tribunal in the course of an, arbitration may apply to the court for the enforcement in accordance with the section 31. [section 19(b-e)]

An arbitrator shall not be liable for his act or omission which is done with due care during the course of arbitration as an arbitrator. (section 20)

(g)Conduct of Arbitral Proceedings

The parties shall be treated with equality and each party shall be given a full opportunity of presenting his case. (section 26)

Without contradicting the provisions of this Law, the parties are free to agree on the procedure to be followed by the arbitral tribunal in conducting the proceedings. Failing such agreement, the arbitral tribunal may conduct the arbitration in such manner as it considers appropriate. And the power conferred upon the arbitral tribunal includes the power to determine the admissibility, relevance, materiality, and weight of any evidence. (section 22)

The parties are free to agree on the place of arbitration. If fails for the place of arbitration, the arbitral tribunal shall determine the place having regard to the circumstances of the case, including the convenience of the parties.

Notwithstanding the above provisions, the arbitral tribunal may, unless otherwise agreed by the parties, meet at any place it considers appropriate for consultation among its members, for hearing witnesses, experts or the parties, or for inspection of goods, other property or documents. (section 23)

Unless otherwise agreed by the parties, the arbitral proceedings in respect of a particular dispute commence on the date on which a request for that dispute to be referred to arbitration is received by the respondent. (section 24)

The parties are free to agree on the language or languages to be used in the arbitral proceedings. Failing such agreement, the arbitral tribunal shall determine the language or languages to be used in the arbitral proceedings. This agreement or determination, unless otherwise specified, shall apply to any written statement by a party, any hearing and any award, decision or other communication by the arbitral tribunal. The arbitral tribunal may order that any documentary evidence shall be accompanied by a translation into the language or languages agreed upon by the parties or determined by the arbitral tribunal. (section 25)

The conditions for the statements of the claim and defence are provided in section 26.

The parties may agree the particulars to be stated in the claim or defence. Failing such agreement, the claimant shall state the facts supporting his claim, the points at issue and the relief or remedy sought, and the respondent shall state his defence in respect of these particulars and apply to the arbitral tribunal within the period of time agreed by the parties or determined by the arbitral tribunal.

The parties may submit with their statements all documents they consider to be relevant and other evidence or may add a reference to the documents they will submit.

Unless otherwise agreed by the parties, either party may amend or supplement his claim or defence during the course of the arbitral proceedings, unless the arbitral tribunal considers it inappropriate to allow such amendment having regard to the delay in making it.

Unless otherwise agreed by the parties, the arbitral tribunal shall decide whether to hold oral hearings for the presentation of evidence or for oral argument, or whether the proceedings shall be conducted on the basis of documents and other materials. However, unless the parties have agreed that no hearings shall be held, the arbitral tribunal shall hold such hearings at an appropriate stage of the proceedings, if so requested by a party. The parties shall be given sufficient advance notice of any hearing and of any meeting of the arbitral tribunal for the purposes of inspection of goods, other property or documents. All statements, documents or other information supplied to the arbitral tribunal by one party shall be communicated to the other party. Also any expert report or evidentiary document on which the arbitral tribunal may rely in making its decision shall be communicated to the parties. (section 27)

Unless otherwise agreed by the parties, if, without showing sufficient cause:

(a) the claimant fails to communicate his statement of claim in accordance with section 26, subsection (a), the arbitral tribunal shall terminate the proceedings;

(b) the respondent fails to communicate his statement of defence in accordance with section 26, subsection (a), the arbitral tribunal shall continue the proceedings.

However, such failure in itself shall not be treated as an admission of the claimant's allegations;

(c) any party fails to appear at a hearing or to produce documentary evidence, the arbitral tribunal may continue the proceedings and make the award on the evidence before it. (section 28)

For the appointment of the expert and for the examination of the expert are mentioned in section 29.

The arbitral tribunal, or a party with the approval of the arbitral tribunal, may apply to the Court for assistance in taking evidence. In the application shall specify the particulars mentioned in section 30 (b). The Court may, within its competence and according to its rules on taking evidence, execute the request that the evidence be provided directly to the arbitral tribunal. The Court may, while making an order, issue the same processes to witnesses as it may issue in suits tried before it. (section 30)

Section 31 provided for the enforcement of interim order of the arbitral tribunal by the court.

(a) relating to arbitration, whether interim order are passed within or outside the State, Courts may enforce such interim orders passed by the arbitral tribunal as if its own order and decision.

(b) in relation to arbitration exercised outside the State, when an applicant file the interim order for enforcement is unable to submit strong evidence that it is the same type of order exercised within the State, the Court shall not approve for enforcement.

(c) When approval is granted according to subsection (a) the Court shall enforce such order.

(d) There shall be no right of appeal upon the Court decision on granting approval according to subsection (a) or upon refusal.

(h)Governing Law

If the place of arbitration is the Republic of the Union of Myanmar:

(1) In domestic arbitration, the arbitral tribunal shall decide the dispute which to be settled by arbitration in accordance with the relevant existing law of the Republic of the Union of Myanmar.

(2) In international commercial arbitration:

aa) The arbitral tribunal shall decide the dispute in accordance with such rules of law as are chosen by the parties;

bb) Any designation of the law or legal system of a given State shall be construed, unless otherwise agreed by the parties, as directly referring to the substantive law of that State and not to its conflict of laws rules;

cc) Failing any designation as per subsection clause (aa) by the parties, the arbitral tribunal shall apply the rules of law which it considers applicable. (section 32)

(i)Decision-making, Settlement and Termination of proceedings

In arbitral proceedings with more than one arbitrator, any decision of the arbitral tribunal shall be made, unless otherwise agreed by the parties, by a majority of all its members.

However, notwithstanding anything contained in subsection (a), questions of procedure may be decided by a presiding arbitrator, if so authorized by the parties orall members of the arbitral tribunal. (section 33)

If, during arbitral proceedings, the parties settle the dispute, the arbitral tribunal shall terminate the proceedings and, if requested by the parties and not objected to by the arbitral tribunal, record the settlement in the form of an arbitral award on agreed terms.

An award on agreed terms shall be made in accordance with the provisions of section 35 and shall state that it is an arbitral award.

Such award on agreed terms has the same status and effect as any other award on the merits of the case. (section 34)

Form and contents of award are mentioned in section 35.

The arbitral proceedings shall be terminated by the final award or by an order of the arbitral tribunal in accordance with subsection (b) of this section.

The arbitral tribunal shall issue an order for the termination of the arbitral proceedings when: the claimant withdraws his claim, unless the respondent objects thereto and the arbitral tribunal recognizes a legitimate interest on his part in obtaining a final settlement of the dispute; the parties agree on the termination of the proceedings; the arbitral tribunal finds that the continuation of the proceedings has for any other reason become unnecessary or impossible.

Subject to the provisions of section 37, the mandate of the arbitral tribunal terminates with the termination of the arbitral proceedings pursuant to the section 34, subsection (a) and this section. (section 36)

Correction and interpretation of award; additional award are specifically mentioned in section 37.

Unless otherwise agreed by the parties, the award made by the arbitral tribunal pursuant to the arbitration agreement, shall be final and binding on the parties and persons claiming under them respectively. (section 38)

(j)Power of the Court relating to Domestic Arbitration

In the part of the relation between the court and arbitration, some functions of the court are already mentioned. This part is concerning the jurisdiction of the court related to domestic arbitral award. In this part provide the initial awards of the court and issue of law, enforcement of domestic arbitral awards, criteria of setting aside of a domestic arbitral award, right of appeal concerning domestic arbitral award, effective on domestic awards of an order of an appeallate court.

Unless otherwise agreed by the parties, the Court may, on the application of a party to the arbitral proceedings who has given notice to the other parties, determine any issue of law arising in the course of the proceedings which the Court is satisfied substantially affects the rights of one or more of the parties.

The domestic award shall be enforced under the Code of Civil Procedure in the same manner as if it were a decree of the court. (section 40)

Section 41 (a) provided that; upon the application for setting aside by one of the party, the court may set aside the domestic arbitral award only if:

(1) a party to the arbitration agreement was under some incapacity; or

(2) the arbitration agreement is not valid under the law to which the parties have agreed or, failing any indication thereon, under the law of the Republic of the Union of Myanmar; or

(3) the party making the application was not given proper notice of the appointment of an arbitrator or of the arbitral proceedings or was otherwise unable to present his case; or

(4) the award deals with a dispute not contemplated by or not falling within the terms of the submission to arbitration, or contains decisions on matters beyond the scope of the submission to arbitration.

(5) the composition of the arbitral tribunal or the arbitral procedure was not in accordance with the agreement of the parties or was not in accordance with this Law.

(6) the subject-matter of the dispute is not capable of settlement by arbitration under the existing law; or

(7) the award is in conflict with the national interest (public policy) of the

Republic of the Union of Myanmar.

A party in dispute may, upon notice to the other parties and to the arbitral tribunal, appeal to the Court on an issue of law arising out of an award made in the proceedings. (section 42)

The Court, if satisfied and agree with the following facts shall accept the appeal:

(1) the decision of the arbitral tribunal of the issue in dispute is substantially affect the rights of a party or upon the parties;

(2) the decision of the arbitral tribunal on the issue in dispute is obviously wrong.

When filing appeal according to this section, the Court can pass any of the following orders: approve the award; amend the award; to return the decision to the arbitral tribunal to review and reconsider the whole or part of the award; set aside the whole or part of the arbitral award.

Appeal can be filed to the Court of competent jurisdiction for following court order:

(1) An order refusing to refer to arbitration according to section 10 subsection (f);

(2) An order granting or refusing to perform one of the interim measures according to section 11;

(3) Court order passing upon the issue of law according to section (39) subsection (a);

(4) An order setting aside or refusing the set aside of domestic arbitral award according to section 41.

Following orders of an arbitral tribunal can be filed for appeal to the Court of Jurisdiction:

(1) Order accepting the application according to section 18 subsection (b) and (c);

(2) Order by the arbitral tribunal that it has jurisdiction or not according to section 18 (e);

(3) Order granting or refusing to perform the any interim measures according to section 19.

There shall be no second appeal upon the order passed from filing of appeal according to this section . (section 43)

(k) Effect of the Appellate Court order upon Domestic Arbitration

The appellate Court, when passing an order relating to the award according tosection 43 subsection (b):

(a) When it is decided to amend the award, such amended decision shall be effected as part of the award;

(b) When the Court pass the order remitting the award in whole or partial to the arbitral tribunal for reconsideration and revision the arbitral tribunal shall revise such matters and pass the decision;

(c) Necessary timing for the arbitral tribunal to review and pass the decision may be recommended. (section 44)

(l) Recognition of Enforcement of Foreign Arbitral Award

Particulars to apply for recognition or enforcement of foreign arbitral award are provided in section 45.

Under section 46, the award shall be enforced under the Code of Civil Procedure in the same manner as if it were a decree of the court.

The court may refuse to recognize the foreign arbitral award if the party against whom it is invoked furnishes to the court proof that:

(1) the parties to the arbitration agreement referred was under some incapacity; or

(2) the said agreement is not valid under the law to which the parties have subjected to it or, failing any indication thereon, under the law of the country where the award was made;

(3) the party against whom the award is invoked was not given proper notice of the appointment of an arbitrator or of the arbitral proceedings or was otherwise unable to present his case; or

(4) the award deals with a dispute not contemplated by or not falling within the terms of the submission to arbitration, or it contains decisions on matters beyond the scope of the submission to arbitration; or

(5) the composition of the arbitral tribunal or the arbitral procedure was not in accordance with the agreement of the parties or, failing such agreement, was not in

accordance with the law of the country where the arbitration took place;or

(6) the award has not yet become binding on the parties or has been set aside or suspended by a competent authority of the country in which, or under the law of which, that award was made;

Enforcement of the foreign arbitral award may be refused if the court finds that:

(1) the subject-matter of the dispute is not capable of settlement by arbitration under the law of the Republic of the Union of Myanmar;or

(2) the enforcement of the award would be contrary to the national interest (public policy) of the Republic of the Union of Myanmar.

Any party to dispute may appeal an order granting or refusing to take any measure under section 10; any order under section 11; an order setting aside or refusing to set aside an award under section 46, subsection (b) and (c);passed by a competent court.

The following orders passed by arbitral tribunal may be appealed to the competent Court:

(1) An order determining whether the arbitral tribunal has jurisdiction or not under section 18, subsection (e);

(2) An order granting or refusing the interim matures under section 19;

Nothing in this Chapter shall prejudice any rights which any person would have had of enforcing foreign arbitral award in the Republic of the Union of Myanmar or of availing himself of such award to the enactment of this Law. (section 48)

Enforcement of foreign arbitral award under this Chapter shall not apply to the enforcement under the Arbitration (Protocol and Convention) Act, 1937. (section 49)

Conclusion

Myanmar Arbitration law is good law for the arbitration system. This law can apply not only for the domestic arbitrtion but also for the foreign arbitration. For the freely appointment of arbitrators and freely choosing of the governing law provisons are also valuable facts for the parties. In respect of the jurisdiction the law mentioned specifically. By promulgating this law the parties easily to finish the enforcement of foreign arbitral awards. Although this law absence the provision for the qualification of arbitrators. The qualification of the arbitrator is important facts of the arbitration procedure, the law should provided that clearly. And Myanmar does not have the arbitration institution or arbitration commission, this point is also arose the difficulty for some procedure; for the choosing of arbitrators, for the choosing the procedure and administrative support. Therefore, to become the perfect arbitration system in Myanmar, the arbitration commision/ institution should be established.

References

1. The Arbitration Law, The Republic of the Union of Myanmar.

2. Arbitration in Myanmar—The Best Option?, William D. Greenlee, Jr. Published in *International Law News*, Volume 45, Number 3, 2017. © 2017 by the American Bar Association.

缅甸仲裁法

Thin Thin Oo[*]

编译　吕蕴谋[**]

摘要:2016年,缅甸联邦会议颁布了仲裁法,进一步明确了投资争端解决的仲裁规则。例如,增加了外国仲裁和外国仲裁的执行两大部分,完善了仲裁的实体内容和程序性框架。自由任用仲裁员和自由选择准据法的规定,对当事人意义重大。司法管辖权和仲裁庭的管辖权之间关系的明晰,便利了投资者对争端解决方式的应用。但此法仍存在不完善的地方,例如仲裁员资格规定的空白,仲裁机构的缺失等问题。笔者认为可以通过建立仲裁机构或仲裁委员会等机构,进一步完善缅甸仲裁制度,以弥补规定空白之处。

关键词:仲裁,司法管辖权,仲裁程序,准据法,承认与执行

引　言

随着缅甸健全的国民经济体系的实施,法律改革也表现出色。在法律改革过程中,缅甸投资法、竞争法、仲裁法的颁布是成就的一方面。为了公平有效地解决国内商业纠纷和国际商事纠纷,通过仲裁解决争议,承认和执行外国裁决,并鼓励通过仲裁方式解决争端,缅甸联邦议会于2016年1月5日颁布了仲裁法。这项新仲裁法的颁布,使得缅甸2013年加入的《纽约公认的承认和执行外国仲裁裁决公约》(纽约公约)生效。新的仲裁法主要是基于联合国国际贸易法委员会(UNCITRAL)的规则制定。贸易法委员会的规则为仲裁程序提供了完善的国际标准。本文的目的是介绍缅甸的仲裁法,换句话说,介

---

* 西南政法大学国际法学院博士生/缅甸联邦最高检检察官。

** 西南政法大学2017级国际法硕士研究生。

绍新仲裁法的基本规定。仲裁法涵盖国内仲裁、外国仲裁和外国仲裁裁决的执行三部分。其具体规定了定义、组织和程序规则、临时措施、仲裁庭的组成、管辖权、准据法和实体法、裁决的效力和执行。

一、缅甸仲裁法的背景

1944 年的仲裁法只规定了国内仲裁的部分，并没有提供承认和执行外国仲裁裁决的程序框架。根据 1944 年仲裁法的规定，缅甸的仲裁裁决一般不能在境外执行，只有在该外方在缅甸境内拥有资产的情况下才可以对国内的该外方执行。理论上讲，外国仲裁裁决可以在缅甸执行；然而，几十年来并没有这样的案例。此外，只有签署了 1923 年《仲裁条例议定书》或 1927 年《执行外国仲裁裁决日内瓦公约》的国家的仲裁裁决可以在缅甸得到执行。根据互惠原则，因缅甸显然未能成功承认外国判决，故缅甸的仲裁裁决一般在境外也得不到承认。

二、适用

关于法律的适用，第 2 条规定如下：

(a)根据第(b)款的规定，无论是在国内还是国外达成的仲裁协议，当约定的仲裁地位于本国时，均适用于本法的规定。

(b)如果仲裁地在缅甸以外的任何国家，或者如果仲裁地没有被指定或确定，则适用第 10 条、第 11 条、第 30 条、第 31 条和第 10 章的规定。

(c)若联邦其他现行法律规定该争议不得以仲裁方式解决，本法的规定不得损害该法的规定。

据上所述，本仲裁法可用于国内仲裁和外国仲裁。外国仲裁规定在第 10 条中，仲裁和法院诉讼适用第 11 条，法院在仲裁程序中的权力规定在第 30 条，要求法院协助调取证据适用第 31 条，关于法院执行仲裁法庭的临时措施也有初步涉及。如果联邦的现行法律限制此种争议适用仲裁解决机制，则所述争议不能通过仲裁解决。

三、仲裁庭的组成

争端各方可以自由确定仲裁员的人数，当不止一个时应为奇数。如果关

于仲裁人数协商不成,则应为一人。关于仲裁员的任命规定在第 13 条中。内容如下:

(a)除争议各方另有约定外,任何国家的公民均可以作为仲裁员。

(b)除第(d)节所载条文另有规定的外,争议各方可自由决定任命一名仲裁员或仲裁员的任用程序。

(c)如果仲裁员的任用程序已经得到争议各方的同意,则应当按照上述程序进行。如果一个缔约方不同意,或者两名指定的仲裁员未能任命第三名仲裁员,或者受委托的第三方或组织未能委任且仲裁协议中没有其他指定仲裁人的方式的情况下,争议方可以向首席法官或由首席法官裁定的任何人或组织提出申请,委任仲裁员。

(d)如果未能按照第(b)节所述确定仲裁员的协议,则

1)在一个需要三名仲裁员的仲裁中,各方应各自指定一名仲裁员,由此任命的两名仲裁员应选择担任仲裁庭首席仲裁员的第三名仲裁员。如果一方当事人在收到另一方的请求 30 日内未指定仲裁员,或者如果两名仲裁员在任命 30 日内未能就第三名仲裁员达成协议,则应当按照由首席法官或其选定的任何个人或机构提出的要求来确定。(在本条中提到的首席法官,是指该地区的高等法院的首席法官或对国内仲裁有管辖权的联邦高等法院首席法官,或国际仲裁联盟的首席大法官。)

2)在独任制的仲裁中,如果一方当事人未能在收到另一方要求指定仲裁员的三十天内任命独任仲裁员,首席法官或其所选择的任何人或机构,可以根据另一方当事人的要求指定独任仲裁员。

(e)首席法官或其选定的任何个人或机构在指定仲裁员时,应适当考虑到双方合意要求仲裁员应具备的资格,和考虑到仲裁员的独立和公正性。

(f)首席法官或其所选择的任何人或机构,可履行本条第(c)段及第(d)段委托他的适当职能。

(g)首席法官或其所选择的任何个人或机构在委任独任或第三名仲裁员进行当事人是不同国籍的国际仲裁时,可以考虑委任除当事人以外的国籍的仲裁员。

(h)在本条第(c)段及第(d)段中,首席大法官或由他选择的任何人或机构在受委托的事项内作出的决定,不得上诉。

关于仲裁庭的组成比例和仲裁员的质疑规定在第 15 条中。内容如下:

(a)当一个人因为可能被任命为仲裁员而被接近时,他应披露任何可能引起合理怀疑其公正或独立的情况。

(b)仲裁员如果没有将这种情况通知第(a)段所述的当事人,则从其被任命时起,在整个仲裁程序中,他应立即向当事各方披露任何此类情况。

(c)仲裁员只有在以下情况下才能受到质疑。

1)存在对他的公正性或独立性产生合理怀疑的情况;或者

2)他不具备当事各方合意约定的资质。

(d)当事人只能因为其在仲裁员的任命之后才知道的事由,对他所指定或参与指定的仲裁员进行质疑。

终止任用和替换仲裁员具体规定在第16条中。

四、法院和仲裁庭之间的关系

仲裁法有许多关于法院在仲裁程序中的作用的规定。最具关联的是第4章仲裁协议、第7章仲裁的进行、第9章国内法院的管辖权和第10章外国裁决的认定和执行。在此处我们只陈述第4章的规定。

有些时候法院和仲裁程序之间会存在很复杂的问题,对此,第10条规定如下:

(a)对于仲裁协议范围之内的事项提起诉讼的,如果当事人在不迟于提交关于争议的实质书面声明的请求之前要求将事项提交仲裁,法院应命当事人提交仲裁,除非发现该协议无效或无法执行;

(b)在本条第(a)款所述诉讼存在的情况下,仲裁程序可能仍然可以开始或继续,并且可以在法院待决的情况下作出裁决;

(c)如果法院拒绝命当事人提交仲裁,在诉讼提起之前作出的与仲裁协议中所涉及的仲裁事项有关的任何裁决,都不影响诉讼;

(d)如果法院命当事人提交仲裁,法院应驳回起诉;

(e)不得对法院依据第(a)款规定的提交仲裁的裁决提出上诉;

(f)允许对法院拒绝提交仲裁的裁决提出上诉。

除非当事人另有约定,如果一方当事人向法院提出请求,法院有权类推自己的管辖权作出以下行为:

(a)调取证据;

(b)保全证据;

(c)对仲裁中的争议财产或与争议标的有关的任何财产通过财产禁令;

(d)检查、拍照取证、保全和调取与争议有关的财产;

(e)对作为或构成争议标的的一部分财产进行取样或对其进行任何形式

的观察或实验;

(f)允许在涉及以上提及事宜的情况下进入争议各方所有或由其控制的房地;

(g)出售作为争议标的的任何财产;

(h)临时禁令或任命接收人。

第11条规定如下:

(a)如果在仲裁中紧急需要临时措施,法院可以根据一方当事人提出的申请,通过有关保全证据和相关财产的命令。

(b)如果临时措施并不紧急,经仲裁中一方当事人提出申请后,法院在向另一方当事人和仲裁庭发出通知后,经仲裁庭批准或者另一方当事人书面同意,可以解除临时措施。

(c)法院仅处理当事人或仲裁机构或其他机构授权人无权或无法有效处理的事项。

(d)本条所作决定可被上诉。

(e)如果仲裁庭作出与本条明确有关的命令,法院作出的命令的效力将全部或部分终止。

五、管辖

管辖权是仲裁程序的重要组成部分之一。为确定管辖权,第18条规定:

(a)除非当事人另有约定,仲裁庭可以自行裁定,包括就仲裁协议的存在或有效性提出异议。[关于仲裁协议,根据第3条第(b)款的规定,书面协议是指:如果双方签署仲裁协议,应当被视为书面形式;如果电子通信中包含的信息是可访问,也可供后来引用的,则此类通过电子通信的仲裁协议应被视为书面形式。仲裁协议可以采用合同中的仲裁条款或单独协议的形式(第9节)]这样做的话:

1)合同中的仲裁条款应视为独立于合同其他条款的协议。

2)仲裁庭作出的合同无效的决定,不影响仲裁条款的效力。

(b)提出仲裁庭不具有管辖权异议的时间,不得迟于提交辩护状。若一方当事人已经任命或参与任命一名仲裁员,也不影响其提出管辖权异议。

(c)在仲裁程序中,仲裁庭超越职权的异议,应该在该争议的越权行为发生之后及时被提出。

(d)如果仲裁庭认为理由正当,可以允许当事人延期提出第(b)款和第(c)

款所述的异议。

(e)仲裁庭可以对第(b)款和第(c)款所述的异议作出初裁或仲裁裁决。如果仲裁庭的裁决认为其具有或者不具有司法管辖权,任何不服该裁决的当事人,可以依照第43条第(d)款第(1)项、第(2)项和第47条第(b)款第(1)项,自收到该裁决之日起30日内向法院起诉。

(f)在第(e)款条件下,若仲裁庭认为其具有管辖权,即使法院尚未判决,仲裁庭也应继续进行仲裁程序并作出裁决。

六、仲裁庭的实行临时措施的权力

根据第19条第(a)款的规定,除非当事各方另有约定,仲裁庭有权对任何一方作出决定、命令和指示:仲裁费用担保;提供文件和质询;提供证人证言;保全,临时监管或出售作为争议标的事项一部分的财产;对作为或构成争议标的的一部分的财产,将其作为取样或任何观察或实验的样本;为诉讼目的,保全和临时保管任何证据;明确争议金额,临时禁令或任何其他临时措施。

仲裁庭不仅可以要求当事人和证人宣誓,也可以在其认为适当的情况下采取纠问式诉讼模式。

仲裁庭不得仅仅因为申请人以下情况,而根据第(a)款命令申请人提供仲裁费用担保:

1)当事人是通常居住在缅甸联邦共和国以外的个人。

2)当事人是根据另一国法律成立或组建的公司或协会。

根据19条第(b)款到第(e)款的规定,仲裁庭在仲裁过程中作出的所有决定、命令或指示均可依照第31条向法院申请强制执行

根据第20条的规定,尽了适当谨慎义务的仲裁员,对于其在仲裁过程中作为仲裁员的作为或不作为不承担责任。

七、仲裁程序的进行

1. 第26条的规定,双方应受到平等的对待,并被给予充分的机会阐释案件

在不违反本法规定的情况下,各方可以自由商定仲裁庭在诉讼中应遵循的程序。根据第22条的规定,没有达成协议的,仲裁庭可以认为合适的方式进行仲裁。而仲裁庭的权力包括确定任何证据的有效性、相关性、实质性和权

重证据力度。

各方可以自由地协商约定仲裁地点。如果不能就仲裁地达成一致，仲裁庭应当根据案件的情况，包括当事人的便利情况，确定仲裁地点。

根据第 23 条规定，尽管有上述规定，除非双方另有约定，否则仲裁庭可以在其认为适合协商的地方在其成员之间举行会议，听取证人、专家或当事人发言，或检查货物、其他财产或文件。

根据第 24 条的规定，除非当事人另有约定，对于特定争议的仲裁程序在仲裁被诉人收到申请仲裁的请求之日开始。

根据第 25 条的规定，双方可以自由地商定在仲裁程序中使用语言。没有达成协议的，仲裁庭应确定在仲裁程序中使用的语言。除非另有规定，本协议或决定适用于任何一方的任何书面陈述、听证会，仲裁庭的任何裁决、决定或其他通知。仲裁庭可以命令双方当事人在一切书面证据中，使用其所商定或由仲裁法庭确定的语言，或附有该语言的翻译。

2. 第 26 条规定了索赔和辩护声明的条件

双方可以就他们在主张或辩护中所言的具体细节达成一致。没有达成一致的，主张人应当举证支持他的主张、所涉及的问题，请求宽限或寻求补救措施。答辩人应就这些内容发表他的辩护，并在双方确定或仲裁庭决定的期限内，将辩护提交仲裁庭。

当事人可以随他们的陈述一起提交他们认为具有相关性的所有文件、其他证据，或者为他们即将提交的文件增加索引。

除非双方另有约定，否则任何一方均可在仲裁程序中修改或补充他的主张或抗辩，除非仲裁庭认为，该修改申请的提出太过延迟，不适宜再进行此类修改。

根据第 27 条的规定，除非当事人另有约定，仲裁庭应决定是开庭听取接受证据或口头辩论，还是以书面和其他材料的形式进行。但是，除非当事各方同意不得进行开庭，否则仲裁庭应当应一方当事人的请求在仲裁的合适阶段开庭审理。如果为了检查货物、其他财产或文件，仲裁庭决定举行听证会或会议，当事人双方应在事前被给予充分的通知。一方当事人向仲裁庭提供的所有陈述、文件或其他信息，都应同时被送交对方当事人。任何专家报告或仲裁庭可能采信的证据文件，均应抄送各方。

根据第 28 条的规定，除非双方另有约定，否则视为没有充分理由：

（a）主张人没有按照第 26 条第（a）款的规定提出他的主张，仲裁庭应终止诉讼程序。

（b）答辩人没有按照第 26 条第（a）款的规定来传达他的抗辩声明，仲裁庭应继续进行诉讼。但是，未按照规定答辩本身不应被视为承认主张人的主张。

（c）任何一方没有出席聆讯或提供书面证据，仲裁庭可以继续进行诉讼，并根据已有证据作出裁决。

3. 第 29 条规定了专家的任命和审查

根据第 30 条的规定，仲裁庭或仲裁庭批准的一方可向法院申请协助调取证据。申请书须载明第 30 条第（b）款所要求的内容。法院可以在其职权范围内，根据其关于取证的规则，执行将证据直接提供给仲裁庭的请求。法院在作出命令的同时，可以向证人告知该过程，因为证人可以在该命令之前对其提出诉讼。

4. 第 31 条规定法院执行仲裁庭的临时措施

（a）在仲裁中，无论临时措施是否在国家内外通过，法院可以如同执行自己的命令和决定一样强制执行仲裁庭通过的临时措施。

（b）涉及裁决的域外执行时，申请人申请强制执行临时措施的，若其无法提交有力证据证明在该国国内有同一类型的临时措施，法院不得批准执行。

（c）当临时措施根据第（a）款获得批准时，法院应强制执行该措施。

（d）不得对法院根据第（a）款作出的批准或拒绝的决定上诉。

八、准据法

根据第 32 条的规定，如果仲裁地是在缅甸联邦共和国境内：

（a）在国内仲裁中，仲裁庭应当按照缅甸联邦共和国现行有关法律，解决涉仲争议。

（b）在国际商事仲裁中：

1）仲裁庭应当按照当事人选择的法律规则决定争议。

2）任何指定某一国家的法律或法律制度，除非双方另有约定外，应解释为适用该国的实体法而不是其法律冲突规则。

3）若当事人双方不能按照本条第 1）款规定达成一致，仲裁庭应适用其认为应当适用的法律规则。

九、仲裁裁决、争议解决和程序的终止

在仲裁员不止一名的仲裁程序中，除非双方同意，否则仲裁庭的任何决定都应经全体仲裁员的多数一致作出。

然而,尽管第(a)款中如此规定,若经双方当事人或所有仲裁庭成员授权,程序问题仍可由主审仲裁员决定。(根据第33条的规定)

若在仲裁程序中,当事人方已解决纠纷的,如果双方要求且仲裁庭不反对,仲裁庭应当终止诉讼程序,并将结果以仲裁裁决的形式记录下来。

认可争议解决协议效力的裁决应按照第35条的规定作出,并应明确说明其具有仲裁裁决效力。

根据第34条的规定,这种认可争议解决协议的裁决,与该案件中其他认定法律依据的裁决具有相同的地位和效力。

该种裁决的格式和内容规定在第35条中。

仲裁程序可以根据最终裁决或仲裁庭应依据第(b)款的命令终止。

在如下情况,仲裁庭应当发出终止仲裁程序的命令:当主张人撤回其主张时,除非答辩人反对其撤回,并且仲裁法庭认为争端解决后其将具有合法利益;双方同意终止诉讼时;仲裁庭认为,由于任何其他的原因,导致继续诉讼变得不必要或不可能时。

根据第37条的规定,仲裁庭的管辖权随着第34条第(a)款和本条规定的仲裁程序的终止一同终止。

裁决的修正和解释,追加裁决书具体规定在第37条中。

除非双方另有约定,否则仲裁庭根据仲裁协议作出的裁决应为终局裁决,对双方当事人及各方主张均具有约束力。

十、法院关于国内仲裁裁决的权力

在法院和仲裁之间的关系章节,法院的一些职能已经被规定。本章节涉及与国内仲裁裁决有关的法院的管辖权。本章节规定了法院的最初裁决和法律的颁布,国内仲裁裁决的执行,撤销国内仲裁裁决的标准,对国内仲裁裁决的上诉权,上诉法院的命令对国内裁定的效力。

除非双方另有约定,法院可应仲裁程序的一方当事人请求,同时该方已向另一方当事人发出通知,确定法院实际上影响一方或多方权利的程序中产生的任何法律问题。

根据第40条的规定,国内裁决应按照"民事诉讼法"的规定执行,执行方式与法院的法令相同。

第41条第(a)款规定:一方当事人提出申请后,法院可以在下列情况下撤销国内仲裁裁决：

（1）仲裁协议的一方无行为能力；

（2）仲裁协议根据当事双方一致适用的法律是无效的或根据缅甸联邦共和国的法律无法确定效力的；

（3）针对仲裁员的任命、仲裁程序，或者以其他妨碍其提出诉讼的事项，提出申请的当事人没有被给予适当的通知的；

（4）该裁决涉及了不属于仲裁条款范围内事项的争议，或包含超出仲裁事项范围的决定；

（5）仲裁庭的组成或仲裁程序不符合当事人的约定或不符合本法的规定；

（6）争议事项根据现行法律无法通过仲裁解决；

（7）该裁决与缅甸联邦共和国的国家利益（公共政策）相冲突。

根据第 42 条的规定，争议当事方可以通知其他各方和仲裁庭，就仲裁程序裁决引起的法律问题向法院提出上诉。

法院如认为满足并认定有以下事实，应接受上诉：

（1）仲裁庭对争议事项的裁决，对一方当事人或当事人的权利产生重大影响；

（2）仲裁庭对争议问题的裁决显然是错误的。

针对根据本条提出的上诉，法院可以作出以下任何一项决定：批准裁决、修改裁决、退回仲裁庭审查并重新作出全部或部分裁决、撤销全部或部分仲裁裁决。

对于下列法院决定，可以向具有管辖权的法院提出上诉：

（1）根据第 10 条第（f）款拒绝提交仲裁的决定；

（2）根据第 11 条，授权执行或拒绝执行其中临时措施的决定

（3）法院根据第 39 条第（a）款，通过命令定性法律问题；

（4）根据第 41 条的规定，撤销或拒绝撤销国内仲裁裁决的决定。

仲裁庭的下列裁决，可以向管辖权法院提出上诉：

（1）根据第 18 条第（b）款和第（c）款接受申请的决定；

（2）仲裁庭依照第 18 条第（e）款的规定，判断其是否具有管辖权；

（3）授权执行或拒绝执行第 19 条中规定的任何临时措施的决定。

针对本条中的上诉法院的决定，不得再次提出上诉。

十一、上诉法院命令对国内仲裁的效力

上诉法院根据第43条第(b)款通过与裁决有关的命令时：

(a)当上诉法院决定修改裁决时,该修改决定作为裁决的一部分,具有同等效力；

(b)当法院决定将全部或者部分的仲裁裁决退回仲裁庭进行重审和修改时,仲裁庭应重新修改此裁决并作出决定；

(c)可以适当考虑给予仲裁庭审查裁决和通过决定必要的时间。

十二、外国仲裁裁决的承认与执行

第45条规定了有关申请承认或执行外国仲裁裁决的内容。

根据第46条的规定,该裁决应同法院的判决一样,遵循《民事诉讼法》的规定执行。

如果反对的一方当事人向法院提供以下证明,法院可以拒绝承认外国仲裁裁决：

(1)所提交的仲裁协议各方属于某种无行为能力；

(2)根据当事人所依据的法律上述协议无效,或根据作出裁决的国家的法律没有法律依据；

(3)针对仲裁员的任命、仲裁程序,或者以其他妨碍其提出诉讼的事项,反对的当事人一方认为其没有被适当的通知的；

(4)该裁决涉及了不属于仲裁条款范围内事项的争议,或包含超出仲裁事项范围的决定；

(5)仲裁庭的组成或仲裁程序不符合当事人的协议,或者未达成协议的,不符合仲裁地国家的法律；

(6)该裁决尚未对当事各方具有约束力,或被该裁决所依据的法律的国家主管当局撤销或暂停。

如果法庭发现如下情况,可以拒绝执行外国仲裁裁决：

(1)根据缅甸联邦共和国法律,争议的主体不能作为仲裁的主体；

(2)执行裁决将违反缅甸联邦共和国的国家利益(公共政策)。

任何争议方可以根据第10条规则授权或拒绝采取任何措施的命令提出上诉；根据第11条作出的命令；根据第46条第(b)款及第(c)款作出的裁定,

撤销或拒绝撤销;由适格法院作出的命令提出上诉。

对于下列仲裁庭通过的命令,当事人可以向主管法院提出上诉:

(1)根据第 18 条第(e)款决定仲裁庭是否具有司法管辖权的命令。

(2)根据第 19 条授权或拒绝执行临时措施的命令;

根据第 48 条的规定,本章任何规定均不得损害任何人在缅甸联盟执行外国仲裁裁决的权利,也不得损害其使其裁决符合本法颁布的目的。

根据第 49 条的规定,根据本章规定执行外国仲裁裁决不适用于 1937 年的仲裁(议定书和公约)下的执行。

结　语

缅甸仲裁法是规定仲裁制度的完备法律。这项法律不仅适用于国内仲裁,也适用于外国仲裁。自由任用仲裁员和自由选择准据法规定,对于当事方来说也是有意义的进步。法律还具体规定了司法管辖权的内容。本法颁布施行后,各方据此可以便利地申请执行外国仲裁裁决。仲裁员的资格是仲裁程序中的重要事项,法律本应明确规定,但是这项法律没有规定仲裁员的资格。而现今缅甸还没有仲裁机构或仲裁委员会,这一点也引发了一些程序的难题,如选择仲裁员、选择程序和行政事务上的支持问题。因此,要进一步完善缅甸的仲裁制度,应当建立仲裁机构或仲裁委员会。

Legal Research on Dispute Settlement Mechanism for Investment in Myanmar

Moe Cho[*]

Abstract：The legal system for foreign investment in Myanmar has developed slowly. Since the Western countries contacted their economic sanctions in 2011, they tried to carry out the old law reform movement. Although a unified foreign investment dispute settlement center has not yet been established. In 2016, Myanmar enacted the Myanmar Investment Law, which provides further protection for investors in resolving disputes. Myanmar's foreign investment dispute settlement mechanism mainly includes litigation, arbitration, negotiation, regulation, etc. This paper analyzes the main problems existing in the investor dispute settlement system, further clarifies the dispute resolution method, and provides guidance for investors to better protect their legitimate rights and interests.

Keywords：Foreign investment, Dispute settlement mechanism, Mediation, Arbitration, Litigation

1. Introduction

After lifting of economic sanctions by the western countries in 2011, the government of Myanmar had conducted the series of reform on the political and economic sectors. Myanmar is, on the one hand, changing its national

---

* Moe Cho, Doctoral Student of School of International Law of SWUPL/Staff Officer, Union Attorney General's Office, Building 25, Nay Pyi Taw, Myanmar, E-mail: m15922771431@163.com.

policy noticeably, on the other hand, trying to reform the old laws since 2011. As there is the fusion between the previous Myanmar Citizen Investment Law and Foreign Investment Law, the new Myanmar Investment Law is promulgated in 2016. According to the section 84 of the above said law, foreign investors are tendered not only exemptions and reliefs but also much guarantee for settling disputes which might be settled by peaceful mean. Currently, Myanmar government and foreign companies are concluding commercial agreements more and more today. In most agreements, disputes settlement mechanism clause is usually included in commercial contracts. If disputes arise, disputing parties are obliged to settle their differences amicably, which of those means are negotiation, mediation, conciliation, arbitration and civil litigation.

The aim of this article is for foreign investors to know and understand how to resolve the arising dispute if mode of settling dispute be embodied in the concluded agreement. Whenever a foreign investor goes to a new country, he is justly concerned with his rights and liabilities under the Law. These concerns are about what remedies will he have whenever there is a breach by the other party, or his liabilities if he breaches the terms of his business transactions? By understanding clearly law, rules and procedures in Myanmar, the foreign investors may become more interested to put more investment in Myanmar.

2. Dispute Settlement Mechanism under Myanmar Investment Law

The law presents some provisions regarding the settlement of investment disputes amicably. Under Section 82, in effectively implementing this Law, the Commission shall establish and manage a grievance mechanism to allow in order to inquire and resolve issues before they become legal dispute disputes and to prevent the occurrence of disputes. An investor may submit notice for his grievance or dispute to the Investor Assistance Committee (IAC) in the following cases; (a) a decision of governmental department in respect of his investment was incorrectly made, (b) that an application for a permit, license, registration or approval was incorrectly refused by governmental department and (c) that any right, protection or approval benefiting him under the law has been frustrated. So MIC must form the IAC to inquire or resolve issues before they become legal disputes. The purpose of formation of IAC is to prevent the occurrence of disputes by offering a mechanism for early detection of issues and grievances and their resolution before they can escalate into a dispute.

The dispute settlement mechanism is stipulated in section 84 of MIL. If the dispute settlement mechanism is not stipulated in the relevant agreement, it shall be complied and settled in court or arbitral tribunal in accord with the applicable law. We must understand this provision that investment disputes shall be settled in a local court or before an arbitral tribunal under the laws of the Union of Myanmar. This provision is in line with the section 9(b) of the Arbitration Law which provides that arbitration agreement may be in the form of and arbitration clause. Under MIL if the dispute settlement mechanism is stipulated in the relevant agreement, it shall be complied and settled in accord with such mechanism. This provision will give investors access to arbitration as opposed to local court because respective individual arbitration agreement will be enforced.

Under this law, the disputing parties including the disputing investor and the Union of government shall initially seek to resolve the dispute through amicably modes including mediation, consultation and negotiation. Such mechanism shall be initiated by a written request for consultations delivered by the disputing investor to the IAC. In this here a foreign investor shall essentially need to notice one that where a dispute is between investors, investors are encouraged to settle their disputes amicably and in accordance with the term of any agreement between them. If, after such settlement, they don't only receive any solution, they may bring it to the court or arbitral proceedings.

And then we find that the MIL does not mention a standing offer to arbitrate. But current existing Myanmar's bilateral investment treaties contain a standing offer to arbitrate. For example, article 9 of the Bilateral Investment Treaty between China and Myanmar provides that when any legal dispute arises between an investor of one contracting party and the other contracting party in connection with in investment in the territory of the other contracting party, it shall, as far as possible, be settled amicably through negotiations. And then if the dispute cannot be settled through negotiation within six months, the investor of one contracting party may submit it to the competent court of other contracting party. Beside it shall be submitted by the request of any party to (a) International Center for Settlement of Investment Disputes (ICSID) and (b) an ad hoc arbitral tribunal. So I want to give well-advises to foreign investors that if they want to make investment contract with Myanmar government, they should incorporate the arbitration clauses into their investment contracts. If they do not put the arbitration clauses in their investment contracts, they may encounter disadvantages in attempting to resolve disputes.

3. Negotiation

Negotiation is the basic form of alternative dispute resolution. A civil dispute arising out of civil and commercial transactions should be attempted to settle by amicable discussions or negotiations between the parties concerned. Usually, whenever arises, both parties tend to settle the disputes through negotiating in friendly manner, in order to resolve the problems quickly and completely.

As there are no laws and regulations regarding the procedures such as settlement by negotiation between the parties concerned, it is not the legal resolution systems of disputes. As a matter of fact, but it is an entirely private means of dispute resolution. The said private civil resolution system of disputes such as mutual negotiations between the parties concerned is the basic means for resolution of civil disputes other than the litigation. However, its framework is not regulated by the laws and its negotiation procedures and result of negotiation are controlled by the parties concerned. The parties may appoint a negotiator to conduct negotiation on his or her behalf. The procedure of negotiation so relatively simple and flexible that it can not only settle the dispute in time smoothly, but also help both parties to maintain their cooperative relationship. Therefore, negotiation is a fundamental form of disputes resolution process and it is the most satisfactory and amicable method of dispute resolution.

This sprit of amicable settlement has its basis in Myanmar history and culture. During the day of the Myanmar kings, settlement of disputes between Myanmar citizens was encouraged. The parties involved settled dispute amicably sometimes face to face. When the dispute is settled, both parties sit down to have salad of tea leaves in the traditional Myanmar manner. This idea is still used by Modern Myanmar jurists and in commercial contracts and amicable settlement is encourage. In modern business transactions, such amicable settlements have proved to be highly successful. Dispute settlements that go to arbitration or courts of law are very small in number as most of them settled amicably.

4. Mediation

Mediation is one of the resolution systems of disputes for reasonable settlement by the mutual concession of the parties concerned. If disputing parties fail in negotiation they may wish to attempt to settle their dispute through mediation before resorting to arbitral or judicial proceeding. Mediation is aimed at resolving the dispute according to an independent agreement between the parties concerned.

"Mediation" means that a neutral third party conducts mediation between the disputing parties so that they can conclude a compromise agreement in order to resolve disputes. The mediator who is selected by both parties shall be the competent person who is trusted by parties. The objective of mediation is to achieve amicable settlement of dispute with the assistance of a neutral person as a mediator appointed by mutual consent. But the mediator has no power to impose a decision on both parties. Any civil and commercial dispute can be settled by mediation but a mediation agreement cannot be enforced by court except with the consent of the other party. However, the mediation system requires less time with lower expenses, compared to civil litigation.

There isa process in which commercial and financial disputes can be resolved at the Union of Myanmar Federation of Chambers of Commerce and Industry (UMFCCI). The UMFCCI has a duty to conciliate disputes between its members and between its members and other individuals and organizations. However, there is no written procedure of mediation. A sub-committee is formed to conciliate for a specific dispute and to call experts and see their opinions if required. Some parties in local disputes seek the help of the committee to reach a settlement before they proceed to court, however this does not occur with international disputes. The findings of the subcommittee with the approval of the Central Executive Committee are pronounced and the parties who do not comply with the findings are blacklisted. This mediation procedure, however, does not appear to be in line with international practices. The decision of the committee has no binding except that the responsible party may be put in blacklist.

5. Arbitration

When disputing parties fail in mediation or cannot use mediation to settle, they might agree to settle their dispute by arbitration or refer to the arbitration agreement that may be made when the contract was concluded. Arbitration is the most common form of Alternative Dispute Resolution (ADR). Arbitration is aimed at attempting to resolve disputes by means of arbitrator's award. Many nations regulate frameworks and procedures of such ADR system, especially arbitration procedures that are established and regulated by the laws. Many countries have separate arbitration laws or incorporate arbitration laws in their civil procedure codes or relevant laws.

"Arbitration" means the determination of a dispute by one or more independent third parties who are arbitrators rather than by a court. Arbitrators are appointed by the parties in accordance with the terms of the "arbitration agreement" or in effort by court. An arbitrator is bound to apply the law accurately.

Arbitration practice in Myanmar has not been well- known for many years although there is an existing arbitration Act 1944. The Act contained seven chapters, 48 sections and First Schedule and Second Schedule for long, it has not been amended at all since its enactment. The Act provided two alternative procedures for arbitration. The parties concerned may choose either of the two alternatives. The first alternative was arbitration without intervention of the court and the second was with the intervention of the court. This Act contained provisions relating to the appointment of arbitrators and umpire and their powers, the supervision by the court for their removal, the enforcement of award in the civil court and appeal from an award to the Supreme Court.

On the other hand, contracts between foreign investors and Myanmar entities or with a reference to Myanmar that establishes Myanmar jurisdiction should always specify the question what institution will decide any disputes and in which language and what national law is to be applied? As stated above, the Arbitration Act 1944 only deals with domestic arbitration. The Act provides that where both disputing parties are from Myanmar, the dispute may only be submitted to domestic arbitration according to the Arbitration Act 1944.

In case there is one party to the dispute having foreign identity, it remains unclear whether a Myanmar party could submit the dispute to foreign arbitration. Under the Myanmar Export Import Law 2012, Myanmar parties in a trade dispute with foreign companies shall resolve that dispute in accordance with the Arbitration Act 1944. Then it is possible that in a non- trading dispute, a foreign party may be permitted to have a foreign arbitration with its Myanmar partner. In this regard, we note that in case laws, it remains unknown whether such foreign arbitration award will be upheld by the Myanmar courts.

With the introduction of the Foreign Investment Law, in order to take full advantage of the arbitration method of dispute settlement, foreign investors are advised to structure the commercial relationship as an investment, obtain necessary investment permits and insert arbitration clause into the agreement. Under the Arbitration Act 1944, the courts have powers to grant conservatory relief in respect of domestic arbitration. However, it is uncertain whether the courts will still grant such assistance to the Myanmar party requesting foreign arbitration proceedings given the lack of an explicit international arbitration act allowing them to do so. On the other hand, foreign investors in Myanmar, as in other developing countries, tend to distrust local courts. They are concerned about impartiality of the judges and corruption. They are also worried about how long it takes to settle the dispute and whether the court proceedings will invite participation of the press, which is normally the case if it is a high-profile dispute. Language used in the proceedings is a barrier for foreign investors as well. However, arbitration in Myanmar has not yet developed. There is no arbitration centre up to now. This means an arbitral award has to be enforced by the court.

In practice, courts in Myanmar often exercise wide discretion in setting aside arbitral awards. Thus, a disaster happens when one party after going through all hard steps to win the dispute in an arbitration proceeding, fails to enforce the arbitral award against the violating party before the local court. A party may then end up with having its dispute re-litigated in court. This happens even in case where parties agree to use arbitration abroad, for example, Singapore International Arbitration Centre. Investors are thus wise not to take such approach if they are already pretty sure that the foreign arbitral awards are worthless in Myanmar. Fortunately, these issues have to end up soon as a result of Myanmar's accession to the New York Convention and the recent promulgation of the new Arbitration Law. The dispute resolution clause will become effective if it is made through a written agreement. This remains to be seen how effective enforcement is in practice but this is a major step towards recognition of Myanmar to be a safe place to make investment and do business. As Advantages of arbitration, the right arbitration centre provides independent decisions and professional competence. It is usually possible to select a pool of arbitrators trusted by both parties in the clause, which might lead to a wider acceptance of a possible arbitrational decision. It is important to consider arbitrator candidates based on their expertise in the relevant business field. Most arbitration centers provide renowned experts for certain fields of work. What is in the new Arbitration Law, the new Arbitration Law is based on widely accepted UNCITRAL Model Law on International Arbitration 1985 ("Model Law"). This is a step to bring Myanmar's legislation towards a level closer to internationally accepted standards in arbitration. The new Arbitration Law is divided into two parts; the first part applies if the place of arbitration is in Myanmar and the second part applies to the enforcement of foreign arbitral awards. Major point to note in the new Arbitration Law is that the arbitration award is defined to include interim awards for enforcement purposes by the Myanmar courts. However, the Arbitration Law is silent on whether the definition includes orders and directions issued by the arbitral tribunal.

On 16 April 2013, Myanmar deposited an instrument of accession with the Secretary- General of the United Nations, expressing its consent to be bound by the New York Convention on the Recognition and Enforcement of Foreign Arbitral Awards. The New York Convention already came into force in Myanmar on 15 July 2013. As a consequence, arbitral awards made in Myanmar should be enforceable in more than 140 parties to the Convention, and awards made in these countries should also be enforced in entire Myanmar.

While Myanmar's Arbitration Act 1944 only provided for domestic arbitration and did not provide a framework for the recognition and enforcement of foreign arbitral awards, the Arbitration Act 1944 has already been replaced by the new Arbitration Law (Union Law No. 5/2016) recently adopted by the Myanmar Union Parliament on 5th January 2016. This legislation is to implement the New York Convention and is positive news for foreign investors who wish to settle their commercial disputes by a neutral, independent and impartial arbitration tribunal outside Myanmar and have the awards enforced in Myanmar. In addition, the new Arbitration Law completes an important piece of the 2012 Myanmar's Foreign Investment Law, part of which stipulates that a foreign investor is entitled to have its commercial disputes settled by foreign arbitration.

We can see some changes in new arbitration law according to the law foreign arbitration means; parties can agree on arbitration for their commercial disputes and choose the seat of that arbitration to be overseas; if so, Myanmar courts must refer to such arbitration proceeding instead of hearing the case when any of the parties applies to the court; Myanmar courts must recognize and enforce a foreign arbitral award, unless one of the limited grounds for refusal in Article V of the New York Convention can be established; all other signatory countries of the New York Convention are under the same obligation to enforce, so you could take your award to any of nearly 160 states for enforcement.

Arbitration law implements these principles with clarity. The legal basis for settling disputes through foreign arbitration in Myanmar is finally there, and its, as far as we can tell right now, pretty much solid as in most New York Convention countries.

Foreign investors should know in advance before investing in Myanmar that Myanmar courts can intervene in arbitration. The arbitration law is not only about foreign arbitration, but also about arbitration with seat in Myanmar under section 3(b). Arbitration law determines which provisions of the law apply to arbitration with a seat outside of Myanmar.

The same combination of domestic and foreign arbitration in one law is not uncommon internationally. But in such case one needs a clear determination which provisions apply to which type of arbitration.

Under section 2, arbitration law does make it clear that the list applies to foreign awards. One of the fundamental rules which is section 7 of Arbitration law which provides that notwithstanding any provision in any existing law, no Court shall intervene in matters carried out under this Law except where so provided in this Law and which is also the equivalent of the article 5 of UNCITRAL Model law. There is no doubt that this provision applies to arbitrations with seat in Myanmar. And there is a very good basis in an ordinary reading of the test to argue that arbitration law should not be read in an exclusionary way.

The arbitration law supports not only Myanmar courts enforcing interim measures issued by the tribunal, including in case of an arbitration with seat outside of Myanmar, and but also parties applying to Myanmar directly for such measures. A party can apply to a Myanmar court for various measures in terms of taking evidence, safeguarding or even selling property, appointing a receiver and other interim measures under section 11of the arbitration law. If the interim measure is needed urgently in arbitration, the court may pass an order relating to preservation of evidence and related properties upon the application of a party as require.

Myanmar law court seems to keep an original jurisdiction for urgent measures relating to the preservation of evidence and property upon the application by a party even in connection with foreign awards. Nevertheless, the Arbitration law has made sure that courts do not intervene in the foreign arbitration too much by limiting its power to urgent cases, and by subjecting the court order to subsequent orders by the tribunal on the same issue. If the interim measure is not needed urgently, upon the application of a party in arbitration, the court shall deal such matter after delivering a notice to the other parties and arbitral tribunal and with the approval of the arbitration tribunal or with the written consent of the other p arty.

Foreign investors should always be aware of the necessity of dispute resolution clauses quite plainly and provides assistance in choosing appropriate alternatives to the Myanmar courts. Why arbitration makers sense and new Arbitration Law is needed.

The Arbitration law also guarantees that a foreign tribunal's decision on jurisdiction or temporary measures be challenged in a Myanmar courts. The obvious provision in the law is that arbitration tribunal has the authority to decide themselves about their own jurisdiction. That is also the case under the Arbitration law. The UNCITRAL model law provides in the possibility for a court to intervene immediately on that decision upon the request of a party. That would almost exclusively be the case in a court in the country where the arbitration takes place. But section 47 (b) of the Arbitration law, recognition and enforcement of foreign arbitral awards, states that a competent court may hear appeals against an order by an arbitration tribunal determining whether it has jurisdiction. The same is provided for an order by the tribunal to grant or refuse temporary measures. The section 46(b) and (c) of the Arbitration law provide that the competent authority to set aside or suspend a foreign award would be the one in the country where it was made.

There may a surprise question: what happens when a claim is lodged before a Myanmar court even though the contract provides in foreign arbitration. It is clearly the key to functioning of the New York convention such a case, the Myanmar court would not allow the court case to proceed, and would just refer to that arbitration mechanism. The Arbitration law provides in the same key principle in the section 10, which applies to arbitrations with seat within and outside Myanmar. For this to happen, one of the parties must bring it up, though. The court cannot bring it up itself.

When the law states or implies that arbitration cannot be used by the parties, the court is allowed not to enforce the award. The Chief Justice of the Union has the authority to appoint arbitrators in foreign proceedings if requested. In respect of domestic proceedings, it is a State Chief Justice or Region Chief Justice who will make the relevant appointment.

The Myanmar courts will be given the power to grant interim measures in support of the arbitration process. Among other provisions that deal with how the Myanmar courts should approach insolvency- related claims, Myanmar courts have discretion to refer insolvency cases to arbitration on application by a party. Myanmar courts have the power to extend a contractual time bar to commence arbitration for arbitrations seated in Myanmar. There is no similar provision in the Model Law or the International Arbitration Act of Singapore.

Arbitrations seated in Myanmar that do not fall within the definition of an "international commercial arbitration" must adopt Myanmar as the substantive law governing the arbitration. Awards made in Myanmar will be enforced, but the court has refused to set aside the award where the application to set aside the award has expired.

A Myanmar court, wishing to continue the court case, would have to find that the arbitration agreement is null and void, or cannot be applied. Such a court decision would, in any event, be subject to appeal. The decision to stay the case is not subject to appeal. The Arbitration law thus has a baked in preference in favor of international arbitration.

This is an issue whether two Myanmar registered companies choose for arbitration overseas instead of arbitration with a seat in Myanmar. In accordance with the letter of law in Myanmar Arbitration law, even two Myanmar national or resident parties can pretty much choose for international arbitration rather than arbitration with a seat in Myanmar. By simply choosing an arbitral site outside of Myanmar, or by expressly ageing that the subject matter relates to more than one country' the arbitration becomes international by definition. As such those power of Myanmar courts which only apply to arbitration proceedings with a seat in Myanmar, are ruled out. For example, a party cannot apply to a Myanmar court in order to set aside an award, or to challenge an arbitrator.

Other laws may prevent Myanmar parties from agreeing to arbitration overseas, or any arbitration at all. At this time, the Myanmar Companies Act 1914 still provides that companies and persons may agree to arbitration under the Myanmar Arbitration Act which until 2016 only provided in arbitration with seat in Myanmar. According to the Myanmar Investment law 2016 if dispute cannot be reached compromise amicably, the disputing parties can submit their case to the competent court or any tribunal to settle their dispute. In this case, such foreign or citizen investors as companies or shareholder can use foreign or domestic arbitration.

It will be better to discuss on the next issue whether two Myanmar registered companies can choose to have their contract governed a foreign law. There are very few Myanmar laws which prescribe the governing law of a contract between two parties, though there are of course contracts that are at least to some extent governed by Myanmar law, regardless what parties have agreed. The Arbitration law brings a potentially high impact new element to this discussion. In Section 32 of the law, it is provided that in case the seat of arbitration is in Myanmar and it is a domestic arbitration, 'The dispute which is to be settled by arbitration in accordance with the substantive law in forced of the Republic of The Union of Myanmar'.

It is important not to read this as if all disputes between Myanmar parties have to be decided under Myanmar law. According to the Arbitration Law, one can perfectly have an international arbitration with a seat in Myanmar. A dispute between a foreign based party and a Myanmar based party, where the parties have chosen for arbitration with seat in Myanmar, is an international arbitration with seat in Myanmar, for example. Those parties may perfectly choose for their contract to be subject to English law. That is just a plain reading application of the section 3 (i) of the Law. Under the Section 3(i) of this law, "international arbitration" means;

(1)if, at the time of execution of the arbitration agreement, if one of the party's place of business and trading activity is situated in another country other than Myanmar; or

(2) if the place stated in the arbitration agreement or the place to conduct arbitration in accordance with the arbitration agreement is situated outside the country in which the parties have their place of business; or

(3) if, among the commercially related business obligations, any place where a substantial part of the obligations is to be performed or the closest place connected to the subject matter of the dispute is situated outside the country in which the parties have their place of business; or

(4) if the parties of the arbitration agreement have expressly agreed that the subject matter relates to more than one country; such arbitration shall mean International Arbitration

It becomes less comfortable when two Myanmar parties have a contract governed under English law, and they chose the arbitral seat in Myanmar and none of the elements defining an international arbitration of the section 3 (i) apply. Because now section 32 says quite clearly that this is a domestic arbitration with seat in Myanmar, and it will have to be decided with Myanmar law as the substantive law. This issued is not dramatic. The same parties can simply opt for international arbitration with seat outside Myanmar to safeguard their application of foreign law to the contract. But if Myanmar wants to develop its own domestic arbitration industry in due course, the legislator might consider fixing this.

The most conspicuous benefit both for foreign investors and Myanmar in the new arbitration law 2016 is Myanmar courts refuse to recognize foreign awards. The courts of any signatory state of the New York Convention can, if they really want to invoke one or more of the grounds for refusal to block the enforcement of a foreign award. The rationale of the New York Convention is that Myanmar courts are obliged to enforce foreign awards, except in case of a limited list of grounds for refusal. That fundamental principle is also found in Myanmar's implementation of the New York Convention. The limited grounds are found in section 46 (b) of the Arbitration Law, and these are essentially just translated from the UN-CITRAL Model Law.

The formal grounds for refusing a foreign award are the following:

(1) one or more of the parties to the arbitration agreement was incapable to conclude such agreement. This could be the case when the person agreeing to arbitration on behalf of a company did so without proper authority as in the example of section 152 of Myanmar Companies Act. Internationally we also often see issues when a party is a state-owned enterprise, but in Myanmar there is no general rule preventing a state-owned enterprise from agreeing to arbitration. This question would presumably have to be decided by a Myanmar court with reference to the choice - of - law rules of Myanmar law.

(2) The arbitration agreement is not valid. This is the most frequent ground for a challenge to arbitration. A party could argue there was no consent, for example pursuant to a misrepresentation or fraud. It is also common of parties to claim that the language of the arbitration agreement is not sufficiently clear and thus inoperative. It is important to note that under the Arbitration law, in following of the UNCITRAL Model law, the validity of the agreement must be tested under the law applicable to the agreement, or under the law of the arbitral seat. So, the law to apply would rarely be Myanmar law.

(3) lack of due process; the party was not given proper notice of the various steps in the arbitration proceedings or was not able to present its case. Failing to show up as such, by intention, obviously does not suffice as long as one was given ample notice.

(4) The award deals with a dispute not contemplated b or not falling within the terms of the matters to be submitted to arbitration, or it contains decisions on matters to be submitted to arbitration, or it contains decisions on matters beyond the scope of those submitted to arbitration. That means the tribunal has decided claims not considered by the parties or outside the arbitration agreement. For example, the award also decided on extra-contractual liability when parties only referred a question on contractual liability to the tribunal, or the award used English law where the arbitration agreement referred to Myanmar law. Another example would be a case where the award was made outside of the time limit set by the parties in the

arbitration agreement.

(5) The composition or proceedings of the tribunal are not in accordance with the arbitration agreement or with the law of the arbitral site. If the a- greement called for an arbitrator with certain qualifications, for example, an architect, a Myanmar court could refuse to enforce the award if this was ignored by the appointing authority. It is not difficult for the losing party to claim that some procedural rule was infringed, but internationally courts do not to enforce an award.

(6) The award is not yet in force or has been set aside. Myanmar courts have the authority under the Arbitration law to adjourn its decision on en- forcement if an application has been made to a court in the arbitral site to set aside.

6. Civil litigation- one of dispute settlement mechanism

Along with the recent raise of economic sanction by European countries to Myanmar, a variety of new investment, both foreign and domestic, there will inevitably be a corresponding increase of diverse litigation, in the future. While many businesses will try to steer clear of Myanmar courts, in some instances commercial litigation simply cannot be avoided in any jurisdiction, including Myanmar, whether as a plaintiff or as a defendant.

Under the 2008 Constitution, the courts of the Union include the Supreme Court of the Union, High Courts of the Region and State, Court of the Self- Administered Division, Courts of the Self- Administered Zone, District Courts, Township Courts and other Court constituted by law; Courts- Martial; and Constitutional Tribunal of the Union (Section 293 of the 2008 Constitution). The Supreme Court of the Union is the highest Court of the Union without prejudice to the jurisdiction of the Constitutional Tribunal of the Union and Courts- Martial (Section 294 of the 2008 Consti- tution).

In Myanmar, according to the 2010 judicial law, there are four court levels relevant to civil cases including commercial disputes. These are as fol- lows;

—The Supreme Court of the Union of Myanmar

—High Courts of the Region or State

—District Courts, Courts of the Self- Administered Division and Courts of the Self- Administered Zone and

—Township Courts

Under section 296(a) of the 2008 Constitution and section 11 of the Union Judiciary Law 2010, the Union Supreme Court is the only one that has original jurisdiction over:

(a)matters arising out of bilateral treaties concluded by the Union,

(b) other disputes except constitutional problems between the Union Government and The Region or State Governments, or among the Regions, among the states, between the Region and The State, and between The Union Territory and the Region or the State,

(c)piracy and other offences committed at ground or international water or airspace by violating international law, and

(d)other matters as prescribed by any law.

The Supreme Court is the court of final appeal and has appellate jurisdiction to decide judgments passed by state and Regional High Courts, and judgments of the other courts in accordance with the law [section 296 (d) of the 2008 Constitution and section 12 of the Union Judiciary Law 2010]. It also has the revisionary power over any judgment or order passed by any subordinate court [section 296 (e) of the 2008 Constitution and section 13 of the Union Judiciary Law 2010]. It is authorized to issue five writs: Habeas Corpus, Mandamus, Prohibition, Quo Warranto, and Certiorari (section 296 of the 2008 Constitution and section 16 of the Union Judiciary Law 2010). The Supreme Court ,the Highest Court in Myanmar, can hear appeals only from High Courts and District Court because disputing parties plaintiff or defendant submit the appeal case of the value which exceed 10 million kyats to the Supreme Court.

The Regional or State High Courts are responsible for the supervision of subordinate courts. And State or Region High courts have jurisdiction over: (1) original civil and criminal cases; (2) appeals cases; (3) revision cases; and other cases prescribed by any law (Section 38 of Union Judiciary Law 2010). The Regional or State High courts which have jurisdiction over suits exceeding 500 million kyat and which can hear appeals from both from Township and District Courts. The District Courts, Courts of the Self- Administered Division and Courts of the Self- Administered Courts have the jurisdiction over suits valued up to 500 million kyats. The Townships courts have jurisdiction over suites valued at 10 million kyats or less and disputes involving not only immovable properties but also movable properties situated in the relevant township.

6.1 Civil Practice and Procedure

Myanmar's legal system is an adversarial system. Matters are heard before a judge or bench of judges and argued by advocates or pleaders. The Code of Civil Procedure provides the main source of Myanmar's procedural rules regarding civil litigation. Advocates and pleaders also refer to the Courts Manual of 1960 and the Evidence Act of 1872. The practices and procedures of Myanmar courts were significantly influenced by English practices and procedures. Currently, Myanmar does not have a developed dispute resolution mechanism, though courts do conduct arbitration. In general, Myanmar courts have jurisdiction to try all civil suits, except certain matters barred by law. The appropriate court in which to commence proceedings in Myanmar is dependent upon the type and value of the claim and the location of the parties or the place the business is in or act in question was carried out.

The next questions for foreign investors who are going to invest in Myanmar whether a foreign entity can sue or be sued in Myanmar. Under section 83 of Civil Procedure Code provide that a foreign national who is staying in the Union with the permission of the President of the Union can sue a civil suit in any courts in Myanmar as if a citizen of Myanmar whether an enemy or friendly nation. But the Transfer of Immovable property act prohibit a foreign national to acquire a immovable property for a term exceeding one year except in the case that a foreign company has relevant beneficial contract with the state.

Moreover, There is no provision in Civil Procedure Code that prevents a foreign person from being sued or sue. The commercial case (called civil case) may take one or two years. It depends on the case nature for example in the case the defendant admits the case, proceeding only last a few months. In our practice we often see that parties may be inclined to settle after receiving a summons or when a temporary injunction is granted, which is generally a matter of a month or two although there are notable exceptions. A claimant to a commercial dispute must file a plaint with the appropriate court. Thereafter, time is given for the defendant to file an answer, a counter claim or clam for set- off against another, and then the plaintiff would have an opportunity to respond by way of written statement, after which the pleadings are closed.

After the pleadings are completed in accordance with the foregoing, the next step is first discovery and inspection of the documents it is also at this stage that a party may file for temporary injunctions and other interlocutory orders. The court will then frame issues based on submissions of the parties. Thereafter if settlement is not reached, there will be a hearing and resulting decree and execution thereof. Appeals may be filed after issuance of a decree.

In Myanmar, disputing party for commercial matter called civil suit submit their complaint to the court as contract breach. In breach of contract action, the proper plaintiff is the person with whom or on whose behalf the contract was made or in whom the rights under the contract were vested (Order I, Rule 1 of the Civil Procedure Code). If an action is to be brought by several co- contractor upon a promise made to them jointly, all parties should be joined.

Who may be jointed as defendants? All persons may be joined as defendants who any right to relief in respect of or arising out of the same act or transaction or series of acts or transactions is alleged to exist, whether jointly, severally or in the alternative, where, if separate suits were brought against such person, any common question of law or fact would arise (Order I, Rule 3 of the Civil Procedure Code). When two or more persons are jointly and severally liable under a contract; all parties must be joined as co-defendants. If only one of the appropriate parties is sued, that party may, on application to the court, have the action stayed until all other relevant person joined as co- defendants.

All objections on the ground of non jointer of miss- jointer of parties shall be taken at the earliest possible opportunity and in all cases where issues are settled, at or before such settlement, unless the ground of objection has subsequently arisen, and any such objection not so taken shall be deemed to have been waived (Order I, Rule 3 of the Civil Procedure Code).

Tort Actions

In a tort action the proper plaintiff is the person injured by the wrongdoer or, in case of death, the person with a vested right to sue. The proper defendant in a tort action is the wrongdoer or the person who is liable for the acts of the wrongdoer. Where several persons are injured by a tort, any one of them may sue without joining the other injured parties. Where there is more than one plaintiff one or more of them may be authorized by the others to appear, plead, or act for them in any proceeding. Where there are more plaintiffs than one, any one or more of them may be authorized by any other of them to appear, plead or act of such other in any proceeding, and in like manner, where there are more defendants than one, any one or more of them may be authorized by any other of them to appear, plead or act for such other in any proceeding. The authority shall be in writing signed by the party giving it and shall be filed in court (Order I, Rule 12 of the Civil Procedure Code).

Every suit shall be instituted by the plaintiff by presenting a plaint to the Court against the defendant. The plaint shall contain the following particulars (Order IV, Rule 1 of the Civil Procedure Code);

(a) the name of the Court in which the suit is brought,

(b) the name, description and place of residence of the plaintiff,

(c) the name, description and place of residence of the defendant, so far as they can be ascertained,

(d) where the plaintiff or the defendant is a minor or a person of unsound mind, a statement to that effect,

(e) the facts constituting the cause of action and when it arose,

(f) the facts showing that the court has jurisdiction,

(g) the relief which the plaintiff claims,

(h)where the plaintiff has allowed a set- off or relinquished a portion of his claim, the amount so allowed or relinquished and

(i) statement of the value of the subject- matter of the suit for the purposes of jurisdiction and of court fees, so far as the case admits.

The Court shall reject the plaint in the following cases:

(a)Where it does not disclose a cause of action,

(b)Where the relief claimed is undervalued, and the plaintiff, on being required by the Court to correct the valuation within a time to be fixed by the Court, fails to do so,

(c)Where the relief claimed is properly valued, but the plaint is written upon paper insufficiently stamped, and the plaintiff, on being required by the court to supply the requisite stamp- paper within a time to be fixed by the Court, fails to do so and

(d)Where the suit appears from the statement in the plaint to be barred by any way.

When a plaint has been filed, a summons is served upon the defendant requesting the defendant to appear and answer the claim. When a suit has been duly instituted a summons may be issued to the defendant to appear and answer the claim on a day to be therein specified and every such summons shall be signed by the judge or such officer as he appoints, and shall be sealed with the seal of the Court (Order V, Rule 1 of the Civil Procedure Code). Besides, every summons shall be accompanied by a copy of the plain (Order V, Rule 2 of the Civil Procedure Code).

Relating the service of the summons in Myanmar, where the defendant resides within the jurisdiction of the court in which the suit is instituted or has an agent resident within that jurisdiction who is empowered to accept the service of the summons, the summons shall be delivered to him or one of his subordinates (Order V, Rule 9 of the Civil Procedure Code). Service of the summons shall be made by delivering or tendering a copy thereof signed by the Judge or an officer as he appoints in this behalf, and sealed with the seal of the Court. However, in a suit relating to any business or work against a person who does not reside within a local limits of the jurisdiction of the Court from which the summons is issued, service on any manager or agent, who, at the time of service, personally carries on such business or work for such person within such limits, shall be deemed good service. For the purpose of this rule the master of a ship shall be deemed to be the agent of the owner or charterer. If the defendant gives the power his lawyer to accept summon service and appear before the court on his behalf, a summons may also be served on the defendant's lawyer.

In relating to substituted service, where the court is satisfied that there is reason to believe that the defendant is keeping out of the way for the purpose of avoiding service, the Court shall order the summons to be served b affixing a copy thereof in some conspicuous place in the Court- house, and also upon some conspicuous part of the house in which the defendant is known to have last resided or carried on business or personal worked for gain, or in such other manner as the Court thinks fit. Where service is sub-stituted by order of the Court, the Court shall fix such time for the appearance of the defendant as the case may require (Order V, Rule 20 of the Civil Procedure Code).

If the defendant is confined in a prison, the summons shall be delivered or sent by post or otherwise to the officer- in- charge of the prison for service on the defendant. If the defendant resides out of the Union of Myanmar and has no agent in the Union of Myanmar empowered to accept service, the summons may addressed to defendant at the place where he is residing and sent to him by post, if there is postal communication between such place and the place where the Court is situate (Order V, Rule 25 of the Civil Procedure Code).

6.2 **Stay of suit**

The Courts of the Union of Myanmar shall have jurisdiction to try shall suits of a civil nature excepting suits of which their cognizance is either expressly or impliedly barred (Section 9 of the Civil Procedure Code). No court shall proceed with the trial of any suit in which the matter in issue is also directly and substantially in issue in a previously instituted suit between the same parties, or between parties under whom they or any of them claim, litigating under the same title, where such suit is pending in the same or any other Court in the Union of Myanmar having jurisdiction to grant the relief claimed, or before the Supreme Court of the Union.

No Court shall try any suit or issue in which the matter directly and substantially in issue has been directly and substantially in issue a former suit between the same parties, or between parties under whom they or any of them claim, litigating under the same title, in a Court competent to try such subsequent suit or the suit in which such issue has been subsequently raised, and has been heard and finally decided by such Court.

Relating to foreign judgment, a foreign judgment shall be conclusive as to any matter thereby directly adjudicated upon between the same parties, or between parties under whom they or any of them claim, litigating under the same title, except the following situations (Section 9 of the Civil Procedure Code):

(a) where it has not been pronounced by a Court of competent jurisdiction,

(b) where it has not been given on the merits of the case,

(c) where it appears on the face of the proceedings to be founded on an incorrect view of international law or a refusal to recognize the law of the Union of Myanmar in cases in which such law is applicable,

(d) where the proceedings in which the judgment was obtained are opposed to natural justice,

(e) where it has been obtained by fraud and

(f) where it sustains a claim founded on a breach of any law in force in the Union of Myanmar.

The court shall presume, upon the production of any document purporting to be a certified copy of a foreign judgment, that such judgment was pronounced by a court of competent jurisdiction, unless the contrary appears on the record but such presumption may be displaced by proving want of jurisdiction. Under the Arbitration Law 2016, a Myanmar court also has the power to stay legal proceeding in some situations, for example the court shall order to stay the suit before the court, if the court refers the parties to arbitration.

7. Conclusion

In conclusion the arbitration law, in following of the UNCITRAL Model Law, provides that if a Myanmar court finds that the subject matter of the dispute is not capable of settlement by arbitration under Myanmar law, the award does not have to be enforced. Myanmar law reserves certain matters for dispute settlement by the judiciary or by administrative proceedings. Such reservations exist in a number of areas such as employment relations, competition, criminal cases and bankruptcy. The question of whether or not to have a dispute resolution clause in contracts in Myanmar can be answered with a clear yes. However, deciding on the right place for dispute resolution can involve much complexity, as a number of factors must be thoroughly taken into account, especially when the arbitration centre in Myanmar has yet been established. There are plans in place to establish such centre in Myanmar and it is highly expected that awareness of international arbitration as an appropriate tool to resolve cross-border disputes will be raised. The Arbitration Law is not merely a positive sign for foreign investors but also beneficial to Myanmar. It demonstrates Myanmar's willingness to position itself as an arbitration- friendly jurisdiction. With the adoption of the Arbitration Law, Myanmar will attract more foreign investment on better terms and from a broader range of sources. The Arbitration Law is also the first step to improve arbitration Myanmar.

Myanmar has become a place where foreign investors should invest as Myanmar is not only rich in natural resources and the sound geographical features with basic infrastructures as roads, waterway but also a good situation in the field of rule of law. Myanmar government is inviting foreign investors by enacting necessary laws as foreign investment law, Myanmar arbitration law and other related laws. In addition Myanmar's court structure and civil procedure has a structure familiar to commercial lawyer s and business people from the Western countries and other common law based jurisdictions. After nearly sixty years of self imposed isolation, Myanmar has at present remerged as a significant and convenient destination for foreign investment.

References

1. Dr Htun Shin, Why Invest in Myanmar? June 2013.

2. Daw Khin Htwe Myint, Alternative Dispute Resolution, Myanmar law journal, Vol. II, No. 2, 2000.

3. Alec Christie, The Rule of Law and Commercial Litigation in Myanmar, Pacific Rim Law and Policy Journal, December 2000.

4. Constitution of the Union of Myanmar 2008.

5. Union Judiciary law 2010.

6. Code of Civil procedure 1908.

7. Arbitration law 2016.

8. Myanmar Investment law 2016.

9. Judicial Decision, Phu Kyaw Wai v. Ah Sein [1958] B. L. R. (H. C.) (Myanmar).

10. Judicial Decision, Daw Yin Yin May Vs. U Min Din 1982, B. L. R (Myanmar).

缅甸外商投资争端解决机制的法律研究

Moe Cho[*]

编译　马逸璇^{**}

摘要:缅甸外商投资法律制度发展较为缓慢,自 2011 年西方国家解除对其经济制裁后,才试图进行旧法改革运动。目前仍未建立解决外商投资仲裁中心,但 2016 年《缅甸投资法》(Myanmar Investment Law,简称 MIC)的实施,为投资者解决争端提供了新的途径和规则。缅甸外商投资争端解决机制主要包括诉讼、仲裁、谈判、调解等,因此,本文通过分析投资者使用这些争端解决方式及其适用中存在的主要问题,进一步明晰缅甸的投资争端解决方式的具体概念和运作程序,为投资者维护其合法权益提供指引。

关键词:外商投资,争端解决,调解,诉讼,仲裁

引　言

自从 2011 年西方国家解除对缅甸的经济制裁后,缅甸政府就开始对政治和经济领域进行了一系列大刀阔斧的改革。一方面,缅甸政府积极改善国家方针政策;另一方面,缅政府从 2011 年开始,就试图进行旧法改革运动。随着《缅甸公民投资法》和《外国投资法》的融合,新的《缅甸投资法》于 2016 年颁布。根据新《缅甸投资法》第 84 条的规定,外商投资者赴缅投资不仅可以获得税收及豁免的优惠政策,而且缅甸政府为投资争端解决提供了保障,力求用平稳和气的方式解决争端。目前缅政府与外国公司达成了越来越多的商业协

---

　*　西南政法大学国际法学院博士生/缅甸联邦最高检检察官。

　**　西南政法大学 2017 级国际法硕士研究生。

议,在大多数协议里,争端解决的条款都附在了商业合同中。一旦争端出现,争端各方应友好解决分歧,目前争端解决方式有谈判、调解、仲裁、诉讼等。

本文的写作目的是让外商投资者了解并熟悉如何运用协议中所列举的方式并更好地去解决争端。外商投资者无论什么时候来到一个新的国家,他们必定会关注在这个国家法律体系下自己的权利和义务。更进一步说,他们想知道当合作双方一方违约时他们该采取何种措施进行救济,或是自己一方违反商业交易条款时应承担多大的法律责任。由此看来,只有更好地理解缅甸法律法规以及投资程序,外商投资者才能更好地在缅甸进行投资。

一、缅甸投资法下的争端解决机制

新的《缅甸投资法》对投资争端的解决有相应的条款,其第 82 条规定,在有效执行该部法律的情况下,投资委员会应当建立并管理一套申诉机制。申诉机制的作用在于方便外商投资者咨询和解决有关投资事项,将纠纷消灭在萌芽状态,避免投资争端的出现。如果出现下面几种情形,投资者可以向投资援助委员会(IAC)提交申诉报告。第一,政府部门关于该投资事项作出错误决定;第二,政府部门自身过错,拒绝受理许可申请、注册申请等;第三,投资者享有的合法权利利益受到伤害。综上,缅甸投资委员会(MIC)有义务建立投资援助委员会,该机构设立的目的就是为投资者搭建平台,让投资者申诉投诉,为投资者提供咨询,做到争端预防、对症下药,将法律纠纷尽早解决。

争端解决机制之所以规定在缅甸投资法第 84 条,原因是如果投资者没有在相应的商业协议里提及争端解决方法,一旦纠纷出现,双方就需要根据适用法律在法庭解决纠纷,而这一机制的优点就在于其符合仲裁法第 9 条第 2 款的规定,仲裁协议可以以仲裁条款的形式进行。在新《缅甸投资法》下,如果投资者在协议中规定了争端解决机制,纠纷出现则应遵循该机制。这一规定将使投资者可以通过仲裁而不是进入当地法庭的方式达到解决纠纷的目的。

依据本法,包括争端的投资者和政府联盟在内的各争端方应首先寻求友好方式解决争端,如调解、斡旋、谈判等。这种争端解决机制应由争端投资者通过向投资援助委员会递交书面请求来发起。因此,如果投资者之间发生了争端,投资者需要注意的是,缅方鼓励争端投资者依据其签订的协议友好解决。如果通过这种方式仍无法解决,他们可以诉诸法院或者仲裁。

我们发现《缅甸投资法》没有提到仲裁的常规要约。但是,目前缅甸现有的双边投资条约中有仲裁的常规要约。例如,《中缅双边投资条约》第 9 条规定,如果缔约一方的投资者与另一方的投资者之间发生了关于投资的法律争端,争端地在另一缔约方的地域内,则该争端应尽可能通过谈判友好解决。如果在 6 个月内通过谈判仍无法友好解决,缔约的一方可诉诸另一缔约方具有管辖权的法院。并且,应由任何一方提交至:(1)国际投资争端解决中心;(2)临时仲裁庭。因此,笔者认为,外国投资者如果与缅甸政府订立投资合同,投资者应该将仲裁条款写入投资合同。否则,外商投资者很有可能会在解决争端的时候碰壁。

(一)谈判

谈判是替代性争端解决的基本方式之一。产生于民商事交易中的民事争端应当尽量由相关当事人通过讨论或谈判的方式解决。通常,无论什么时候发生了争端,双方都应当试图通过友好谈判来解决,这样解决问题既快速又全面。

由于没有法律法规规定相关当事人通过谈判解决争端的程序,所以谈判并不是在缅甸法律框架体系下的争端解决方式。事实上,谈判是一种国际上常用的私下解决争端的方式。所谓私下民事争端解决体系是指不采用诉讼来解决民事争端。因为法律并没有规定谈判的基本框架,所以谈判的程序和结果也完全掌握在争端双方当事人手中。当事人可以以其名义指定谈判员进行谈判。谈判的优点是程序相对简单灵活,不仅能够快速及时地解决争端,还能使双方当事人维持其合作关系。因此,谈判是争端解决程序的基本形式,也是最令人满意并友好的争端解决方式之一。

这种友好解决争端的精神根植于缅甸的历史文化中。在缅甸王统治的时期里,鼓励公民积极自力解决纠纷。在缅甸传统文化背景下,相关当事人有时面对面友好地解决争端,争端解决之后,双方要坐下来一起喝茶吃点心。在现代社会,缅甸陪审员仍持有这种友好解决争端的思想,商业缔约中也鼓励当事人友好解决争端。事实证明,在现代商务交易中,这种友好解决能带来巨大的成功。正因为很多争端都友好地得到了解决,所以通过仲裁或者在法院解决的争端数量很少。

(二)调解

调解是双方当事人通过相互让步来合理解决争端的一种方式,也是争端解决体系中的一种方式。如果争端双方无法谈判,在诉诸仲裁或司法程序前,他们可能会倾向于通过调解来解决争端。调解旨在依据相关当事人之间的独立协议来解决争端。

调解是指中立的第三方在争端双方之间主导调和，从而使他们能够订立一份让步协议来解决争端。调停者由双方当事人选出，其应为适格的，双方当事人均信任的人。调解的目标是通过经双方同意而指定的中立人员作为调停者，来协助友好解决争端，但是调停者不能为双方作决定。任何民商事争端都可以通过调解的方式解决，但调解协议不会在法院产生强制执行力除非另一方同意。尽管如此，调解与民事诉讼相比，其所需要的时间更少，成本更低。

针对特殊商业和金融纠纷，缅甸联邦工商业联合会也可以解决争端。缅甸联邦工商业联合会（UMFCCI）有义务调解其成员之间以及其成员与其他个人与组织之间的争端。对于调解，缅甸也没有任何成文的程序释明。成立小组委员会是为了调解某一具体争端，并在必要时召集专家听取他们的意见。在缅甸某些地方，纠纷的当事人会在诉诸法院之前寻求委员会的帮助以达成解决办法。然而，在国际争端中不会出现这种情况。经中央执行委员会批准，小组委员会的调查结果将会予以公布，不遵守调查结果的当事人会被列入黑名单。然而，这一调解程序似乎并不符合国际惯例。委员会的决定不具约束力，但责任方可能会被列入黑名单。

（三）仲裁

如果争端双方未能达成调解或者无法使用调解的方式来解决争端，他们可以通过仲裁或参考仲裁条款来解决纠纷（仲裁条款可能在他们缔结合同的时候就有）。仲裁是替代性争端解决最常用的形式。仲裁旨在通过仲裁员的裁决来解决争端。许多国家都规定了此类替代性争端解决的框架和程序，特别是法律规定的仲裁程序。许多国家也有独立的仲裁法或将仲裁纳入其民事诉讼法或相关法律。

仲裁是指由一个或多个独立的第三方仲裁员裁定争端而不是通过法院解决问题。仲裁员由各方当事人依据"仲裁协议"的条款指定或由法院任命。仲裁员必须准确地适用法律。

尽管缅甸有 1944 年的现行《仲裁法》，但缅甸的仲裁条例多年来一直不为人所知。该法共有 7 章、48 条和附表一、附表二，并且自生效以来，该法就从未进行过修正。该法规定了仲裁的两种替代性程序。相关当事人可选择任何一种。第一种仲裁程序没有法院的介入而第二种仲裁程序有法院的介入。该法规定了仲裁员和裁判员的指定方式以及他们的权力，还规定了法院对其任免职事项，民庭中裁决的生效和裁决诉至最高法院的上诉事项的监督。

另一方面,外国投资者与缅甸主体缔结的合同尤其是有关确立缅甸管辖权的条款里,投资者应当始终明确如下问题:"什么机构解决争端?用哪种语言?适用哪国的法律?"如前所述,1944 年的《仲裁法》仅涉及国内仲裁。该法规定,如果争端双方均来自缅甸,那么争端只能依据 1944 年的《仲裁法》提交缅甸国内仲裁。

如果争端的一方拥有外国身份,那么缅甸的这一方是否可以将争端提交外国仲裁,这一点该法没有予以明确。根据 2012 年的《缅甸进出口法》的规定,缅甸当事人在贸易中与外国公司发生争端的,应当依据 1944 年的《仲裁法》解决。那么在非贸易争端中,外国当事人可以与其缅甸合伙人进行外国仲裁。在这方面,我们注意到,在判例法中,缅甸法院是否会维持这种外国仲裁裁决,尚不得而知。

根据《外国投资法》的介绍,为了充分利用仲裁这种争端解决方式,建议外国投资者将商业关系构建为一项投资项目,获得必要的投资许可,然后在协议中加入仲裁条款。依据 1944 年的《仲裁法》,法院有权就国内仲裁给予保全救济。然而,鉴于缺乏明确的国内仲裁法规定,法院是否仍向请求外国仲裁程序的缅甸当事人提供这种援助或允许他们这样做,目前尚不确定。另一方面,与其他发展中国家一样,缅甸的外国投资者往往不信任当地法院。他们担心法官由于贪污腐败导致判决有失公正性。他们还担心解决争端的时间长短,以及法院的诉讼程序是否会被媒体舆论导向,如果这是一场引人注目的争端,通常就是这种情形。此外,程序中使用的语言也是外国投资者的一个障碍。然而,缅甸的仲裁仍尚未发展,目前还没有仲裁中心。这意味着仲裁裁决将由法院予以生效。

在实践中,缅甸法院在撤销仲裁裁决时往往会行使广泛的裁量权。因此,当一方在仲裁程序中经历了数个艰难的步骤赢得争端时,却未在法院将仲裁裁决予以确认使之产生执行力,那所做的一切都将前功尽弃。一方当事人最终可能会在法庭上重新提起诉讼。即使当事人同意在国外使用仲裁,如新加坡国际仲裁中心,也会发生这种情况。因此,如果投资者已经相当肯定外国仲裁裁决在缅甸毫无价值,最好还是不要采取这种做法。幸运的是,由于缅甸加入了《纽约公约》,最近也颁布了新的《仲裁法》,这些问题必定很快就会结束。争端解决条款如果是通过书面协议订立的,则该条款将生效。但是实际执行是否有效,仍有待观察,但这是向打造缅甸安全投资环境迈出的重要一步。关于仲裁的优势,完美的仲裁中心提供了独立的裁决和专业的仲裁能力。通常来说,其实可以在该条款中选择一批双方都信任的仲裁员,这可能会使得纠纷双方更广泛地接受并认同仲裁决定。仲裁中心根据不同的业务领域和专业知识来考虑仲裁员候选人是很重要的,大多数仲裁中心都为某些工作领域提供知名专家。新的《仲裁法》有哪些内容呢?新《仲裁法》是在1985年《联合国国际贸易法委员会仲裁规则》基础上制定出来的,联合国国际贸易法委员会仲裁规则被国际和社会广泛接受,这也就标志着缅甸的仲裁立法向着国际公认仲裁标准迈进了一步。新《仲裁法》分为两个部分。第一部分是关于仲裁地是否在缅甸的问题,第二部分适用于执行外国仲裁裁决。新《仲裁法》中要注意的一点是,仲裁裁决被界定为包括由缅甸法院执行的临时裁决。然而,《仲裁法》并没有提及定义中是否包含仲裁庭作出的命令和指示。

2013年4月16日,缅甸向联合国秘书长交存加入书,表示同意接受《纽约公约》中关于承认及执行外国仲裁裁决的约束。纽约公约已于2013年7月15日在缅甸生效。因此,缅甸的仲裁裁决应该可以在140多个公约成员国中执行。在这些国家中作出的仲裁裁决也应在整个缅甸内生效并得到执行。

尽管缅甸1944年的《仲裁法》仅规定了国内仲裁,并没有为承认和执行外国仲裁裁决提供框架,但1944年的《仲裁法》已被2016年1月5日缅甸联邦议会通过的新《仲裁法》(第5/2016号联盟法)所取代。该项立法就是为了与执行《纽约公约》。对于希望通过缅甸境外中立、独立和公正的仲裁法庭解决商业纠纷并在缅甸执行裁决的外国投资者来说,这是一个利好消息。此外,新《仲裁法》也就成了2012年缅甸"外商投资法"的重要部分。其中,部分规定外国投资者有权通过外国仲裁解决商业纠纷。

依据外国仲裁手段,我们可以看到新《仲裁法》有所变化:当事人可就商业争端仲裁事宜达成一致,并选择海外国家作为仲裁地;如果这样做,缅甸法院必须遵循此类仲裁程序而不是当事人向法院申请时直接审理案件;此外,缅甸法院必须承认并执行外国仲裁裁决,除非出现《纽约公约》第5条中所列举的限制理由;《纽约公约》的成员国都有同样的执行仲裁裁决的义务,因此投资者可以将裁决带到近160个国家的任何一个执法部门进行执行。

缅甸新《仲裁法》明确规定了所有仲裁原则及规则。这也标志着在缅甸进行外国仲裁解决争端的法律基础再一次完善。就笔者现在所见,它与大多数加入《纽约公约》的国家一样,仲裁规则非常稳固。

在投资缅甸之前,外国投资者应事先知道缅甸法院可以介入仲裁。《仲裁法》不仅涉及外国仲裁,而且涉及根据第3(B)条在缅甸的仲裁事由。《仲裁法》决定哪些法律条款可以适用于在缅甸境外的仲裁机构。

国内外仲裁结合出现在一部法律中在国际上并不多见。但在这种情况下,需要明确规定哪些条款适用于哪种类型的仲裁。

根据第 2 条的规定,《仲裁法》确实清楚地表明适用于外国裁决的清单。《仲裁法》第 7 条规定,即便任何现行法有所规定,除本法规定的情况外,法院不得干预本法所执行的事项,这也和《联合国国际贸易法委员会仲裁规则》第 5 条的规定一样。毫无疑问,这一规定适用于将缅甸作为仲裁地的纠纷双方。而且对于普通投资者来说,他们在解读仲裁法时也不会排他性地进行阅读。

《仲裁法》不仅支持缅甸法院执行仲裁庭发布的临时措施,包括在缅甸境外进行仲裁的情况,而且还支持直接向缅甸提出此类措施的当事人。根据《仲裁法》第 11 条的规定,当事人可以向缅甸法院申请各种措施采集证据、财产保全、变卖财产以及指定接管人和其他临时措施。在仲裁中临时措施急需采取的,法院可以视情况根据要求在当事人申请时作出证据保全与财产保全。

缅甸法院似乎保留了原来的紧张措施管辖权,即便涉及外国裁决,一方当事人也可申请证据保全和财产保全的临时措施。尽管如此,《仲裁法》确保法院不能过度干涉外国仲裁,通过将其权利限制于紧张案件,并且规定将法院的命令服从仲裁庭就同一问题作出后续命令。如果不需要施行紧急临时措施,则当事人申请仲裁时,法院应在向其他当事人和仲裁庭发出通知,并经仲裁庭批准或经另一方书面同意后处理此事。

外国投资者应清醒地意识到争端解决条款的必要性,并友好协商提出除了走缅甸法院诉讼程序以外的替代争端解决方案。为什么仲裁以及仲裁法显得如此有必要且有意义呢?

这是因为《仲裁法》能够保证外国仲裁法院对管辖权适用或临时措施的仲裁裁决权威免受缅甸法院的质疑。仲裁法明确规定了仲裁庭有权决定自己的管辖权。《联合国国际贸易法委员会仲裁规则》规定,法院只有基于当事人一方的要求,可以干预仲裁决定。这是唯一一种经过仲裁后又在法院上呈现的情形。但《仲裁法》第 47(b)条承认和执行外国仲裁裁决,适格法院可以审理针对仲裁庭作出的确定其是否有管辖权的决定的上诉。仲裁庭作出批准或拒绝临时措施的命令也是如此。《仲裁法》第 46(B)条和第 46(C)条规定,主管当局撤销或暂停外国裁决是其所在国的裁决。

可能有一个意外的问题:即使纠纷在外国仲裁中裁决,在向缅甸法院提出索赔时会发生什么情况呢? 显然这是《纽约公约》运作的关键,缅甸法律不会允许法院继续审理案件,而只是提及了该仲裁机制。《仲裁法》在第 10 条中提出了同样的关键原则,该原则适用于缅甸境内外的仲裁。但是,这一点的实现需要当事人一方提出,法院不能主动释明。

当法律规定或暗示当事人不能使用仲裁时,法院可不执行该裁决。如果有要求,联邦首席大法官有权在外国程序中任命仲裁员。关于国内诉讼,是由州首席大法官或地区首席大法官进行相关任命。

缅甸法院将有权发布临时措施支持仲裁程序。对于缅甸法院如何处理相关破产索赔案件,法律规定缅甸法院可酌情在一方当事人提出申请的情况下将破产案件提交仲裁。缅甸法院有权延长诉讼时效以便于开始在缅甸进行仲裁。《联合国国际贸易法委员会仲裁规则》和《新加坡国际仲裁法》中没有类似的规定。

在缅甸进行的不属于"国际商事仲裁"定义的仲裁必须采用缅甸法律作为仲裁的实体法。在缅甸作出的裁决将得到执行,但法院可以驳回已过执行时效的裁决。

如缅甸法院希望继续审理该案件,必须认定仲裁协议无效或无法在国内适用。这种法院判决,在任何情况下都可以提出上诉。保留此案的决定不受上诉使得《仲裁法》优先于国际仲裁。

在缅甸注册的两家公司选择在国外进行仲裁还是在缅甸进行仲裁,是一个重要的问题。依据《缅甸仲裁法》的规定,即使是两个缅甸国民或居民当事人也可以选择国际仲裁,而不是在国内仲裁。通过简单地选择在缅甸以外的仲裁地,或明确陈述该纠纷涉及多个国家,则仲裁将根据事由定义成为国际仲裁。因为缅甸法院的权利只适用于在缅甸的仲裁,其他的则排除在外。例如,在外国仲裁下一方不能向缅甸法院申请撤销裁决或提起对仲裁员的挑战。

其他法律可能也会阻止缅甸当事人同意在海外仲裁,或者采用仲裁方式解决争端。目前,1914 年的《缅甸公司法》仍规定,公司和个人可同意进行仲裁,但是只能选择在缅甸仲裁。依据 1916 年的《缅甸投资法》,如果争端不能友好地达成妥协,争端各方可将其案件提交主管法院或任何法庭解决。在这种情况下,外国或缅甸公司及其股东可以选择到外国或在缅甸进行仲裁。

在讨论缅甸注册的两家公司是否可以选择将他们的合同适用外国法律之前,笔者想阐述以下背景知识。缅甸几乎没有规定双方合同应适用哪国法律的法律规定,尽管双方合同至少在某些方面必须受到缅甸法律的约束。但是新《仲裁法》为此作出部分有意义的规定。该法第 32 条规定,如果仲裁地在缅甸,而且是国内仲裁,则双方当事人必须适用缅甸联邦共和国实体法,通过仲裁解决争端。

如果双方都是缅甸人进行争端解决,毫无疑问适用缅甸法律即可。但是根据仲裁法,外商投资者作为当事方完全可以选择缅甸为仲裁地进行国际仲裁。例如,纠纷双方一方为缅甸人,一方为外国人,若双方当事人选择缅甸作为仲裁地,那么这是一种以缅甸为仲裁地的国际仲裁。这些当事人完全可以选择适用英国法律。这只是本法第3条第(i)款的字面意思。而根据该法第3条第(i)款,国际仲裁意为:

(1)如果在执行仲裁协议时,一方的营业地和交易行为地其中之一位于缅甸以外的另一个国家;或者

(2)仲裁协议中规定的地点或者根据仲裁协议进行仲裁的地点,位于当事人的营业地所在国之外的;或者

(3)如果在与商业有关的经营义务中,履行实质部分义务的地点或与争议事项有最密切联系的地点位于当事人营业地所在国家之外;或者

(4)仲裁协议当事人是否明确表示该事项涉及多个国家,则这种仲裁意味着是国际仲裁。

但当缅甸的两个当事方订立了一个适用英国法律的合同并选择了缅甸为仲裁地,却没有符合第3条(i)款中规定的要素,这就显得不太适用。因为现在第32条清楚地规定,这种情况是仲裁地在缅甸的国内仲裁,并且必须以缅甸法律作为准据法。但是这个问题并不严重,如果出现该种情况,当事方可以很容易地选择缅甸境外作为仲裁地,以此来确保他们的合同适用外国法律。但是,如果缅甸适时发展自己的国内仲裁业,立法者就应当考虑解决这个问题了。

在2016年的新仲裁法中,对外国投资者和缅甸两者最显著的利益是,缅甸法院拒绝承认外国裁决。如果其真的想要援引一项或多项拒绝阻止执行外国裁决的理由的话,纽约公约任何签署国的法院都可以阻止外国裁决的执行。纽约公约的理论基础是缅甸法院有义务执行外国裁决,除非援引其拒绝执行的限制理由。缅甸执行纽约公约时也确立了这一基本原则。仲裁法在第46条第(b)款中规定了拒绝执行的限制理由,这些理由实际上都是从《联合国国际贸易法委员会仲裁规则》中翻译而来的。

拒绝执行外国裁决的正式理由如下:

(1)仲裁协议的一方或多方无权签署此类协议。比如,如果代表公司同意进行仲裁的代表,并无缅甸公司法第152条所举的例子那样拥有适当的权限。在国际层面上,我们也经常看到一方当事人是国有企业的情况,但在缅甸并无阻止国有企业同意仲裁的一般规则。这个问题有必要由缅甸法院根据缅甸法律中的冲突规则来决定。

(2)仲裁协议无效。这是质疑仲裁最常见的理由。一方可以主张未达成

合意,如受到虚假陈述或欺诈行为的影响。还有一种普遍情况就是,各方会主张仲裁协议因其语言不够清晰而无效。值得注意的是,根据《仲裁法》和《联合国国际贸易法委员会仲裁规则》的规定,仲裁协议的有效性必须根据协议适用的法律或仲裁地的法律来进行判断。所以,缅甸法律很少被适用。

(3)缺乏正当程序:当事方没有收到关于仲裁程序中各步骤的适当通知,或无法出席其案件。若当事一方收到通知,但故意无法出席,当然不能认为是程序不当。

(4)该裁决涉及未提交或提交不属于仲裁事项的条款范围内的纠纷,或包含关于提交仲裁事项的决定,或包含有关提交仲裁范围之外事项的决定。这意味着仲裁庭已经受理了当事各方没有考虑或仲裁协议以外的诉求。例如,当事人仅向仲裁庭提交了有关合同责任的问题时,该裁决还决定了合同责任以外的事项,或者在仲裁协议决定适用缅甸法律时,裁决适用了英国法。另一个例子是,裁决是当事人在仲裁协议中设定的期限以外作出的。

(5)仲裁庭的组成或程序不符合仲裁协议或仲裁地的法律。如果协议要求具有某种资格的仲裁员(如要求建筑师资格),如果负责选择仲裁员的当局忽视了这一点,缅甸法院可拒绝执行该裁决。败诉方很容易就会宣称裁决违反了一些程序性规则,但国际性的法院不会执行裁决。

(6)该裁决尚未生效或已被废除。根据仲裁法的规定,如果撤销一项仲裁裁决的申请已向仲裁地的法院提出,则缅甸法院有权决定暂缓执行。

二、民事诉讼——争议解决机制之一

随着近期欧洲国家对缅甸经济制裁的提高,各种新形式的国内外投资相关的各类诉讼,也将不可避免地同比增加。尽管许多企业设法规避缅甸法院,但在某些情况下,无论是作为原告还是被告,包括缅甸本地人在内的任何投资者都无法避免需要提起商业诉讼。

根据2008年宪法第293条的规定,联邦法院包括联邦最高法院、地区和州高等法院、自治区法院、自治地带法院、地方法院、乡镇法院和其他依法设立的法院、军事法庭和联邦宪法法院。根据第294条的规定,联邦最高法院是联邦的最高法院,但不影响联邦宪法法院和军事法庭的管辖权。

在缅甸,根据2010年司法法的规定,涉及民事案件(包括商业纠纷)的法院分为四个级别。分别如下所述:缅甸联邦最高法院;该地区或州的高等法院;地方法院、自治区法院和自治地带法院;乡镇法庭。

根据 2008 年宪法第 296 条第(a)款和 2010 年联邦司法法第 11 条的规定,对下列事项,联邦最高法院是唯一具有原始管辖权的法院:

(a)由联邦缔结的双边条约引起的事端。

(b)联邦政府与地区或各州政府之间;或各地区之间;各州之间;地区与州之间;以及联邦直辖区与地区或州之间除宪法问题之外的其他争议。

(c)海盗以及其他在陆地或国际水域或空域犯下的违反国际法的罪行。

(d)其他由法律规定的事项。

最高法院是最终上诉法院,对州和地区高等法院通过的判决以及其他法院依法判决拥有上诉管辖权[2008 年宪法第 296 条(d)款和刑事诉讼法第 12 条及 2010 年联邦司法法]。它还具有修改任何下级法院判决或命令的权力[2008 年宪法第 296 条第(e)款和 2010 年联邦司法法第 13 条]。它有权发布五个令状:人身保护法令、书面训令、禁止令、调查令和调卷令(2008 年宪法第 296 条和 2010 年联邦司法法第 16 条)。最高法院是缅甸的最高法院,其只能受理高等法院和地方法院由于争端原告或被告向法院提交的标的价值超过 1000 万缅元而提起的上诉案件。

地区或州高等法院负责监督下级法院。地区或州高等法院对下列事项拥有管辖权:(1)初审的民事和刑事案件;(2)上诉案件;(3)复审案件以及任何法律规定的其他案件(2010 年联邦司法法第 38 条)。地区或州高等法院对超过 5 亿缅元的诉讼拥有管辖权,其也可以受理乡镇法庭和地方法院的上诉案件。地方法院、自治区法院和自治地带法院有权处理标的价值最高 5 亿缅元的诉讼。乡镇法庭对标的价值 1000 万缅元或以下的诉讼,以及涉及位于该乡镇的不动产和动产的纠纷,拥有管辖权。

(一)民事诉讼实践和程序

缅甸的法律体系是一种对抗式的体系。案件由独任法官或合议庭受理,并由辩护律师或答辩者辩论。民事诉讼法是缅甸民事诉讼程序规则的主要法律渊源。辩护律师和答辩者还要遵守 1960 年的法院规则和 1872 年的证据法。缅甸法院的实践和程序很大程度上受英国实践和程序的影响。目前,虽然法院确实在引导纠纷双方进行仲裁,但缅甸仍没有一个发达的争端解决机制。一般来说,缅甸法院有权审判所有的民事诉讼,但法律禁止的某些事项除外。在缅甸,判断是否为受理诉讼的管辖法院要根据主张标的的种类和价值,以及当事方的住址或营业地或争议行为发生地。

对于那些准备在缅甸投资的外国投资者而言,下一个问题是,外国实体是否可以在缅甸提起诉讼或被起诉。根据民事诉讼法第 83 条的规定,经联邦主席许可留在联邦的外国公民(无论来自敌国还是友邦),都可以在缅甸的任何法院如同缅甸公民一样提起民事诉讼。但是,不动产交易法禁止外国公民取得不动产超过一年期限,除非外国公司与州签有相关的利益合同。

此外,民事诉讼法没有规定禁止外国人起诉或被起诉的条款。商事案件(在缅甸被称为民事案件)可能需要花费一年或两年时间。这取决于案件的性质,如在被告认可的情况下,程序仅持续几个月。在实践中,我们经常看到,当事人可能会在收到传票后或者在获得临时禁令时就倾向于解决问题了,这基本上就是一两个月的事情,虽然有明显的例外情况存在。商业纠纷的原告必须向适当的法院提起诉讼。此后,给予被告时间提出答辩、反诉或者主张与其他人进行抵销,然后原告可以以书面声明的方式作出回应,然后终止诉讼。

根据上述规定完成诉讼程序之后,下一步就是证据开示并检查诉讼文件,现阶段当事方也可以提出临时禁令和其他中期命令。法院将根据当事方提交的意见定性争议。此后,如果没有达成和解,将会有听证会并作出判决和执行命令。宣判后当事方可提出上诉。

在缅甸,能够被称为民事诉讼的商业争端的争议方在合同违约时向法院提起诉讼。存在违反合同行为时,适格的原告就是签订合同的,或被代表签订合同的,或合同中的权利所归属的人(民事诉讼法第 I 号令第 3 条)。如果一个行为是由多个共同缔约方根据他们共同的承诺作出的,则应将所有方纳入其中。

谁可以被列为被告?对所有因与同一交易行为或关联行为有关的,原告认为可以寻求权利救济的人均可以被列为被告。无论是列为共同被告还是分别列为被告,或以其他方式,比如在单独的诉讼中针对该人提出任何常见的法律或事实问题(民事诉讼法第 I 号令第 3 条)。若根据合同,两人或两人以上承担连带责任的;各方必须以共同被告的身份加入诉讼。如果只有一个适当的当事方被起诉,那么该当事方可以向法院申请暂停该诉讼,直到所有其他相关人员被列为共同被告为止。

除非反对理由是随后出现的,否则所有以共同当事方未被列入为理由提出的反对意见,都应尽早在所有已解决或尚未解决此问题的案件中提出。但未提出任何此类反对意见不应被视为放弃提出此异议的权利(民事诉讼法第 I 号令第 3 条)。

(二)侵权行为

在侵权行为中,适格原告是被侵权者伤害的人。在死亡的情况下,适格原告是拥有诉讼权利的人。侵权行为的适格被告是不法行为人或对不法行为人负有责任的人。如果有多人因侵权行为而受伤,他们中的任何一人都可以单独起诉而不必加入其他受害方。凡有多于一个原告人的情况,其中一人或多人可以被他人授权在任何诉讼中出庭、提出请求,或采取诉讼行动。并且同样的,在被告人数多于一人的情况下,他们中的任何一人或多人可以被其他任何人授权出庭,为诉讼中的其他人辩护或采取行动。该种授权应以书面形式作出,签字并提交给法院(民事诉讼法第 I 号令第 12 条)。

所有诉讼都应始于原告针对被告,向法院提起诉讼。起诉书应包含以下内容(民事诉讼法第 IV 号令第 1 条):

(1)提起诉讼的法院名称;(2)原告人的姓名、名称及居住地;(3)被告人的姓名、名称及居住地点(只要能够确定);(4)如果原告人或被告人是未成年人或心智不健全的人,就此种情况的声明;(5)构成诉讼缘由的事实,以及发生的时间;(6)证明法院具有管辖权的事实;(7)原告主张的救济;(8)如果原告允许抵偿或放弃其部分债权,则允许的数额;(9)就本案所涉及的情况而言,诉讼标的的价值和法院的诉讼费用。

下列情况法院将拒绝受理:

(1)如果其没有揭示诉讼的原因;(2)在主张的救济估值偏低的情况下,原告在法院确定的时间内未能纠正估价;(3)如果主张的救济估值正确,但是这种陈述是写在未加盖的纸上的,并且原告未能在法院确定的必要时间内提供加盖的文件的;(4)如果诉讼是在禁止声明中以任何方式被禁止的。

当起诉状被提交时,也同时向被告送达传票,要求被告出庭并答辩。当诉讼正式开始时,可发出传票给被告,以便在指定的日子出庭并应诉,并且每一张传票都应由法官或其指定的工作人员签字,并应盖法院印章(民事诉讼法第 V 号令第 1 条)。此外,每份传票均须附有一份原件副本(民事诉讼法第 V 号令第 2 条)。

在缅甸,关于传票的送达,如果被告居住在受理诉讼的法院的管辖范围内,或者在该司法管辖区设有有权接受传票送达的代理人,则传票应递交给他或他的一个分支机构(民事诉讼法第 V 号令第 9 条)。送达传票应递交或投递由法官或他指定的官员代其签署并由法院印章加盖的副件。但是,在涉及企业和工作的诉讼中,针对不居住在发出传票的法院管辖地区范围内的人,将传票送达给当时为其在该区域的企业或工作的任何管理者或代理人,应被视为已送达。就本规则目的而言,船舶的船长应被视为船东或租船人的代理人。如果被告授权他的律师接受传票并代表他出庭,传票也可以送达被告的律师。

在与替代送达有关的情况下,如法庭有理由相信被告一直在躲避送达,则法院应通过将一份复印件贴在法院显著位置,以及已知被告最后居住地或营业地或个人工作地的某些显眼部分,或以法院认为合适的其他方式完成公告送达。如果是通过法院命令送达的,法院应根据情况确定被告出庭的时间(民事诉讼法第 V 号令第 20 条)。

如果被告人被关押在监狱内,传票应通过递交或邮寄或其他方式送交监狱主管人员送达被告。如果被告居住在缅甸联邦之外,并且在缅甸联邦没有授权接受送达的代理人,则传票可以送至被告居住的地点并通过邮寄方式寄给他,前提是法院所在的地点和上述地点有邮政通信服务(民事诉讼法第 V 号法令第 25 条)。

(三)诉讼的维持

缅甸联邦法院有权审判民事性质的诉讼,但明示或默示禁止的诉讼除外(民事诉讼法第 9 节)。任何法院都不得受理,先前已在同一当事人之间或在他们或任何一方主张的当事方之间提起的诉讼中涉及直接或实质的事项,如果同一案由的诉讼正在缅甸联邦的同一法院或任何其他法院进行审理,该法院有权救济当事人的诉求,或在联邦最高法院之前审理。

如果一案件或争议,在先前已由相同当事人直接并实质性主张权利或诉讼,或者经适当法院进行了此类后续诉讼,或之后提出此类问题进行诉讼,已由该适当法院审理并最终作出裁决的,法院不得再次受理。

关于外国判决,直接裁决了在相同当事人之间事项的,或主张诉讼了相同案由的当事方之间事项的外国判决具有终局性,除了以下情况外(民事诉讼法第 9 条):(1)有管辖权的法院并没有宣判;(2)没有就案情的实体问题作出判决;(3)在诉讼过程中发现了明显违反国际法的现象,或者在案件中拒绝接受缅甸联邦可适用的法律;(4)审判的程序与自然法公正原则相抵触;(5)判决是通过欺诈获得的;(6)支持了违反缅甸联邦任何强制性法律的主张。

法院应根据任何具有外国判决的合格副本外观的文件推定,该判决是由具有司法管辖权的法院作出的,除非有相反的记录证明。但这种推定可能因证明了缺乏管辖权而推翻。根据 2016 年仲裁法的规定,缅甸法院在某些情况下也有权维持管辖。例如,如果是法院将当事人提交仲裁的,则法院有权命令继续在法院进行诉讼。

三、结论

根据《联合国国际贸易法委员会仲裁规则》的规定，如果缅甸法院发现争议事由，根据缅甸法律不能通过仲裁解决，则该裁决无须强制执行。缅甸法律保留了一些只能由司法或行政程序解决的特定事项。这种保留存在于雇佣、竞争、刑事案件和破产等领域。缅甸的合同可以设有争议解决条款。然而，确定最适当的争议解决方式可能很复杂，因为在其中必须要考虑诸多因素，特别是在缅甸仲裁中心尚未建立的情况下。目前有计划在缅甸建立这样的中心，预计此举会提高投资双方采取国际仲裁作为跨境争端解决适当手段的意识。仲裁法不仅对外国投资者是一个积极信息，对缅甸也是个有利因素。这表明缅甸愿意将自己定位为对仲裁友好的法区。随着仲裁法的通过，缅甸将以更优惠的条件和更多元的渠道吸引更多的外国投资。仲裁法也是改善缅甸仲裁机制的第一步。

缅甸已经成为外国投资者投资的理想地点。因为缅甸不仅自然资源丰富，地理环境良好，陆路、水路等基础设施完善，法治环境也处于良好状态。缅甸政府正在通过完善必要的法律体系（如外国投资法、缅甸仲裁法和其他相关法律）以吸引外国投资者。此外，缅甸的法院体系和民事诉讼程序对来自西方国家和其他普通法系的商事律师和商人并不陌生。在近 60 年的自我封闭之后，缅甸目前已被重新视为外国投资的理想便利之地。

Legal Review Relating to Marriage System in Myanmar

Luo Yuan Yuan[*]   Moe Cho[**]

Abstract：In Myanmar，marriage is not based on the nationality，but on the religion of both parties. Although there are many religions in Myanmar，Buddhism，Hinduism，Christianity and Islam are the main ones. Marriage between religious believers and marriages between non-religious and religious believers，and even marriages between foreigners and Burmese religious believers，must be based on religious rules and customs，and also comply with the Monogamy Law of Myanmar 2015. This article intends to provide relevant legal knowledge and advice to foreigners who have entered into a marriage relationship with Myanmar citizens in Myanmar.

Keywords：Enter into a marriage，Monogamy，Religion，Customary Law of Myanmar

1. Introduction

In Myanmar，Marriage amongst Myanmar Buddhist has not concerned with any religious character it might have and at the present day it is purely civil and consensual contract. Both Myanmar Buddhist men and women

---

* Luo Yuan Yuan，Program Director of China-ASEAN Legal Research Center，E-mail：yuanyuanandeleven@hotmail.com.

** Moe Cho，Doctoral Student of School of International Law of SWUPL/Staff Officer，Union Attorney General's Office，Building 25，Nay Pyi Taw，Myanmar，E-mail：m15922771431@163.com.

enjoy equal rights in all legal aspect, social aspect and cultural aspect. Marriage amongst Myanmar Buddhist men and women not only determines the questions of legitimacy and inheritance but imposes a liability on the husband to maintain his wife and children and to remain faithful to wife. Regarding the marriage in Myanmar, it does not base on the nationality of the parties, it bases on the religion of the parties. Although there are many religions in Myanmar, the Buddhist, Hindu, Christian and Islam are the four main religions. Under the Constitution of the Republic of the Union of Myanmar, every citizen is entitled to freedom of conscience and the right to freely profess and practice religion subject to public order, morality or health and to the other provisions of this Constitution. Although the Hindus, Christians and Muslims may contract the marriages in accordance with their relevant laws and customs, they shall also comply with the Monogamy Law of Myanmar 2015. This article intends to give the legal knowledge regarding to marriage in Myanmar for foreigner who want to contract the marriage with Myanmar citizens. And it will also give the suggestions for foreigners who intend to contract the marriage with Myanmar citizens.

2. Marriage Styles in Myanmar

Marriage is a civil institution into which the Buddhist religious element enters not at all. Social life in Myanmar, and for that matter in the Southeast Asian of the majority, is so wrapped up in religious ethics that the absent of priests and religious elements from the ceremony of marriage becomes all the more remarkable. Here no members of the Buddhist clergy officiate because the love is of a profane nature and the contract purely a social one. Certain requirement are prescribed by custom for a valid marriage, the parties must be capable as regards age and mind. The Dhammathats do not fix the age of competence for marriage, though they suggest that parents should give their sons and daughters in marriage when they reach the age of 15 or 16. It is generally accepted that a boy attains competence with puberty and a girl when she reaches the age of 20 before which she needs parents consent.

For a woman to enter into a valid marriage, she must not have a subsisting marriage tie. A window or a divorce can marry, and indeed such a woman, being emancipated from parental control by a previous marriage, does not need parental consent even if she should be below the age of 20, when she marries again. This requirement, however, does not apply to men, for polygamy among Burma Buddhists is beyond dispute, "observed the Privy Council," and that it is sanctioned by the Dhammathats is also beyond dispute. Polygamy, however, is not a popular institution. It is legal, but except among officials and the wealthy, is seldom practiced. In ordinary life a man with more than one wife is talked of as not being a very respectable person. However, at present, Myanmar practices the Monogamy system, One Husband and One Wife, under the Myanmar Monogamy Law 2015.

The most important element of Burmese marriage, which is commonly described as a "consensual contract" is consent. The consent of the parents or guardian is needed, as we have seen, if a girl is below the age of 20 and not yet emancipated. No longer can a father give away an unwilling minor daughter into marriage. Mutual consent of the parties freely given, by tests laid down in see 14 of Contract Act, and where the parties are of sound mind as tested by section 12 of the Act, is the indispensable ingredient. Consent of the parties to marry, their intention to enter the status of husband and wife, are the large factors in a marriage proof of which therefore turns on conduct showing the consent and the intention. Where there is a dispute, and proof of marital status has to depend only on habit and repute, then the facts have to be carefully examined, and a bare statement by a witness that the couple is husband and wife is held insufficient. It has become popular and fashionable with the young people these days to go to a judge and sign affidavits, in the presence of a few friends and elders, stating their competence and intention to marry. The affidavit is then kept by the parties, the young man keeping the young woman's and vice versa, as "certificate" of marriage and proof. This procedure saves the expense of big ceremonies and receptions, is quicker, and looks more "legal" in that there are documents to keep which bear stamps and seals and signatures. Now this legal practice is used widely and it is very popular practice in Myanmar.

Under Myanmar customary law, women are tenants-in common in respect of properties. They jointly own the property accumulated during the period of marriage together with their spouses.

3. The laws relating to Marriage in Myanmar

In Myanmar, Marriage amongst Myanmar Buddhist has not concerned with any religious character it might have and at the present day it is purely civil and consensual contract. In its juridical aspect, marriage is both a contract and an institution in as much as it creates a status the incident if which are quite independent of volition of parties. Both Myanmar Buddhist men and women enjoy equal rights in all legal aspect, social aspect and cultural aspect. Marriage amongst Myanmar Buddhist men and women not only determines the questions of legitimacy and inheritance but imposes a liability on the husband to maintain his wife and children and to remain faithful to wife. Regarding the marriage in Myanmar, it does not base on the nationality of the parties, it bases on the religion of the parties. Although there are many religions in Myanmar, the Buddhist, Hindu, Christian and Islam are the four main religions. Under the Constitution of the Republic of the Union 2008, the Union recognizes special position of Buddhism as the faith professed by the great majority of the citizens of the Union. In addition the Union also recognizes Christianity, Islam, Hinduism and Animism as the religions existing in the Union at the day of the coming into operation of this Constitution 2008.

Section 13(1) of the Burma (Myanmar) Laws Act 1898 provides that where in any suit or other proceeding in the Union of Burma (Myanmar) it is necessary for the Court to decide any question regarding succession, inheritance marriage or caste, or any religious usage or institution;

(a) the Buddhist law in cases where the parties are Buddhists,

(b) the Muhammadan law in cases where the parties are Muhammadan and

(c) the Hindu law in cases where the parties are Hindus,

shall form the rule of decision, except in so far as such law has by enactment been altered or abolished, or is opposed to any custom having the force of law.

243

However, the Pyidaungsu Hluttaw hereby enacts the Monogamy Law in 2015 in order to help legally married couples set up peaceful and pleasant families on the basis of loyalty by practicing monogamy, to protect women from being co-wives, and to prevent crimes arising from polygamous acts of men. This law concerns all those who are living in Myanmar, Myanmar citizens who live outside of Myanmar, and foreigners who marry Myanmar citizens while in Myanmar. Unless contrary to the provisions of this law, any man or woman may legally enter into a marriage with any person in accordance with the relevant existing law or religious or custom.

3.1 Marriage Laws for Buddhist Persons

Regarding the marriage amongst Myanmar Buddhist men and women under the Burma Law Act 1898, it has been governed by the Buddhist Law. Myanmar Customary Law is the Customary Law of Myanmar Buddhists, Customary law gradually came to be confided to affairs of Myanmar family mainly, and religious usages and institutions. Because the British Administers identified it as having force among the Myanmar who professed the Buddhist faith they called it "Myanmar Buddhist Law" and the name has passed into common use. The Customary Law of Myanmar also identified as "Personal Law" because prima facie a Buddhist in Myanmar, irrespective of what his nationality is, and irrespective of where he comes, is governed by the Myanmar Customary Law, i.e., by the Dhammathats and precedents in matters of marriage, inheritance and succession, unless he can prove that he is governed by a custom which has the force of Law in Myanmar which is opposed to the Myanmar Customary Law. Before British's occupation, the Myanmar Customary Law is the social and irreligious law based upon the custom and usage that were historically accepted by the ancient Myanmar. After 13 years of occupation of Upper Myanmar, the British colonial government enacted the Myanmar Laws Act in 1898 which is still law today. From that time, we firstly see the word "Buddhist Law" in this Act. Most of the prominent jurists of Myanmar said that the term "Buddhist Law" in reference to the Customary Law of the Myanmar is a misnomer. They urged to mean the Myanmar Buddhist law as Myanmar Customary Law. The case, U Thein Pe Vs U Pe, is expressly accepted that name in each particular case. In Lim Chin Neo Vs Lim Geok Soo, U Chan Tun Aung, Chief Justice of High Court, decided in a civil proceeding that " Myanmar Buddhists" is meant the "Customary Law of Myanmar Buddhists" U Mya Sein, the prominent author of 'Myanmar Customary Law', advised that the Myanmar Buddhist law should be called and meant as "Myanmar Customary Law".

Sources of Myanmar Customary Law are as follows:

(a) The Dhammathats

(b) Custom

(c) Judicial precedents

(d) Legislation or the legislative enactments.

(1) The Registration of Kittima Adoption Act.

(2) The Buddhist Women's Special Marriage Law 2015.

Regarding the marriage of Myanmar Buddhists, there are two kinds of marriage. One is marriages contracted between the Buddhist women and Buddhist men. Another is marriages contracted between the Myanmar women and non-Buddhist men.

If the Buddhist women and Buddhist men contract marriages, they shall comply with the Myanmar Customary Law and the Monogamy Law of Myanmar. Under the Myanmar Customary Law, the essentials of marriage are as follows:

(a) The man should be attained his puberty.

(b) The woman should be a spinster above 20 years of age, a widow, a divorcee or a spinster under the age of 20 years who has obtained her parents' or guardian's consent.

(c) The parties must be mentally competent to contract according to section 11of the contract Act, 1872. (Both parties must not be unsound mind).

(d) The parties must give their mutual and free consent with intend to become husband and wife presently.

(e) The woman must not have a subsisting valid marriage. (polygamous system)

(f) In the absence of direct proof, marriage may be assumed from the conduct of the parties or established by reputation. They should live together as husband and wife openly.

In the marriages contracted between the Myanmar Buddhist Women and non—Buddhist men, they shall comply with the Myanmar Buddhist Women's Special Marriage Law 2015 and the Monogamy Law of Myanmar 2015. The Pyidaungsu Hluttaw enacts the Myanmar Buddhist Women's Special Marriage Law in 2014 in order to enable the enjoyment of equal rights by Myanmar Buddhist Women and non-Buddhist men with respect to marriage, divorce, partition and guardianship of children and to give effective protection. The disputes relating to marriage, divorce, partition, succession and guardianship of children of Myanmar Buddhist women and non—Buddhist men shall, subject to the provisions of the Monogamy Law of Myanmar 2015, be decided in accordance with this law. Under the Myanmar Buddhist Women's Special Marriage Law 2015, a non—Buddhist man, who has attained the age of 18, and a Buddhist woman, who has attained the age of 18, may contract a valid marriage if the following facts are fulfilled:

(a) both parties shall not be of unsound mind.

(b) consent to marry shall be voluntary and free from seduction, inducement, coercion, undue influence, fraud or misrepresentation.

(c) if the woman has not attained the age of twenty, the consent of parents, or if they are dead, of the guardian de facto or of the guardian de jure, if any, shall be obtained.

(d) in the case of a woman, no valid marriage shall subsist, and

(e) in the case of a man, no valid marriage shall subsist.

In comparing the marriageable ages for women between the marriage of Buddhist women and Buddhist men and the marriage of Buddhist women and non—Buddhist men, there is difference. Under the Myanmar Customary Law, the woman, who will marriage, should be the 20 years of age and under the Myanmar Buddhist Women's Special Marriage Law 2015, the woman, who will marriage, has attained the 18 years of age. We see that the Myanmar Buddhist Women's Special Marriage Law 2015 contrary with the Myanmar Customary Law. The Dhammathat do not specify the exact age when a boy or girl could validly become husband and wife. In 1928 the Yangon High Court decided in Maung Thein Mg vs Ma Saw case that at

Myanmar Buddhist youth is competent to contract a valid marriage at any time the is physically competent of marriage and no consent of his parents or guardian is necessary. In the case Ma E Sein vs Maung Hla Min7 Myanmar Buddhist Law minor spinster whether capable of entering into a contract of marriage without consent of guardian or not, was held that no minor girl under the age of twenty can contract a valid marriage without the consent or against the will of her parents or guardians, or of the relation under whose protection she is living. Nowadays when a couple marries in the court, the marriage age is fixed at 18 years at which age the consent of the parent or guardians are needed. Hence, there is a difference in age limits, according to the Myanmar Customary Law and the Court of Law. Therefore we should define to fix the age limit.

3.2 Christian marriage laws in Myanmar

Every marriage between persons, one or both of whom is orare a Christian or Christians, shall be solemnized in accordance with the provisions of the Christian Marriage Act 1872. This marriage may be solemnized:

(a) by any person who has received Episcopal ordination, provided that the marriage be solemnized according to the rules, rites, ceremonies and customs of the Church of which he is a Minister.

(b) by any clergyman of the Church of Scotland, provided that such marriage be solemnized according to the rules, rites, ceremonies and customs of the Church of Scotland.

(c) by any Minister of Religion licensed under this Act to solemnized marriages.

(d) by, or in the presence of, a Marriage Registrar appointed under this Act, and

(e) by any person licensed under this Act to grant certificated of marriage between Native Christians.

If a Myanmar Buddhist embraces Christianity and marries a Christian in a valid way and subsequently reverts to Buddhist, he or she is not thereby entitled to contract a second marriage with a Myanmar Buddhist so long as the tie of Christian marriage remains intact. Nowadays, the Christian man and Christian woman contracts the marriage in the presence of a Marriage Registrar appointed under the Christian Marriage Act 1872. They shall also comply with the provisions of the Monogamy Law of Myanmar 2015. In addition, the Christian men who intend to marry with Myanmar Buddhist women shall only contract the marriage under the Myanmar Buddhist Women's Special Marriage Law 2015.

3.3　Islam Marriage Laws in Myanmar

For Muslims, marriage is called *Nikah*, the Arabic word, which literally means marriage or matrimony. Muslim man and Muslim woman may make the marriage of contract under the Islamic Family Law of Myanmar. Under the Islamic Family Law of Myanmar, the essentials of the valid marriage are capacity, contract of the marriage and free from all the prohibitions. Every Muslims of sound mind, who has attained puberty, may enter into a contract of marriage. As the majority of the Myanmar Muslims are Sunni Hanafi, Myanmar Islamic family law follows the Sunni Hanafi law in most but it cannot be contravened with the enacted laws of Myanmar. Sunni Hanafi law accepts that a boy or a girl who reaches to the 15 years of age shall be recognized as the capacity of marriage if there is no evidence the date of puberty. However Myanmar does not allow it because the Child Marriage Restraint Act 1929 provides that a person who, if a male is under eighteen years of age and if a female is under the sixteen years of age, is defined as a child. At present, the Muslims men and Muslims women make the contract of marriage under the Myanmar Islamic Family Law. In addition, they shall comply with the Monogamy Law of Myanmar 2015 relating to their contracts of Marriage.

As Myanmar Buddhist are not kitabic (followers of any revealed religion believing in one God), so no marriage is valid between a Mohammedan and a Myanmar Buddhist unless the latter embraces the Mohammedan faith or any other revealed religion believing in one God and the marriage is celebrated according to the rites of the Mohammedan faith. Nowadays, if the Muslims men, however, intent to make the contract of marriage with the Myanmar Buddhist women, they shall only make the contract of marriage under the Myanmar Buddhist Women's Special Law 2015.

3.4 **Hindu Marriage Laws in Myanmar**

Under the Hindu Customary law, the marriage contracted between the Hindu man and Hindu woman will only be the valid marriage if this marriage was held with the Religious ceremony in accordance with customs of the Hindu. Under the Anand Marriage Act 1909, all marriages which may be or may have been duly solemnized according to the Sikh marriage ceremony called Anand and it shall be deemed to have been with effect from the date of the solemnization of each respectively, good and valid in law. Regarding the Hindu Widows' Re-Marriage, no marriage contracted between Hindus shall be invalid, and the issue of no such marriage shall be illegitimate, by reason of the woman having been previously married or betrothed to another person who was dead at the time of such marriage, any custom and any interpretation of Hindu law to the contrary notwithstanding.

However, a Hindu cannot contract a legal marriage with any woman unless she belongs to his own caste. There are four kinds of Hindu caste such as the Brahmins, Kshatriya, and Vaisya. So, a Hindu of the Brahmins, Kshatriya, and Vaisya or Oudra caste cannot contract a valid marriage in the orthodox style with a Myanmar Buddhist. At present, the Hindus shall comply with the Myanmar Monogamy Law 2015 relating to their marriage amongst Hindus. In addition, the Hindus may marry with Myanmar Buddhist women in accordance with the Myanmar Buddhist Women's Special Law 2015.

4. Can the foreigners marry with Myanmar Citizens?

There is no restriction relating to the rights of the foreigners to marry with Myanmar citizens. Although there is no restriction for foreigners to marry with Myanmar citizens, the foreigners shall contract the marriages in accordance with the respective customs of Myanmar and shall comply with the existing laws of Myanmar relating to marriage. In Myanmar, the marriage does not base on the nationalities of the parties, it only base on the religions of the parties. If the foreigners intend to contract the marriage with the Christians of Myanmar, they can only contract the marriage in accordance with the Christian Marriage Act and Christian Custom.

In addition, the foreigners want to contract the marriage with the Muslims of Myanmar, they can only contract such marriage in accordance the Myanmar Islam Family Law. Similarly, they also intend to marriage with the Hindus of Myanmar, they can only contract such marriage in accordance with the Myanmar Hindus Family Law. It means that the foreigners can contract the marriage with the Myanmar Christians, Muslims and Hindus in accordance with the relevant laws and customs. However, this part of the article points out the marriage between the Myanmar Buddhists citizens and the foreigners. Like as the above mentioned, the foreigners can contract the marriages with the Myanmar Buddhist citizens. We will explain in the following parts that how to contract the marriage between the foreigners and Myanmar Buddhist citizens and which laws should the foreign notice in contracting the marriages with Myanmar Buddhist citizens?

4.1 How to contract the marriage between the foreigners and Myanmar Buddhist citizens?

Regarding the Myanmar Buddhist citizens, there is no restriction for Myanmar Buddhist men to contract the marriage with the foreign women. However, if the Foreign Buddhist men or the Foreign non—Buddhist men intend to contract the marriage with the Myanmar Buddhist women, they shall comply with the existing laws of Myanmar and Myanmar Customary Law. The Supreme Court of the Union has issued the Directives regarding the matter concerning the marriage of Myanmar women and foreigners. Because many foreigners from foreign countries have come to Myanmar through various means, and some foreigners have connections with human brokers from Myanmar and try to lure Myanmar women to marry them by swearing an oath in court and take them abroad. These women who have been taken abroad through this process have faced unseemly problems even before they have arrived overseas, and also when they do arrive overseas, they lose their characters and have various problems. Devoid of national spirit, they lure Myanmar women with promises of money and are making plans to transport them form Myanmar by marring them to foreigners. As this situation, the Supreme Court of the Union strove to protect Myanmar's women lives from the dangers that threaten them. Therefore the Supreme Court of the Union had issued the Directive No. 2/1998 in 1st July 1998 for all Staffs of Courts that none of the staff is empowered to accept any oath or application of marriage of a Myanmar woman to a foreigner nor marry any Myanmar woman to any foreigner.

However, as the courts did not accept any oath or application of marriage of a Myanmar woman to a foreigner, there were difficulties for the foreigner and the Myanmar woman who really wanted to marry and there were loses for Myanmar woman. Therefore, the Supreme Court of the Union has withdrawn the Directive No 2/1998 by the Directive No 1/2012. Under the Directive No. 1/2012, the courts are empowered to accept any oath or application of marriage of the foreigners and Myanmar women. If, besides, the foreign Buddhist man intends to contract the marriage with Myanmar Buddhist woman, they shall only contract the marriage before the District Courts. Although, under the Directive No. 1/2012, the court had the power to accept the marriage of foreign non—Buddhist man and Myanmar Buddhist woman, this power of the courts was withdrawn by the Directive No. 494/2016. Under the Directive No. 494/2016, the courts is empowered an y oath or application of marriage of a Foreign non—Buddhist man and Myanmar Buddhist woman, because the Pyidaungsu Hluttaw enacts the Myanmar Buddhist Women's Special Marriage Law in 2015 and under this law, Township Administrative Officers of the Township General Administration Department shall be the Registrars of Marriages between a non—Buddhist man and a Myanmar Buddhist woman. Whenever a non—Buddhist man and a Buddhist woman intend to contract a marriage, one of them shall apply in writing in the prescribed form to the Registrar within the jurisdiction where one of them is residing. The application shall be accompanied by an affidavit, admitting that the facts provided under this law are fulfilled.

4.2 What should the foreigners who intend to contract with Myanmar Buddhist women notice?

This article gives suggestions to the foreigners, both Buddhist foreigners and non—Buddhist foreigners, who intend to contract the marriage with the Myanmar Buddhist women. Firstly, the Buddhist foreigners who intent to contract the marriage with the Myanmar Buddhist women shall comply with the Myanmar Customary Law and the existing laws of Myanmar including the Monogamy Law of Myanmar 2015 and they may only contract the marriage before the District Courts. Disputes concerning marriage, divorce, partition, succession and guardianship of children of Buddhist women and Buddhist men shall be decided in accordance with Myanmar Customary Law.

Secondly, the non—Buddhist foreigners who intend to contract the marriage with the Myanmar Buddhist women shall comply with the Myanmar Buddhist Women's Special Marriage Law 2015 and the existing laws of Myanmar including the Monogamy Law of Myanmar 2015 and shall contract the marriage before the Township Administrative Officers of the Township Administrative Departments. The disputes concerning marriage, divorce, partition, succession and guardianship of children of Buddhist women and non—Buddhist men shall be decided in accordance the Myanmar Buddhist Women's Special Marriage Law 2015 subject to provisions of the law relating to the practice of Monogamy System. In addition, a non—Buddhist man, who has contracted or deemed to have contracted a marriage with Myanmar Buddhist woman under this law, shall observe the following provisions relating to the religious faith of the Buddhist woman:

(a)to allow the Buddhist woman to profess the religion freely according to her faith.

(b) to allow the children born from the marriage with the Buddhist woman to profess their religion freely according to their faith.

(c)to allow the Buddhist woman to keep Buddha status and images at their home.

(d) to allow the Buddhist woman to donate according to religion, to worship, to recite to ward off evil (Payeik), to tell (one's) beads, to listen to religious sermons, to practice religious meditation, to visit Pagoda and Monasteries, to fast, to read and study literature relating to Buddhism.

(e)not to cause the Buddhist woman to relinquish the Buddhist faith by using various means, and to convert her to his religion.

(f) not to destroy or damage or to defile the place of worship or the thing which is sacred with an intent to insult Buddhist and

(g) not to insult, in words or in writing or though visible representation or gesture, with bad intention to cause bitter feeling to the Buddhist.

Notwithstanding any provision contained in law and custom, if a non—Buddhist man, who has contracted a marriage with Myanmar Buddhist woman under this law, violates any fact in the above mentioned, the Buddhist woman can divorce the non—Buddhist man. In addition, if the Buddhist woman would divorce the man due to that reason,

(a) the man shall waive the portion that he is entitled to from the property owned by both, and pay compensation to the Buddhist woman.

(b) the guardianship of all children shall be with the Buddhist woman and

(c) the man shall pay maintenance for children who are minors.

If the non—Buddhist man violates the following provisions of the Myanmar Buddhist Women's Special Law 2015:

(a) to allow the Buddhist woman to profess the religion freely according to her faith.

(b) to allow the children born from the marriage with the Buddhist woman to profess their religion freely according to their faith.

(c) to allow the Buddhist woman to keep Buddha status and images at their home and

(d) to allow the Buddhist woman to donate according to religion, to worship, to recite to ward off evil (Payeik), to tell (one's) beads, to listen to religious sermons, to practice religious meditation, to visit Pagoda and Monasteries, to fast, to read and study literature relating to Buddhism.

He shall be punished with imprisonment for a term which may extend to 6 months, or with fine not more thanKyats 500, 000 (about US $ 400), or with both. If the non—Buddhist man violates the provision of this law which is that "not to cause the Buddhist woman to relinquish the Buddhist faith by using various means, and to convert her to his religion", he shall be punished with imprisonment which may extend to 3 years, and shall also be liable to a fine. Besides, if the non—Buddhist man violates the provisions of this law which are that "not to destroy or damage or to defile the place of worship or the thing which is sacred with an intent to insult Buddhist and not to insult, in words or in writing or though visible representation or gesture, with bad intention to cause bitter feeling to the Buddhist", he shall be with imprisonment for a term which may extend to 2 years, or with fine or with both.

Regarding the marriage in Myanmar, Myanmar practices the Monogamous System, One Husband and One Wife System under the Monogamy Law of Myanmar 2015. This law concerns all those who are living in Myanmar, Myanmar citizens who live outside of Myanmar, and foreigners who marry Myanmar citizens while living in Myanmar. Any marriage between a man and a woman in accordance with any law or any religion or any custom shall be legitimate only if monogamous. Any man or woman who is already married with one spouse or more than one spouse in accordance with a law or a religion or a custom shall not enter, while the original union is still legally recognized, into another marriage with another person or conduct an illegal extramarital affair and that person shall be deemed to commit the act of polygamy or conjugal infidelity under section 494 of the Penal Code and shall be punished with imprisonment which may extend to 7 years and shall also liable to a fine.

Any man or woman who is already married in accordance with a law or a religion or a custom shall not enter, while the original union is still legally recognized, into another marriage with another person or conduct an illegal extramarital affair and that person shall be deemed to commit the act of polygamy or conjugal infidelity under section 494 of the Penal Code and shall be punished with imprisonment which may extend to 7 years and shall also liable to a fine. Any man or woman, if he or she was previously married, can enter into another marriage with another person, only after declaring the previous marriage and showing evidence of legal divorce with his or her previous spouse, and that shall be deemed to commit a crime under section 495 of the Penal Code and shall be punished with imprisonment which may extend to 7 years and shall also liable to a fine.

Under the Monogamy Law of Myanmar 2015, if any husband or wife, while the original union is still legally recognized according to a law or a religion or a custom, marries another person, that person is deemed to commit matrimonial crime. Despite whatever contradictories with an existing law or religion or custom, if any husband or wife, while an original union is still legally recognized, marries another person, he or she is deemed to commit a matrimonial crime, and his or her spouse has the right to seek divorce. In such divorce, the person who commits a matrimonial crime shall forfeit all his property rights.

5. Conclusion

Regarding the marriage in Myanmar, it does not base on the nationality of the parties, it bases on the religion of the parties. Although there are many religions in Myanmar, the Buddhist, Hindu, Christian and Islam are the four main religions. Under the Constitution of the Republic of the Union 2008, the Union recognizes special position of Buddhism as the faith professed by the great majority of the citizens of the Union. In addition the Union also recognizes Christianity, Islam, Hinduism and Animism as the religions existing in the Union at the day of the coming into operation of this Constitution 2008. In addition, under the Myanmar Law Act 1898, where in any suit or other proceeding in the Union of Myanmar it is necessary for the Court to decide any question regarding succession, inheritance marriage or caste, or any religious usage or institution;—the Buddhist law in cases where the parties are Buddhists, the Muhammadan law in cases where the parties are Muhammadan and the Hindu law in cases where the parties are Hindus, shall form the rule of decision, except in so far as such law has by enactment been altered or abolished, or is opposed to any custom having the force of law. However every person, any religion or both man and woman, who want to contract the marriage with any person, any religion or both man and woman, shall comply with the Monogamy Law of Myanmar 2015. If the foreigners want to contract the marriage with any religious person except the Myanmar Buddhist women, shall contract the marriage in accordance with their relevant Family Law and shall also comply with the

Monogamy Law of Myanmar 2015. The foreign Buddhist man may contract the marriage with the Myanmar Buddhist woman in accordance with the Myanmar Customary Law but he shall also comply with the Monogamy Law of Myanmar 2015. In addition，the foreign non—Buddhist man may contract the marriage with Myanmar Buddhist woman in accordance with the Myanmar Buddhist Women's Special Law 2015 and he shall also comply with the Monogamy Law of Myanmar 2015. Therefore，this article will give the legal knowledge relating to the Myanmar marriage system and the suggestions for foreigners who intend to contract the marriage with Myanmar citizens.

References

1. U MayOung，A Selection of Leading Cases on Myanmar（Myanmar）Buddhist Law，Part（1），Second edition，Burma(Myanmar) Press，Yangon 1926.

2. Dr. Maung Maung, Law and Custom in Burma and the Burmese Family，The Hague：Martinus Nijhoff，1963.

3. UMya Sein，Myanmar Customary Law，Fourth Edition,1968.

4. Lahiri，S C，Principles of Modern Myanmar Buddhist Law，6th Edition 1957.

5. UThein Pe vs U Pe 3 LBR 175(186) F. B.

6. Lim Chin Neovs Lim Geok Soo 1956 B. L. R 248(H. C).

7. Ma AyeSein vs. Mg Hla Min 4 BLJ 258.

8. UTun Yin Vs. Maung Ba Han，1949 BLR 443（HC）.

9. AyeKyaw，Religion and Family Law in Burma.

10. The Administration on Islamic Law of Marriage in Myanmar.

11. The Constitution of the Republic of the Union of Myanmar 2008.

12. The Myanmar Customary Law.

13. The Hindu Family Law.

14. The Islamic Family Law.

15. The Christian Marriage Act，1872.

16. The Monogamy Law of Myanmar 2015.

17. The Myanmar Buddhist Women's Special Law 2015.

18. The Hindu Widows' Re-Marriage Act 1856.

19. TheAnand Marriage Act 1909.

20. TheKazia Act 1880.

21. The Foreign Marriage Act 1903.

22. The Contract Act 1872.

23. The Myanmar (Burma) Law Act 1898.

24. Directive No. 2/1998 of the Supreme Court of the Union.

25. Directive No. 1/2012 of the Supreme Court of the Union.

26. Directive No. 494/2016 of the Supreme Court of the Union.

缅甸婚姻制度法律评论

罗媛媛* Moe Cho**
编译 郭雅菲***

摘要：在缅甸，婚姻不以双方国籍为基础，而是以婚姻双方的宗教为基础。虽然缅甸有众多的宗教，但佛教、印度教、基督教和伊斯兰教是四大主要宗教。宗教教徒之间的婚姻以及非宗教人士与宗教教徒之间的婚姻，甚至外国人与缅甸宗教教徒的婚姻，既要依据宗教的相关规则和习俗缔结婚姻，也要遵守缅甸 2015 年《缅甸一夫一妻法》的规定。本文拟对在缅甸与缅甸公民缔结婚姻关系的外国人提供相应的法律知识和建议。

关键词：缔结婚姻，一夫一妻制，宗教，缅甸习惯法

引　言

在缅甸，缅甸佛教徒之间的婚姻并不涉及任何宗教性质，如今，这是一种纯粹的民事行为和协商一致的契约。缅甸佛教男女教徒在法律、社会和文化方面享有平等权利。缅甸佛教男女之间的婚姻不仅决定着合法性和继承性，还要求丈夫承担赡养妻子和子女的责任，对妻子保持忠诚。缅甸的婚姻不以婚姻双方的国籍为基础，而是以婚姻双方的宗教为基础。虽然缅甸有很多宗教，但佛教、印度教、基督教和伊斯兰教是四大宗教。根据《缅甸联邦共和国宪法》的规定，在遵守公共秩序、道德或健康以及宪法的其他规定的情况下，每个公民都享有意识自由和宗教信仰自由的权利。尽管印度教徒、基督教徒和穆斯林教徒可能根据他们的相关规则和习俗缔结婚约，但他们也将遵守 2015 年

---

* 中国-东盟法律研究中心项目官员，西南政法大学中国-东盟法律研究中心。
** 西南政法大学国际法学院博士生/缅甸联邦最高检检察官。
*** 西南政法大学 2014 级本科法学专业涉外人才实验班。

的《缅甸一夫一妻法》。本文拟对在缅甸与缅甸公民缔结婚姻关系的外国人提供法律知识和建议。

一、缅甸婚姻风格

婚姻是一种民间习俗,根本不存在佛教的宗教元素。缅甸的社会生活,以及在大多数东南亚国家的社会生活,都被宗教伦理所包含,以至于没有牧师和宗教元素的结婚仪式变得更加引人注目。这里没有佛教神职人员的主持,因为爱是世俗的,而契约纯粹是社会的。习俗对有效婚姻有特定的要求,双方必须有结婚的能力,如年龄和精神上。缅甸的达马蔡法典并没有规定固定的婚姻能力年龄,尽管其建议父母在 15 岁或 16 岁的时候应该允许他们的儿子和女儿结婚。人们普遍认为,男孩在青春期和女孩达到 20 岁之前就能获得父母的同意。

对于女人来说,要想缔结有效婚姻,她就不能是已婚妇女。寡妇或离异妇女可以结婚,解放父母控制的之前的婚姻,不需要父母同意,即使当她再次结婚时在 20 岁以下。然而,这一要求并不适用于男性,因为在缅甸佛教徒中,一夫多妻制是无可争议的,"观察枢密院"说,"它被达马蔡法典认可,这也是无可争议的"。然而,一夫多妻制并不是一个受欢迎的机制。这是合法的,但除了官员和富人之外,很少有人实践。在日常生活中,有不止一个妻子的男人被认为不是一个非常值得尊敬的人。然而,根据 2015 年《缅甸一夫一妻法》的规定,目前缅甸实行一夫一妻制。

缅甸婚姻最重要的因素,通常被称为"协商一致的契约",即同意。父母或监护人的同意是必要的,正如我们已经提到的那样,如果女孩低于 20 岁,还没有获得解放,父亲再也不能把不情愿的未成年女儿送进婚姻。根据《合同法》第 14 条所规定的测试,双方当事人之间的相互同意以及该法第 12 条规定的双方的意思表示是不可缺少的组成部分。结婚双方的同意,他们想要获得丈夫和妻子身份,是婚姻证明中的一个重要因素。因此,在婚姻证明中,表明同意和意图。在有争议的地方,婚姻状况的证明只能依赖于习惯和名誉,那么事实就必须经过仔细的审查,并且有证据表明这对夫妇是夫妻是不够的。如今,在年轻人中,他们会在一些朋友和长辈面前签下宣誓书,以陈述结婚的能力和意愿,放在年轻人中很流行,也很时髦。然后由当事人保留宣誓书,男子保留女子的,反之亦然,作为婚姻和证明的"证书"。这一程序节省了大型仪式和招待会的费用,而且更快、看起来更"合法",因为有文件可以保存,包括印记、印章和签名。这一法律实践得到了广泛应用,在缅甸非常流行。根据缅甸习惯法的规定,妇女在财产方面是分权共有人。他们共同拥有在婚姻期间与配偶共同积累的财产。

二、缅甸有关婚姻的法律

根据 2008 年《缅甸联邦共和国宪法》的规定,联邦承认佛教的特殊地位,因为它是大多数合众国公民所宣称的信仰。此外,该联盟还承认基督教、伊斯兰教、印度教和万物有灵论,这是在 2008 年《宪法》生效之日在联邦中存在的宗教。

1898 年《缅甸法》第 13(1)条规定,在缅甸联邦的任何诉讼或其他程序中,法院有必要决定任何有关继承、继承婚姻或种姓,或任何宗教用途或机构的问题:

(a)佛教法律中,当事人是佛教徒;

(b)在双方是伊斯兰教徒的情况下的穆罕默德法;

(c)印度法律中,双方是印度教徒。

除非颁布的法律被改变或废除,或违反任何具有法律效力的习俗,应形成制定的规则。

然而,Pyidaungsu Hluttaw[①] 在 2015 年颁布一夫一妻制的法律,以帮助合法夫妻在忠诚的基础上建立和平和幸福的家庭,通过实行一夫一妻制,保护女性不成为共同的妻子,并防止男性的一夫多妻行为引发犯罪。这条法律涉及所有生活在缅甸的缅甸人、缅甸以外的缅甸公民以及在缅甸与缅甸公民结婚的外国人。除非违反本法规定,任何男女均可依照有关现行法律、宗教或习俗,依法与任何人缔结婚姻。

(一)佛教人士的婚姻法

缅甸的佛教男女在 1898 年的《缅甸法》中的婚姻,受佛教法律的管辖。缅甸习惯法是缅甸佛教教徒的习惯法,习惯法逐渐向缅甸家庭的事务和宗教习俗和制度逐渐渗透。因为英国官员认为其在缅甸对于佛教信仰者是有法律效力的,普遍称之为"缅甸佛教法"。缅甸的习惯法也被认为是"个人法",因为在

---

① 缅甸地名。

缅甸,不管其国籍是什么,不论他来自哪里,都是由缅甸习惯法规定的,即婚姻、继承和继承问题上的达马蔡法典和先例,除非能证明受缅甸法律的约束,而这一习俗违背缅甸法。在英国占领之前,缅甸习惯法是一种基于习俗和惯例的社会和非宗教法,历史上被古代缅甸所接受。经过 13 年对上缅的占领,英国殖民政府于 1898 年颁布了《缅甸法》,至今仍是法律。从那时起,我们第一次看到"佛教法"这个词。缅甸的大多数著名法学家都说,"佛教法"一词指的是缅甸习惯法,这是用词不当。他们敦促缅甸佛教法律是缅甸的习惯法。案例 U Thein Pe Vs U Pe 中都被明确地接受了这个用语。在 Lim Chin Neo Vs Lim Geok Soo,U Chan Tun Aung 案中,最高法院首席大法官,在民事诉讼中判定,"缅甸佛教徒"意味着遵守习惯法中的缅甸佛教徒,U Mya Sein,"缅甸习惯法"的杰出作者,建议缅甸佛教法律应该被称为"缅甸习惯法"。

缅甸习惯法的法源如下:

(a)达马蔡法典;

(b)习俗;

(c)司法先例;

(d)立法或立法规定。

(i)《Kittima 收养法》的登记;

(ii)2015 年佛教妇女特别婚姻法。

关于缅甸佛教徒的婚姻,有两种婚姻。一种是佛教妇女教徒和佛教另性徒之间的婚姻。另一种是缅甸妇女和非佛教徒之间的婚姻。

如果佛教妇女和佛教另性徒缔结婚姻,他们遵守缅甸的习惯法和缅甸的一夫一妻制。根据缅甸习惯法的规定,婚姻的基本要素如下:

(a)男人应该达到青春期;

(b)妇女应是 20 岁以上的未婚者、寡妇、离婚人士或 20 岁以下的未婚者,并获得父母或监护人的同意;

(c)根据 1872 年《合同法》第 11 条的规定,双方必须有精神上的合意(双方都不能有不健全的头脑);

(d)双方必须在双方自愿同意的情况下成为夫妻;

(e)妇女不得存在有效的婚姻(一夫多妻制);

(f)在没有直接证据的情况下,可以从当事方的行为或以声誉建立婚姻,他们应该公开地以丈夫和妻子身份生活在一起。

在缅甸佛教妇女与非佛教另性徒之间的婚姻中,他们将遵守 2015 年《缅甸佛教妇女特别婚姻法》和 2015 年《缅甸一夫一妻法》。2014 年,Pyidaungsu

Hluttaw 颁布了缅甸佛教妇女特别婚姻法,以使缅甸佛教妇女和非佛教男性在婚姻、离婚、分割和监护子女等方面享有平等权利,并给予有效的保护。缅甸佛教妇女和非佛教徒儿童的婚姻、离婚、分割、继承和监护等争议,依照 2015 年《缅甸一夫一妻法》的规定决定。2015 年《缅甸佛教妇女特别婚姻法》规定,一名年满 18 岁的非佛教男子和年满 18 岁的佛教妇女,如果符合以下事实,可以订立有效的婚姻:

(a)双方不得有不健全的精神;

(b)同意结婚是自愿的,不受引诱、胁迫、不正当的影响、欺诈或歪曲;

(c)如果妇女尚未年满 20 岁,未获得父母的同意,或如果他们已死亡,则应获得监护人的事实或监护人的同意;

(d)在妇女的情况下,任何有效的婚姻都不能维持;

(e)在男子的情况下,任何有效的婚姻都不能维持。

佛教女性与佛教男性的婚姻与佛教女性与非佛教男性的婚姻之间的适婚年龄存在差异。根据缅甸习惯法的规定,即将结婚的女人,应该是 20 岁。根据 2015 年《缅甸佛教妇女特别婚姻法》的规定,女方结婚已达到 18 岁。2015 年《缅甸佛教妇女特别婚姻法》与缅甸习惯法相悖。Dhammathat 没有具体说明男孩或女孩能成为夫妻的确切年龄。1928 年,仰光高等法院决定在 Maung Thein Mg vs Ma Saw 的案例中发现,在缅甸佛教青年有能力在任何时间签订有效的婚姻,而不需要他的父母或监护人同意。在 Ma E Sein vs Maung Hla Min7 案中,缅甸佛教法律中对于年轻未婚女性未经监护人同意是否能够缔结婚姻合同,认为没有父母或监护人,或者在其保护下的人的同意或遭到反对,20 岁以下的小女孩合同不可以缔结有效的婚姻。现在,当一对夫妇在法院结婚时,结婚年龄是固定在 18 岁,在这个年龄,父母或监护人的同意是需要的。因此,根据缅甸习惯法和法院的规定,年龄限制是有区别的。因此,我们应该明确统一年龄限制。

(二)缅甸的基督教婚姻法

每个人之间的婚姻,一个或两个是基督徒,都应依照 1872 年《基督教婚姻法》的规定举行。这段婚姻可能会很隆重。

(a)任何接受主教任命的人,只要婚姻是按照他作为牧师的教会的规则、仪式和习俗举行的;

(b)苏格兰教会的任何神职人员,只要按照苏格兰教会的规则、仪式和习俗进行隆重的婚礼;

（c）任何宗教部长根据本法案授权举行庄严的婚姻；

（d）根据本法所指定的婚姻登记官，或在其在场的情况下；

（e）根据本法案获得许可的任何人，授予在当地基督徒之间的婚姻证书。

如果一位缅甸佛教徒信奉基督教，并以有效的方式与基督徒结婚，随后皈依佛教，那么他或她就没有资格与缅甸佛教徒缔结第二次婚姻，只要基督教婚姻存续。如今，基督教徒和基督教妇女在婚姻登记官的见证下，根据1872年《基督教婚姻法案》的规定缔结婚姻，他们还应遵守2015年《缅甸一夫一妻法》的规定。此外，打算与缅甸佛教妇女结婚的基督教男性，也只能在2015年《缅甸佛教妇女特别婚姻法》下缔结婚约。

（三）缅甸的伊斯兰婚姻法

对穆斯林来说，婚姻被称为"尼卡"，阿拉伯语，字面意思是婚姻或婚姻。穆斯林男子和穆斯林妇女可以根据缅甸的伊斯兰家庭法缔结婚约。根据《缅甸伊斯兰家庭法》的规定，有效婚姻的基本要素是能力、婚姻契约和不受所有限制。每个进入青春期的心智健全的穆斯林，都可以缔结一份婚姻契约。缅甸的大多数穆斯林都是逊尼派的哈纳菲，缅甸的伊斯兰家庭法在大多数情况下都遵循着逊尼派的哈纳菲法，但它不能与缅甸制定的法律相抵触。逊尼派的哈纳菲法承认，男孩或女孩到15岁，如果没有证据表明青春期的日期，他们将被认为具有婚姻能力。然而，缅甸不允许这样做，因为1929年的《儿童婚姻限制法》规定，如果一名男性未满18岁，而女性在16岁以下，则被定义为儿童。目前，穆斯林男子和穆斯林妇女根据《缅甸伊斯兰家庭法》订立婚约。此外，他们应遵守2015年《缅甸一夫一妻制》。

缅甸佛教不是kitabic（任何揭露宗教的追随者相信一个神），所以没有有效婚姻的伊斯兰教徒和缅甸佛教，除非后者接受伊斯兰教的宗教信仰或其他显示相信一个神和婚姻庆祝仪式的伊斯兰教的信仰。如今，如果穆斯林男子想要与缅甸的佛教妇女缔结婚约，那么他们只能在2015年《缅甸佛教妇女特别婚姻法》下缔结婚约。

（四）缅甸的印度教婚姻法

根据印度教习惯法的规定，如果这段婚姻是按照印度男教的习俗举行的，印度教徒和印度教妇女之间的婚姻就只能是合法的婚姻。在1909年的《Anand婚姻法》中，所有可能是或可能已被正式隆重举行的在婚姻都被称为Anand，它将被认为是在各自的庄严仪式的日期起生效的，在法律仪式上是好

263

的和有效的。关于印度教寡妇的再婚，印度教徒之间没有婚姻合同无效，并没有这样的婚姻应当是非法的问题，因之前的女人已经结婚或与另一死了的人订婚过，而该人是在这种婚姻的时候，任何习俗和对印度教法的解释都是相反的。

然而，印度教徒不能与任何女人签订合法婚姻，除非她属于他自己的种姓。印度教的种姓有四种，如婆罗门（Brahmins）、刹帝利（Kshatriyas）和维赛亚。因此，印度教的婆罗门、刹帝利、吠舍（Vaishyas）和首陀罗（Shudras）种姓不能与缅甸佛教徒签订正统婚姻。目前，印度教徒应遵守 2015 年关于他们与印度教徒结婚的一夫一妻制。此外，印度教徒可以根据 2015 年《缅甸佛教妇女特别婚姻法》与缅甸佛教妇女结婚。

三、外国人能和缅甸公民结婚吗？

法律没有限制外国人与缅甸公民结婚的权利。外国人与缅甸公民结婚不受限制，但外国人应当按照缅甸有关风俗缔结结婚，并遵守缅甸现行有关婚姻的法律。在缅甸，婚姻并不是以婚姻双方的民族为基础，而是以双方的宗教为基础。如果外国人打算与缅甸的基督徒签订婚约，他们只能按照有关基督教的婚姻法和基督教习俗来签订婚约。

此外，外国人想要与缅甸的穆斯林签订婚约，他们只能按照《缅甸伊斯兰家庭法》缔结这样的婚姻。同样，外国人如果打算与缅甸的印度教徒结婚，他们只能按照缅甸的印度教家庭法来签订这样的婚姻。这意味着外国人可以根据相关法律和习俗与缅甸基督教徒、穆斯林和印度教徒签订婚约。然而，文章的这一部分指出了缅甸佛教徒和外国人的婚姻。就像上面提到的，外国人可以与缅甸佛教公民缔结婚姻。我们将在以下几个部分中解释如何与缅甸佛教公民缔结婚约，以及在与缅甸佛教公民缔结婚姻时应注意哪些法律。

（一）外国人与缅甸佛教公民的婚姻如何签订？

对缅甸佛教公民，缅甸佛教男子与外国妇女结婚没有任何限制。然而，如果外国佛教人士或非佛教人士打算与缅甸佛教妇女签订婚约，则应遵守缅甸现行法律和缅甸习惯法。联邦最高法院颁布了关于缅甸妇女和外国人婚姻问题的规定。因为许多来自国外的外国人通过各种途径来到缅甸，一些外国人与缅甸的中间人有联系，并试图通过在法庭上宣誓并把他们带到国外来引诱缅甸妇女嫁给他们。这些经过这一过程被带到国外的妇女甚至在出国之前就已经面临着不体面的问题,而且当她们来到海外时,她们也会失去她们的人格,出现各种各样的问题。由于缺乏民族精神,他们用金钱的承诺引诱缅甸妇女,并计划将他们从缅甸运到外国人手中。在这种情况下,联邦最高法院努力保护缅甸妇女的生命免受威胁。因此联邦最高法院发布的指令第 2/1998 号,针对 1998 年 7 月 1 日起所有法庭成员,没有官员被授权接受任何缅甸女人对外国人婚姻的誓言或程序,双方不得结婚。

然而,由于法院不接受任何一名缅甸妇女嫁给外国人的誓言或申请,外国人和真正想要结婚的缅甸妇女和缅甸妇女面临着困难。因此,联邦最高法院在第 1/2012 号指令中撤销了第 2/1998 号指令。根据第 1/2012 号指令,法院有权接受外国人和缅甸妇女结婚的任何宣誓或申请。此外,如果外国佛教徒打算与缅甸佛教妇女签订婚约,他们只能在地区法院签订婚约。虽然,在第 1/2012 号指令下,法院有权接受外国非佛教人士和缅甸佛教妇女的婚姻,法院的这一权力被第 494/2016 号指令撤销。在指令篇 494/2016 号下,法院授权非佛教男人和缅甸佛教女人的涉外的婚姻誓言或程序,因为 Pyidaungsu Hluttaw 制定 2015 年《缅甸佛教妇女特别婚姻法》,和本指令规定,乡镇行政官员中的乡一般行政部门的婚姻登记官负责登记非缅甸佛教的男人和女人。非佛教人士和佛教妇女拟结婚时,其中一人应以规定的形式向其所在地的司法常务官提出书面申请。申请书应附一份宣誓书,承认本法律规定的事实已经履行。

(二)欲与缅甸佛教妇女缔结婚姻契约的外国人应注意什么?

对于打算与缅甸的佛教妇女结婚的外国人,包括信仰佛教的外国人和非信仰佛教的外国人权建议如下。第一,打算与缅甸佛教妇女结婚的信仰佛教的外国人,应遵守缅甸习惯法和缅甸现行法律,包括 2015 年《缅甸一夫一妻法》,他们可能只在地区法院前签订婚约。关于佛教妇女、佛教徒子女的婚姻、离婚、分割、继承、监护等争议应依照缅甸习惯法作出裁决。

第二,打算签订契约婚姻的非信仰佛教外国人与缅甸佛教女性应当遵守 2015 年《缅甸佛教特别婚姻法》和缅甸现行法律,包括 2015 年《缅甸一夫一妻法》,乡的乡镇行政人员签订契约婚姻。根据《缅甸佛教妇女特别婚姻法》和 2015 年《缅甸一夫一妻法》的规定,有关婚姻、离婚、分割、继承和监护权的争议,应依照《缅甸佛教妇女特别婚姻法》的规定确定。此外,一名非信仰佛教男子,因其与缅甸佛教妇女订立婚约或被认为与缅甸佛教妇女缔结婚约,应遵守下列有关佛教妇女宗教信仰的规定:

(a)允许佛教妇女根据自己的信仰自由地信奉宗教;

(b)允许与佛教妇女结婚的孩子根据信仰自由地公开他们的宗教;

(c)允许佛教妇女在家中保持佛像地位和形象;

(d)允许佛教妇女根据宗教信仰崇拜、吟诵、辟邪、念珠、听宗教布道、练习宗教冥想、参观佛塔和寺院、斋戒、阅读和学习与佛教有关的文学作品;

(e)不使用各种手段使佛教妇女放弃佛教信仰,并使她皈依他的宗教;

(f)不破坏或破坏或玷污敬拜的地方或以侮辱佛教徒为目的的神圣之物;

(g)不要侮辱、用文字或书面表达,也不要用有形的表示或姿态,恶意地给佛教徒造成痛苦的感觉。

虽然法律和习俗中都有规定,如果一名非佛教徒与缅甸佛教妇女缔结婚约,违反了上述任何事实,佛教妇女可以与非佛教徒离婚。另外,如果佛教徒因为这个原因而与他离婚:

(a)该男子将放弃他有权从双方拥有的财产中获得的部分,并向佛教妇女支付补偿;

(b)所有儿童的监护应裁决给佛教徒妇女,并且;

(c)男子应支付未成年人的抚养费。

如果非信仰佛教徒违反了2015年《缅甸佛教妇女特别婚姻法》的规定,即

(a)允许佛教妇女根据自己的信仰自由地信奉宗教;

(b)允许与佛教妇女结婚的孩子根据信仰自由地公开他们的宗教;

(c)允许佛教妇女在家中保持佛像地位和形象;

(d)允许佛教妇女根据宗教信仰崇拜、吟诵、辟邪、念珠、听宗教布道、练习宗教冥想、参观佛塔和寺院、斋戒、阅读和学习与佛教有关的文学作品。

他将被处以监禁,刑期可延长至6个月,罚金不得超过50万缅元(约400美元),或两者皆可。如果非信仰佛教人违反本法规定,"不能通过使用各种手段逼迫信仰佛教的女子放弃佛教信仰,使之信仰他自己的宗教",监禁处罚可能延长到3年,而且还应当承担罚款责任。除此之外,如果非信仰佛教人违反本法的规定,"不破坏或损坏或污秽的敬拜地或神圣物品,侮辱佛教,或者不是侮辱,但用文字或书面或其他可见表示或姿态,对佛教徒造成痛苦的感觉",监禁可能延长2年,或罚款,或两者兼而有之。

关于缅甸的婚姻依据2015年缅甸《一夫一妻法》,缅甸实行一夫一妻制。这条法律关系到所有生活在缅甸的缅甸人、缅甸以外的缅甸公民以及在缅甸生活的外国人。根据任何法律或任何宗教或任何习俗,男人和女人

之间的任何婚姻,只要一夫一妻制,都是合法的。依照法律、宗教或者风俗,已经与配偶或者其他配偶结婚的男女,不得结婚,原婚姻关系仍被依法认定的,缔结另一个婚姻与另一个人或进行非法婚外情和那个人应被视为一夫多妻或配偶不忠的行为,根据《刑法》第 494 条,处罚监禁可能延长到 7 年,还应当承担罚款。

依照法律或宗教或习惯结婚的任何已婚男人或女人,在原来的婚姻关系仍受法律认可时不得再婚,或有非法婚外情,否则那个人应被视为一夫多妻或配偶不忠的行为,根据《刑法》第 494 条,处罚监禁可能延长到 7 年,还应当承担罚款。任何人,如果他或她以前结过婚又再婚,应当宣布之前的婚姻结束和展示与他或她之前配偶法律离婚的证据,否则应被视为触犯第 495 条犯罪的刑法,处罚监禁可能延长到 7 年,还应当承担罚款。

在 2015 年的《缅甸一夫一妻法》中,如果任何丈夫或妻子,而最初的婚姻关系仍然根据法律或宗教或习俗依法被承认,而与另一个人结婚,这个人被认为是婚姻犯罪。如有丈夫或妻子与另一个人结婚,而最初的婚姻关系仍在法律上被承认,无论与任何与现行法律或宗教或习俗相抵触,他或她被认为是婚姻犯罪,而他或她的配偶有权离婚。在这种离婚中,犯婚姻罪的人将丧失其所有的财产权利。

四、结论

关于缅甸的婚姻,它不以婚姻双方的国籍为基础,而是以婚姻双方的宗教为基础。虽然缅甸有很多宗教,但佛教、印度教、基督教和伊斯兰教是四大宗教。根据 2008 年《联邦共和国宪法》的规定,联邦承认佛教的特殊地位,因为它是大多数合众国公民所宣称的信仰。此外,该联邦还承认基督教、伊斯兰教、印度教和万物有灵论,这是在 2008 年《宪法》生效之日在联邦中存在的宗教。此外,缅甸 1898 年法案,在任何诉讼或其他程序在缅甸联邦法院有必要决定关于继承,继承,婚姻或等级或使用任何宗教或机构的任何问题;——佛教法律在这种情况下,当事人是佛教徒;伊斯兰教的法律在这种情况下,当事人是伊斯兰教徒教徒;印度法律在这种情况下,当事人是印度教徒,形成规则的决策,除非法律的颁布被修改或废除,或反对任何具有法律效力的习俗。然而,任何人、任何宗教,无论男女,希望与任何人,任何宗教的男人和女人缔结婚约,应遵守 2015 年的《缅甸一夫一妻法》。如果外国人想与除缅甸佛教妇女以外的任何宗教人士缔结婚约,则应按照其有关家庭法缔结婚约,并遵守

2015 年《缅甸一夫一妻法》。外国佛教徒可以按照缅甸习惯法与缅甸佛教妇女签订婚约,但他要遵守 2015 年的《缅甸一夫一妻》。此外,外国非信仰佛教人士可根据 2015 年《缅甸佛教妇女特别婚姻法》与缅甸佛教妇女签订婚约,并遵守缅甸 2015 年《缅甸一夫一妻制》。因此,本文提供了有关缅甸婚姻制度的法律知识,以及对打算与缅甸公民结婚的外国人的建议。

图书在版编目(CIP)数据

中国-东盟法律评论. 第 7 辑/张晓君,[缅甸]吴温敏主编. —厦门:厦门大学出版社,2017.12
ISBN 978-7-5615-7029-6

Ⅰ.①中… Ⅱ.①张…②吴… Ⅲ.①法律-中国、东南亚国家联盟-文集
Ⅳ.①D92-53②D933-53

中国版本图书馆 CIP 数据核字(2018)第 153569 号

出 版 人	郑文礼
责任编辑	李　宁
封面设计	李嘉彬
技术编辑	许克华

出版发行 厦门大学出版社

社　　　址	厦门市软件园二期望海路 39 号
邮政编码	361008
总 编 办	0592-2182177　0592-2181406(传真)
营销中心	0592-2184458　0592-2181365
网　　　址	http://www.xmupress.com
邮　　　箱	xmup@xmupress.com
印　　　刷	厦门集大印刷厂

开本	720 mm×1 000 mm　1/16
印张	17.75
插页	3
字数	302 千字
版次	2017 年 12 月第 1 版
印次	2017 年 12 月第 1 次印刷
定价	86.00 元

本书如有印装质量问题请直接寄承印厂调换

厦门大学出版社
微信二维码

厦门大学出版社
微博二维码